LIBRAR...

Telephone (0...00)...

Please return this book on or before the last date stamped
below.

Fines will be charged on books returned after this date.

CROSS-TRAIN YOUR HORSE

Also by Jane Savoie

More Cross-Training:
Build a Better Performance Horse with Dressage

That Winning Feeling!
Program Your Mind for Peak Performance

That Winning Feeling! Audios
Tape 1: *Choose Your Future*
Tape 2: *Learning Relaxation and Imaging Skills*

The Half Halt–Demystified! Videos
Tape 1: *Learning the Half Halt*
Tape 2: *Putting Your Horse on the Bit*

CROSS-TRAIN YOUR HORSE

BOOK ONE

Simple Dressage for Every Horse, Every Sport

JANE SAVOIE

PHOTOGRAPHS RHETT B. SAVOIE
DRAWINGS SUSAN E. HARRIS AND PATRICIA PEYMAN NAEGELI

J.A. Allen
London

First U.K. edition published in Great Britain in 1998 by

J.A. Allen & Company Limited

1 Lower Grosvenor Place

Buckingham Palace Road, London, SW1W 0EL

First published in the United States of America in 1998 by

Trafalgar Square Publishing, North Pomfret, Vermont 05053

The author has made every effort to obtain a release from all persons appearing in the photographs used in this book. In some cases, however, the persons may not have been known and therefore could not be contacted.

Susan Harris' drawings reprinted with permission of Macmillan General Reference, from *Horse Gaits, Balance and Movement* by Susan E. Harris. A Howell Book House publication. Copyright © 1993 by Susan E. Harris.

Disclaimer of Liability:

The author and publisher shall have neither liability nor responsibility to any person or entity with respect to any loss or damage caused or alleged to be caused directly or indirectly by the information contained in this book. While the book is as accurate as the author can make it, there may be errors, omissions, and inaccuracies.

British Library Cataloguing-in-Publication Data

A catalogue record for this book is available from the British Library.

ISBN: 0-85131-719-7

Cover and book design by Carrie Fradkin, C Design

Typeface: Poppl-Pontifex and Tiepolo

Printed in Hong Kong by Dah Hua International Printing Press Co., Ltd.

Dedication

In loving memory of my father, Benjamin Elkind.
Not a day goes by without thoughts of you.

Table of Contents

Acknowledgements

A project like these two books is rarely done alone and this one is no exception. It's my distinct pleasure to thank all of the talented people who helped me with their time, effort, skill and support.

To the gifted riders and gracious owners who generously allowed themselves and their horses to be photographed showing both the "do's" and the "don'ts:"

Michele Bump
Carole Ann Cahill
Lynda Cameron
Jamie Cripps
Deborah Dean-Smith
Amy Foss
Christopher Hickey
Ruth Hogan-Poulsen
Gerri Jenkyn
Renate Kundrun
Claire Talbot
Kelly Weiss

To my husband, Rhett Savoie, for his skill behind the camera and his unfailing patience during this massive project. Rhett, you can finally walk through the living room again without having to tiptoe through the wall-to-wall carpet of manuscript pages, photographs, and illustrations.

To my publisher, Caroline Robbins, who sweated shoulder to shoulder with me for six years over the creation of these books. During that time she worked tirelessly as my editor, conscience, supporter, and most importantly, my friend. I could always count on her to be the voice of reason when I couldn't see things clearly.

To Martha Cook of Trafalgar Square Publishing for her many contributions to this project. She wears many hats and they all fit comfortably. Thank you, Martha, for all your efforts but especially for your special ability of always making me feel that I was your most important project even when you were buried in something else.

To Lynn Palm Pittion-Rossillon and Anne Kursinski for agreeing to write forewords for Book One and Book Two, respectively. I consider it a great honor as I have tremendous admiration for both the skill and training philosophies of these two women.

To the following trainers who I have had the very great privilege of working with:

Linda Jaskiel-Brown, for introducing me to the joy of dressage

Robert Dover, my "brother", for being the major influence in my education by teaching me the priniciples as well as the art of dressage

Cindy Sydnor, whose elegance I constantly strive to emulate and whose teaching style set the pattern for my own

Pam Goodrich, for helping me to think creatively

The late Herbert Rehbein, for his pure genius on a horse

Sue Blinks, for inspiring me with her loving approach to training. She's a shining example that excellence and kindness do, in fact, go hand in hand.

To Susan Harris, for generously allowing us to use her brilliant drawings from her book *Horse Gaits, Balance and Movement.*

To Patty Naegeli, whose lighthearted illustrations not only educate but also remind us that riding is supposed to be fun.

To my dear friend Ann Kitchel, who graciously allowed me to take over her arena at Huntington Farm during the photo shoots.

To all my friends who supported and commiserated with me through each "final" rewrite. I love you all.

Foreword

When I was young I was taught that the word "dressage" meant "training"—training for any breed performing any discipline of riding. In fact, I can still remember my instructor, Bobbie Steele, telling me this at her dining room table where I would hang out after riding lessons when I was a teenager. Mrs Steele was a performer with the Ringling Bros. and Barnum & Bailey Circus for more than ten years and she was trained by a famous German classical dressage rider, Captain William Heyer, who was brought over to America to train the circus horses, and teach the riders. In fact, she was the only rider who didn't give up under his strict, European disciplinary methods. She persevered, learned how to ride using his methods, and in 1946, *Life Magazine* featured her as "The First Woman to Ride Classical Dressage in America", when she developed her two horses for exhibition at top horse shows, such as in New York City at Madison Square Garden.

I was very lucky to have spent nearly twenty years under Mrs Steele's guidance. Her whole life was about horses, and more specifically, the connection between horse and rider. She explained it as "going as one." She took me to watch trainers who were "whip and spur" riders, pointing out how tense and hurried their horses became, and how "forced" they looked. These horses were never happy, and it showed. The riders were "demanding" of the horses and there was no sense of unity.

I learned that the longer you take to "make" a horse, the better the product you'll have in the end. I remember Nick Nack, a Quarter Horse-Saddlebred cross that I started riding as a three-year old. It took six years of working with him and Mrs Steele before she felt I was good enough to compete in a dressage competition, or ready do an exhibition at the local show. She made me realize the importance of the rider learning to be absolutely balanced and centered, and the necessity of building Nick Nack's muscles, and the flexibility of his joints, slowly. At the end of every lesson he got a reward whether it was a good or poor session, and my reward was my new-found understanding as a rider and knowledge of how to develop a horse's body to eventually achieve collection.

A little later in life I became more interested in Quarter Horses because of their versatility. I applied my dressage knowledge to train them for many Western events (Western pleasure, trail, horsemanship and reining), as well as hunter seat classes (hunter under saddle, hunter hack, working hunter), and even pleasure driving. There was no difference except in the position of my hands. The basics were the same as the ones I had been taught in dressage, and training came easily. I was fortunate to have some wonderful horses who were very successful.

So now today I am reading Jane's book and see that it echoes Mrs Steele's principles exactly. Jane's goal of achieving her three "golden rules"—Clarity, Consistency, and Kindness—match mine. This book is not complicated. It is full of common sense and will teach you a natural way to communicate with your seat, legs and hands.

Horses of all breeds have different habits, characteristic traits, instincts, behavior, attitude, and conformation, but a common denominator to training them is classical, elementary dressage, and Jane explains how to do it. Read her book, work hard with determination, practice with passion, and you will achieve the ultimate with your horse—a true bond as you work together as one.

LYNN PALM PITTION-ROSSILLON
Four-time winner of the
American Quarter Horse Association
"World Champion Superhorse" title.

Author's Note

Welcome to the fascinating world of classical training—that is, training your horse the way it has been done for hundreds of years. I've written two books, Book One *Cross-Train Your Horse: Simple Dressage For Every Horse, Every Sport* and Book Two *More Cross-Training: Build a Better Performance Horse with Dressage.* These books are not only for the beginning dressage enthusiast, but also for those of you who have no intention of ever setting foot inside a competitive dressage arena, but want to do dressage to help you clearly communicate with your horse and develop his body and movement so that over time he becomes more beautiful and athletic. I want you to have the tools to give him a solid foundation from which you can easily branch off into any riding discipline.

All riders will find that this is a simple, non-mysterious system of training that places a high priority on the horse's physical and mental well-being. You will also discover how cross-training with dressage can give you the edge to excel in your chosen specialty.

Here's what's in store for you. First, you'll get the inside scoop from experts—both professionals and amateurs in all different riding disciplines. You'll see how as "horse people" we're not as different as you might think at first glance. And, you'll hear how riders from all "trots of life" have discovered the secret that there are countless benefits to cross-training with dressage.

Chapter Four starts your horse's formal education with a discussion of longeing technique and your job as rider and trainer. I am making certain assumptions, even at this initial stage, about the level of training of both you and your horse. Specifically, I'm addressing horses that have been started under saddle and riders who have some control over their position as well as the skill to comfortably walk, trot, and canter.

Starting in Chapter Six I explore the heart of training—work under saddle. Here, I introduce the first two of my Four Stages of training (Stages Three and Four will be introduced in Book Two). The information in Stages One and Two is for all riders, and every horse regardless of his natural ability, talent, or eventual career.

I call Stage One, "Dressage 101," because it is reminiscent of my freshman year in college when my schedule was filled with introductory (101) courses. As with any good introductory course, its discussion of "the Basics" provides you with a solid background from which you can easily progress to the next level.

Stage Two includes the "Nuts and Bolts" of training—all the transitions, school figures, and movements you'll need to cross-train with dressage.

Keep in mind that this is work that you can incorporate into your everyday schooling. You don't need to devote certain days to "dressage," and you certainly don't need a fancy dressage arena. You can practice this basic work anywhere, whether you're out on the trail or in a field. However, for some of the exercises described in Nuts and Bolts you will find it helpful to set up a rectangle and some markers when you work in your ring, arena, field, or schooling area. You don't need to outline the entire perimeter of your rectangle—you can just define the corners with some poles or perhaps mow a rectangular area in your field so that the taller grass forms a clear boundary. Then designate the middle of each short and long side with four markers, such as small road cones or plastic milk containers filled with sand. That's it—your cross-training office is open for business. (Just in case you do want to set up a proper arena, you'll find diagrams of both small and standard dressage arenas in an appendix.)

I also want to mention that in this first book I'll be describing distances in feet. In *More Cross-Training*, however, I'll switch to the more traditional system of measuring in meters to help you get in a dressage mode.

I do have a few additional comments about the material in both books. First, you'll discover that I refer to all the riders as "she" and all the horses as "he." I'm hoping my male readers and mare owners will not take offense at my arbitrary choice of pronouns. I am not being sexist here! I'm simply trying to avoid cumbersome references to "he and she" and the impersonal sound of calling your horse "it."

Also, in the interest of clarity, you'll notice that nearly all of the movements and exercises are described with your horse traveling to the left—counterclockwise. When you go to the right, all you need to do is reverse the aids.

I believe that you'll find the explanations and descriptions "reader-friendly." They are basically a reflection of my own learning style. By nature I'm a very left-brained, methodical, analytical person who eventually learned how to unleash and blend some right-brained creativity into my established system. So that's what you'll find when you get to the movements. Every exercise will be broken down and clearly explained in a step-by-step manner.

And, if some of the words and expressions sound new or foreign, don't worry because you'll find a glossary of terms in an appendix. In fact, each time I introduce a new dressage word or phrase, I'll put it in bold type so you'll know that the term is defined in the glossary.

You'll also find lots of imaging in this book to help you tap into your creative side and strive for peak performance. After all, practice doesn't make perfect. Perfect practice makes perfect. And in your imagination, you never miss!

Some of you will be content to stop after you finish Book One. That's fine because with the information you have at that point, your horse should be obedient and fun to ride.

However, many of you will be excited to hear that the material in Book Two, which includes Stages Three and Four, picks up where this book leaves off. Specifically, in Stage Three, you'll learn about "The Professional's Secret"—how to give a half-halt and how to put your horse "on the bit." Knowing how to give a half-halt will improve the quality of all the work that you already do as well as increase your horse's ridability and your level of comfort.

Then, once you're really bitten by the bug, I know you'll want to learn what you can do next. So for those of you who become intrigued with dressage, I've included some "Fancy Stuff" in Stage Four. This material is not solely reserved for the rider who wants to specialize in dressage. I believe it's also well within the capacity of most horses. A word of caution here, though. You'll probably find that the more you know about dressage, the more you'll want to know. So, although the whole process of training classically can become endlessly fascinating and addictive, bear in mind that no horse should be schooled in a ring every day. All horses need play days and hack days to preserve their sanity and their joy in their work.

Whether you're a recreational rider or an aspiring professional, cross-training with dressage can give you a choice. You don't need to be victimized by a tense, flighty, uncooperative horse or a lazy, sullen, heavy-on-the-forehand type who you have to kick and pull to make stop, go, and turn. You can discover the joy of riding a calm, responsive animal who responds happily and willingly to the most invisible cues.

Convinced? I hope so because you're about to embark on an exciting adventure of a lifetime of learning. Any horse with three acceptable paces—one that can walk, trot, and canter in a regular rhythm—can do this program. And, don't panic. There aren't any secrets or complicated theories to absorb. What I do is simply training—clearly presented and kindly executed. I'll be giving you a clear-cut, non-hocus-pocus system that's straightforward and easy to incorporate into your work. Ready? Have fun!

J.S.

SETTING THE STAGE FOR CROSS-TRAINING

CHAPTER ONE

Dressage—What's in it for You

When I'm asked what kind of riding I do, I sort of mumble the word dressage and hope no one notices. That's because I know there are a lot of misconceptions about dressage. But now, in this book, I'm going to come right out and admit it up front. I'm what's known (condescendingly) as a "DQ"–dressage queen–and I have been one for nearly twenty-five years. But, please don't hold it against me!

Don't put the book down, and bolt for the door. Indulge me for a little while by keeping an open mind. Not only will you discover that we dressage riders aren't the humorless, snooty, elite bunch you might have imagined, but you might just find that you get excited about the prospects of including a little dressage in your training program. I'm convinced that by cross-training your endurance, reining, hunter, jumper, combined training, pleasure, saddleseat, or _____ (you fill in the blank) horse with dressage, you can open up a whole new world of possibilities.

Let's take a moment to talk about some of those misconceptions. In the past, we dressage riders have been given a bad rap. We've been accused of being snobs who only allow certain (and expensive!) breeds of horses into our very exclusive club. We've been charged with riding endlessly around in circles in a ring, boring our horses to death. Even the very word "dressage" often invites comments accompanied by a knowing nod such as, "Oh, she does dressage. She never sets foot outside her ring!"

These generalizations really don't surprise me. I mean, after all, even after more than two decades devoted exclusively to dressage, when I tell my own mother I'm competing the following weekend she says,"That's nice, dear. Are you going to jump?" I really can't blame her. Jumping certainly seems a lot more exciting than riding around in circles.

1.1

Deb Dean-Smith and Galen are featured in many of the photos throughout this book. Here, you can see just what cross-training with dressage has done for this pair. Galen is calmly and enthusiastically doing her job on the cross-country course of a combined training event. Photo: Terri Miller.

On the other hand, every time you turn around lately you've probably heard how riders from all different disciplines have been incorporating dressage into their training programs. If it sounds intriguing and you think, "How about me?" "Can I?" "Will I like it?" "Will it help?" "How do I get started?" "Do I need special equipment or clothing?" "Is my horse the right type?" "Am I qualified?," then this book is for you.

Is Dressage for You?

According to the American Horse Shows Association (AHSA) rulebook, the ultimate purpose of dressage is the harmonious development of the physique and ability of a horse. It makes a horse calm, supple, attentive and keen, thus closer to achieving perfect understanding with his rider. Does this sound like something that might appeal to you?

Would you like your horse to be relaxed, obedient, and more of a pleasure to ride? Wouldn't it be fun to have a horse that willingly and enthusiastically responds to refined, invisible signals? Dressage will enable you to develop a nonverbal language—a way to clearly communicate with your equine partner so that you begin to function as one.

Is the idea of helping your horse become more of an athlete appealing? Consider a horse when he's free. Even the most common animal is fascinating and beautiful to watch when he gets the wind under his tail on a crisp spring morning or when he cavorts with his friends while being pursued by imaginary enemies.

The catch here, however, is that horses aren't designed to be ridden. And, as much as you might love your horse, you really are a burden to him. You bring this proud creature in from the field, put a saddle and your weight on his back, and suddenly he doesn't move in the same lofty way. Instead of showing himself off with a "Hey! Look at me! I'm hot stuff!" attitude, he either lazily shuffles along or stiffens his body and moves with tension. Fortunately, this is where dressage holds the key to unlock his potential; you can give back to the horse that is being ridden the beauty of movement he has when he's at liberty.

Now let's consider some physical and balance problems. Is your horse ever so sore, stiff, or weak that he can't do his job? I'm not talking about fancy maneuvers here. I mean real nitty gritty stuff like the quality of the basic paces—such as the horse who is so unathletic that he can barely

Ted Zajac and Jettagair show the kind of harmony and balance you can achieve with a solid background of classical training.

canter and ends up switching leads behind, dragging his hind feet along the ground or simply breaking back into the trot. With a program of systematic training like the one presented in this book, a horse like that can become a strong and capable athlete.

Are you a jumper rider who finds that your horse is so "locked" or "blocked" in his body that he's difficult to turn? He's so hard, in fact, that you wonder if you'll be able to stay in the ring, let alone negotiate a corner in order to have a decent approach to the next fence. Or maybe you go for a so-called "pleasure" ride and return exhausted because your horse has been pulling your arms out of their sockets for an hour? Cross-training with dressage enables you to become your horse's physical therapist, so you can loosen, strengthen, unlock, unblock, supple, rebalance, and teach your friend to carry himself.

If all this doesn't entice you, consider the fact that proper physical training can prolong your horse's useful years. Most of the world's top dressage horses peak in their teens when many other competitive types are getting ready to retire.

You'll also discover the joys of learning from, and communicating

1.3

A pretty picture in harness! Amy Foss and Special Effects show the result of their ridden dressage work. This pair is featured in many of the technical photos in this book. Photo: Reflections of Killington.

with, your partner. Horsepeople often say, "I wish my horse could talk so he could tell me what's wrong." Well, horses do talk. We just need to learn how to listen to what they're saying—that is, we need to learn how to interpret their body language and behavior. Dressage training creates a mutual awareness that improves performance in whatever is your chosen discipline.

Beginning at the End

Before we get started with the specifics of training, let's examine the ultimate aim which, for me, is the development of a happy, athletic horse. I'm convinced that dressage provides the system and technique to do just that for horses of all ages, shapes, sizes, and abilities.

The proof of this for me was that when I started teaching, I began to see all different types of horses, from many diverse backgrounds, change right before my eyes. Tense horses became relaxed. Stiff horses became more supple. Tight horses started taking longer, looser strides and swinging through their backs.

What fun! I was inspired and thus began my new mission. My goal during lessons and now with these two books is to give riders in all disciplines the tools they needed to develop happy and athletic horses. I want them to understand and appreciate their horse's uniqueness while bringing out the personal best in each.

Cross-training with dressage can show you how to build the self-esteem of the shy horse and make him feel as if he can do anything. It can help the lazy horse discover that going forward is fun. It encourages the tense horse to put his trust in his rider and learn to relax, nurses the timid fellow along until he becomes more confident and brave, and even transforms the rogue into an agreeable, cooperative sort.

I have found that to reach this goal, training needs to follow three golden rules: Clarity, Consistency, and Kindness. These form the basis of the philosophy you'll find permeating these two books. Occasionally, force or domineering styles of training will produce competent athletes, but I'd be willing to bet that these approaches rarely create happy horses that have joyful partnerships with their riders.

1.4
Robin Merrill's cutting horse shows the self-carriage that enables him to do his job keenly and effortlessly. Photo: David Stoecklein, courtesy of the American Paint Horse Association.

CLARITY

When I first started teaching lessons and clinics, I found that there was a distinct advantage to my left-brained, list-making learning style. Since I had needed to break things down into a step-by-step process for myself, I was able to do the same thing for others.

I discovered that many riders were confused about the "how to" of things. As a result, their horses often struggled to understand what they wanted. Signals for movements seemed to be chosen by "multiple

1.5

Scott McCutcheon's sliding stop is a testament to one of the goals of dressage—maximum power controlled by minimum signals. Photo: courtesy of the American Paint Horse Association.

choice" and responses were, inevitably, haphazard.

I found out just how vague riders were because I'd ask them questions like, "How do you ask for a transition to the canter?" They'd reply, "Well...." and then there would be a long pause. Or they'd say, "Sometimes I'll do this and sometimes I'll try that." No wonder it took so long to train—there was no clarity or consistency in the language between horse and rider. In response I started to use "recipe riding" to teach: if you blend this with this and then add a pinch of that, you'll get a certain result! I wanted my students to understand cause and effect before they tried to get creative.

I discovered that with my formulas I was able to make things clear enough to riders that they could follow through with a program after I had left. This was important to me if the clinics were going to have any value. I thought it was fairly useless to stand in the middle of the ring and say, "Now use your left leg" or "Slow down there." That might help for the moment, but would not leave a rider understanding why or when to do anything when she was on her own.

I tried to get the point across that training questions shouldn't have multiple choice answers. One signal means one, and only one, thing. When you want to ask for something else, you must have a completely different cue. With this kind of clarity, you can eliminate a lot of confusion, and training can progress more smoothly.

You start by teaching the young or unschooled horse basic "words" like "go," " stop," "turn left," "turn right." Then, you develop his vocabulary one word at a time. Eventually he has an extensive understanding of a nonverbal language that allows you to communicate through subtle variations of signals.

CONSISTENCY

If communicating can be so straightforward and clear, you might wonder why it takes one rider three times as long as another equally able rider to train her animal. It often boils down to *consistency*. It's important to understand that every second you're on your horse you're either *training* or *untraining* him.

For example, if one day you insist that your horse walk energetically under his own steam without any urging from you, and then the next day you start using alternate leg aids to keep him going, you're being inconsistent. Or, let's say you've decided to train your horse to slow down when you brace your back; you do your homework diligently while in the ring, and he's really starting to understand what it means when you "still" your seat. But then you head off on a trail ride and find yourself pulling on the reins to slow him down instead of using your back. This is the kind of inconsistency that *untrains* him.

KINDNESS

The signals that you use to communicate with your horse are called "aids", and that's exactly how I'd like you to think of them. You'll communicate with your horse by *aiding* or *helping* him to understand rather than regarding your signals as rigid commands.

To explain what the aids mean, you'll need to use the basic principles of behavior modification. This is a method that can be used to train any animal most efficiently. When you shape behavior, you give a stimulus—the aid—which the animal will respond to with either a correct or an incorrect response. You must reward the correct response or "punish" the incorrect one.

Since you presumably want the correct behavior to be repeated, reward this response. You can do this in any number of ways—patting, verbally praising with a "Good Boy!" or "Good Girl!", or taking a short break by walking on a long rein. My system emphasizes training with reward because I believe that this is the way to nurture a happy and cooperative partnership.

In order to change the incorrect response, you "punish" your horse. I must stress, however, that the word "punish" does not imply severity in any way. Punishment can be as mild as

1.6

Cross-training with dressage builds the well-developed, muscular hindquarters that allow this endurance horse to do his work easily and athletically. Photo: Nancy Loving, DVM.

simply repeating an exercise or perhaps as strong as a few taps with the whip, but it should never be harsh or abusive.

It's important to keep in mind that when you're teaching a new behavior you must reward every slight effort your horse makes toward doing it right, or else you'll discourage him. *Absence of reward* is the same as punishment: it will take him much longer to understand what you want if you skimp on the praise.

Robert Dover, a four-time Olympian in dressage, says, "Remain patient, reward your horse's every effort, and every day look for harmony and joy in your ride. If you do, you will be rewarded by his becoming ever more beautiful."

Obviously I'm really sold on the advantages of classical training. But you don't need to take my word for it. In the next two chapters I'll report on how some experts and amateurs from other riding disciplines have discovered that cross-training with dressage can give them the edge they need to achieve peak performance.

KEY POINTS

- No matter what type of riding you do, there is a place for dressage in your program.

- Dressage can help your horse become relaxed, obedient, fun to ride, more athletic, and it can prolong his useful life.

- To develop a happy, athletic horse, training should be *clear, consistent,* and *kind.*

CHAPTER TWO

Just What the Doctor Ordered

I n this chapter, you'll have a chance to see one of the many uses of dressage: as physical and emotional therapy for horses in every riding discipline. As you read the following stories, you'll discover that cross-training with dressage can help any horse become stronger, more comfortable, and more athletic, as well as calm, confident, and secure. I'm hoping you'll be able to recognize the inevitable similarities between your horse's needs and the ensuing accounts of how experts—both professionals and amateurs—in many different fields have discovered the benefits of dressage as therapy.

Physical Therapy

Several years ago a student brought her combined training horse to me for some lessons. This horse had a chronic sore back, and his rider was at a loss as to how to make him better. She had explored several different avenues—injecting his back, massage, therapeutic pads, and different saddles. Everything helped a little, but she was determined to get him one hundred percent pain-free.

She knew that all of the "solutions" she had tried were merely "bandaids." If she was going to make him totally comfortable, she'd have to stop treating the symptoms and pay closer attention to the cause.

I looked at his physique and guessed that his weak and underdeveloped back muscles were the source of his problem. Strengthening these muscles became our objective. To do this, we worked him with his hindquarters coming well under his body and his head and neck placed very long and low. Initially, we kept him in that "deep" position (which I more thoroughly explain in Book Two) for the entire session. All of his school figures, transitions, and movements were done in this **frame.**

2.1

The "ugly duckling" becomes a "swan." Judi Whipple's Homer proudly shows off his strong, muscular body—the end product of cross-training with dressage as physical therapy.

(Note that Homer's noseband has slipped too low—it should never interfere with a horse's air passage.)

While "deep," his back was raised rather than dropped and hollow, so the right muscles developed. Within a couple of months, his back was so much stronger that he was able to do his work easily.

The physical therapy was a temporary measure. Eventually his rider was able to ride him "deep" for just his warm-up and cool-down. The rest of his work was done in a frame appropriate for the work he was doing in competition.

A SWAN EMERGES

If you really need to be convinced that dressage is great physical therapy, you need to meet Judi Whipple and Homer (photo 2.1). Judi's first love was dressage but she was horseless until a kindly neighbor gave her his pet. The first time I saw Homer, I groaned (inwardly) for Judi. What a project! This nine-year-old Appaloosa had no paces. He crawled in the walk, shuffled in the trot and was so unbalanced in the canter that he couldn't make it around one large circle without breaking to the trot or cross-cantering. Plus, he was very weak behind, had no desire to go forward, and all these problems were complicated by his quick temper.

But, Judi was up to the challenge. She worked her "dressage magic," and within a relatively short period of time, Homer was transformed. I still shake my head in wonder every time I see him. This "90 pound weakling" blossomed into "The Incredible Hulk!" His body is muscular and strong and he is willingly schooling some fairly advanced dressage movements. He goes sideways easily and his extensions are developing. But the most amazing thing is to see this horse–who couldn't even canter–now doing a balanced counter-canter and starting flying changes.

The Collection Connection

The next few stories illustrate how, by first **connecting** your horse–also known as putting him "**on the bit**" and later **collecting** him–that is, asking him to carry himself by shifting his center of gravity more toward his hind legs–you can help him become more of an athlete. Although I don't get into the actual aids and exercises to produce these two important qualities until Book Two, I want to introduce them to you and discuss them a little here to give you an inkling of what they can do for your horse.

Learning to connect your horse is desirable because it makes your horse more physically comfortable (and more comfortable for you to sit on!), as well as better able to do many of the things you'll want to do with him. Plus, connection is a prerequisite if you want to go on to the ultimate athletic goal of collecting your horse.

Collection, or **self-carriage**, is the icing on the cake. Not only does it allow you to prolong the useful life of your horse by transferring some of his weight off his front legs, but it also makes him more maneuverable, athletic, and easier to ride.

Before I get ahead of myself with this talk about *collection*, let's first take a look at what my experts had to say about *connection*. I found out that although the semantics might vary, the need to *connect* your horse is a constant throughout all the disciplines.

WHAT'S THE CONNECTION?

Think of connection as the concept of the horse's back being the "bridge" between his hind legs and his front legs. The horse's power, his "engine," is in the hindquarters. You need to connect him over his back so that the energy can travel from the hind legs, over the back, through his neck, into the rider's hands, and then be recycled back to the hind legs.

We dressage riders call this connection phenomenon "**on the bit**." You might also hear connection being described as "**throughness**," "**roundness**," "packaged," "over the back," "round outline, shape, or **frame**," or "moving from the hind legs into the hands." These are phrases that sometimes create a lot of confusion. (To add to the mix-up, we also have all sorts of ways to describe a horse who isn't connected such as "disconnected," "hollow," "in two parts," "dropping his back", or "off the bit.")

2.2

Compare the frame (outline or silhouette) of my horse, Eastwood (also known as Woody) in these two photos. In this photo, Woody is not connected. His hind legs are lazy, his back is low and hollow, his neck is high, and he is pulling against my hand.

2.3

Here, Woody is connected and his frame is "round." His hind legs step well under his body, his back just behind the saddle looks raised and convex, his neck is long and arched, and he is seeking a comfortable contact with my hands.

Basically, a horse's **frame,** (which is the outline or silhouette of his body) is described as **round** when his hind legs step well under his body so that his back is raised and looks convex rather than dropped and concave, his neck is long and arched, and he stretches toward the contact. The top of his body resembles the curve of a bow when it is tightly strung (photos 2.2 and 2.3).

2.4

Davina Whiteman riding Peter Esq., a champion lightweight working hunter in England, clearly shows the desirable "bridge," or "connection," over his back. Notice how the area right behind the saddle looks round and convex, rather than dropped and concave. The energy coming from his hindquarters can flow unimpeded over his back, through his neck, and into her hands to produce the beautiful shape to his body that we see here. Photo: Pleasure Prints.

Davina Whiteman is the Chairman of the Ponies Association in the United Kingdom and is one of Britain's top authorities in the field of showing horses and ponies (photo 2.4). Ms. Whiteman was a student of dressage master Egon von Neindorff, one of three recipients of the German Cross for achievements in horsemanship. Her classical background is evident in that her main interest is to develop her animals to fulfill their potential through correct, systematic training and muscle development.

She discusses the importance of that bridge or connection over the horse's back regardless of the horse's showing discipline. Ms. Whiteman explains that she considers basic dressage training essential in developing the natural balance of horse and rider in every discipline. Schooling horses on the bit promotes "the formation of the skeletal muscles, particularly those of the longissimus in the back and the infraspinatus in the neck from which the outline or shape gradually begins to form."

All the experts I consulted strive to build a better equine athlete (and all riders should do the same). It's a fact that "use makes the muscle" and the horse that's connected or on the bit will develop a rounded, muscular, and therefore, beautiful "topline." The horse that carries himself with a stiff, hollow back and an upside-down neck will develop the muscles under the neck and the "bottomline." At best, this can lead to the horse moving with choppy, short strides that are uncomfortable for both horse and rider. At worst, the horse's back becomes weak and eventually painful.

Master horseman Ray Hunt from Idaho describes his goal of working connected horses by proclaiming to his students, "I don't know why you have a bridle on that horse if it isn't to try to bring the life in the body up from the hindquarters, through the back and mouth, to the feet." He believes in the importance of "shaping up" a horse's back, neck, and poll through the use of mind, seat, legs, and hands before ever calling for any specific movement (photo 2.5).

Three-time World Champion endurance rider Becky Hart (photo 2.6) says that "as far as I'm concerned, all endurance horses need to learn to go on the bit, round their backs, and to move in a round frame. This makes any horse move better."

2.6

Three-time World Champion endurance rider Becky Hart teaches all her horses to work "off their hind ends" and "round" their backs so that they move more efficiently. Photo: Terry Grand.

This frame is a particular challenge for Becky's horses, who are predominantly Arabians that tend to carry themselves with their backs hollow and their heads up. She teaches them to work off their hind ends and round their backs so that they learn to use their hindquarters to push themselves up hills. If they use their shoulders to pull themselves uphill, they get very tired. If they don't have their hind legs underneath them for support when going downhill, they pound their front legs and feet a lot harder. So Becky feels that working on the bit is vital not only from an efficiency standpoint, but it helps prevent the many front end lamenesses associated with the endurance horse.

COLLECTION: THE ULTIMATE GOAL

As I said earlier, collection is the icing on the cake. Only when a horse is in self-carriage is he able to dance. As Sally Swift, in her wonderful book *Centered Riding* said, "When the horse has self-carriage, with each stride he reaches the hind leg well under his belly, giving the body increased support, thus lightening the whole forehand and lending liveliness and gaiety to his appearance and movements."

The difficulty in achieving self-carriage is that by nature a horse's center of gravity is more towards his front legs. But when a rider starts to collect a horse, she shifts his center of gravity more toward the hindquarters. The horse does this through **engagement**–bending and flexing the joints of the hind legs. This flexing and closing of the joints causes the hindquarters to lower and a corresponding elevation and lightening of weight on the forehand. When the horse is correctly collected, you'll notice that a comparison of the relative height of the horse's withers to the croup shows that the withers look higher.

Collection helps the endurance horse to lighten his forehand so there are fewer front-end injuries caused by pounding along the miles; it helps the jumper to turn handily and to rock back on his hocks so he can propel himself over fences; it enables the dressage horse to become more beautiful and expressive in his movement; and lets the pleasure horse carry himself so that the contact with the rider's hand is light and pleasant.

This last benefit reminds me of a rider I met at one of my teaching clinics. This girl was obviously not a dressage rider so I asked her why she was there. She explained that her horse was so heavy on the forehand that riding him made her arms and back sore. He really wasn't much of a pleasure to take out on a ride. So we discussed the idea of self-carriage as a long-range goal. And, in order to reach it, we decided on exercises and short term goals that would head her horse on that path.

She left the clinic armed with exercises to help her balance her horse and with full knowledge that it would take time to develop the strength of his hindquarters. Since the horse wasn't used to carrying weight behind, the muscles would have to be built up very gradually. She needed to understand that to demand immediate results would be like expecting herself to do five hundred deep knee bends while carrying one hundred and fifty pounds on her back. By the time she reached seventy five (or even twenty five!), her muscles would be screaming, and she'd be unable to do even one more.

I saw this girl and her horse a year later. She had done her homework, and her horse had been transformed. Through her diligence and patience, her partner was now light in her hands and truly fun to ride.

I'll explain the technique to produce collection in detail in Book Two. But for the moment, I'd like to share some more responses from experts in fields other than dressage when I asked them if connection and self-carriage had any relevance to their discipline. The answer from all was an unqualified yes, and here's what they had to say.

2.7

Rob Byers uses classical techniques to teach his Saddlebred champions to drive off their hocks and free up their shoulders. Here, we see his World and National Five-gaited Champion Face Card clearly showing power and athletic ability. Photo: Linda Quillen Wollaber.

Rob Byers from Kentucky has trained many World and National Three- and Five-gaited Saddlebred champions (photo 2.7). Rob is aware that the innately high head carriage of the Saddlebred can lead to in-correct collection and overflexion. So he's careful to teach connection first by encouraging his horses to seek the contact with a lower head and neck. He does want his horses "up" in the bridle, but only after correct connection has been achieved. He talks about wanting his gaited horses to move fluidly forward in a regular rhythm. And eventually, his goal is "to encourage that animal to drive off his hocks and as a result free up the shoulders." The higher head carriage should be the result of the engagement of the hindquarters.

Once upon a time, Dennis Reis earned his living on the Professional Rodeo Cowboys Association circuit. Dennis was a cowboy who trained horses for a living and discovered he had been doing dressage without knowing it. As his ability to communicate with his animals evolved and his talent was noticed by his neighbors, who were mostly dressage riders, he found himself in the unusual position of being asked to reschool upper-level dressage horses who were brought to him with specific problems. The dressage riders sought him out even though he had no classical training himself.

When asked about collection, Dennis is quick to point out that it's not just a "head-set." "Collection isn't conforming to a preconceived notion of a frame or a picture of what it should look like. It's not a reduction in speed or a shortening of frame. It's a posture that generates deep inside the body. The horse is round, balanced, engaged, off the forehand, and his back and neck are turned off—not braced." In dressage terms, when the horse's back and neck is "turned off," the energy that originates in the hindquarters can flow to the forehand without meeting any stiffness or restriction caused by the sustained contraction of the back muscles.

Dennis is enthusiastic about the joys of riding a horse who is in self-carriage. "The movements are fluid and elastic, transitions are flowing and soft, the horse is light and easy to guide and willingly yields his body to the rider."

Regardless of the breed and the specific challenges that go with different types of horses, the experts agree that self-carriage is a worthwhile goal if only because it can prolong the horse's useful life by reducing wear on his forelegs.

Lynn Palm Pittion-Rossillon is a four-time winner of the American Quarter Horse Association "World Champion Superhorse" title—the highest achievement possible in the performance portion of the Quarter Horse industry. She realizes that her Quarter Horses are built with their balance more to the forehand than other breeds. But this type of conformation doesn't preclude her striving for collection. She constantly asks the forehand to come up higher, not with gadgets or harsh bits, but by riding with her seat and leg up to her hand. She feels that a good "circle" routine helps to promote self-carriage.

On the other side of the ocean, Davina Whiteman's show horses aren't built with their balance as much to the forehand as Lynn's Quarter Horses. However, their naturally long strides make it difficult for them to shift their weight onto the hindquarters, so it's a challenge to collect them. Ms. Whiteman finds classical dressage exercises "really helpful as they encourage the engagement of the inside hind leg and the horse to 'sit down behind'."

Tennessee Walking Horse trainer Diane Sept explains why she incorporates dressage into her work and about the importance of self-carriage (photos 2.8). She explains that many Walkers are sickle-hocked and therefore, give the impression of stepping under the body with the hind legs. However, this "stepping under" can be merely an optical illusion, and the horse is not really working from behind, rounding his body, and carrying himself.

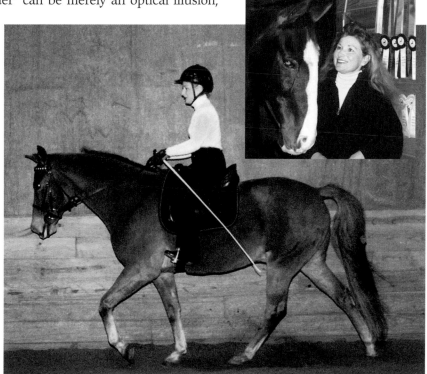

"Because our primary pace is the walk—both the flat-footed walk and the running walk (an extension of the flat-footed walk)—our horses tend to get ground-laden and heavy. Most people who ride Walkers don't trot their horses, and I suppose I'm a bit unorthodox, but I do. I find that by schooling my horses at the trot much as a dressage rider would, I'm able to teach them about suspension and to make them more athletic. Using trot work as a gymnastic exercise greatly improves the walk."

She goes on to say, "I want all my horses to be in self-carriage. Ideally, a Walker should be able to halt from the running walk and hold his position in balance without hanging on the rider. A running walk done in balance and self-carriage is the most glorious blending of strength and smoothness."

Both in teaching and in training, show jumping Olympian, Anne Kursinski does it all (see photo 3.2). In order to make her mounts straight, responsive, and more supple with the end result of being better able to "sit down behind," she incorporates all of the traditional collecting exercises such as shoulder-in, haunches-in, half-pass, and counter-canter, as well as lengthening and shortening in all different combinations. (I'll describe all of these exercises in detail in later chapters and in Book Two.) Because of this work, Anne says, "In between fences on course, my horses are quite responsive. I can make adjustments in pace and balance with a minimum amount of effort so they can fully concentrate on the fences."

2.8 a and b

In a mid-winter session, Tennessee Walking Horse trainer Diane Sept schools Strike Gold with classical training techniques. Inset: Diane, with Diamond Chips T. Photos: Nicole R. Hamilton.

Emotional Therapy

I could go on and on with stories about how dressage is useful for every horse physically. I've seen horses with one weak hind leg develop strength and become even behind, and I've seen horses who just wouldn't turn become handy and maneuverable. But, I don't want to ignore the emotional benefits of dressage for horses. Not only can it turn an insecure, dangerous animal into a calm and confident partner, as you'll see in the story of Eli that follows, but it can add to your horse's fun by giving him a base from which he can enjoy a wide variety of activities.

A ROGUE TURNED PARAGON

The greatest example of what dressage can do for a horse's brain is illustrated by the story of Sue and Eli. The first time I saw Eli he was six years old and standing on his hind legs. According to the man who was riding him, he was a rogue who had temper tantrums and rearing was part of his repertoire. I found out he had been sent up and down the East Coast. At each new home the rider became discouraged and he'd be shuffled off cheaply to another barn.

Sue went to see him because the price was right and she was struck by the fact that he was attractive and had three good paces. She felt she might be able to overcome his bad habits. When the curious asked her about her new horse, she would laughingly call him her "reclaimer."

The first four months were a delicate balance between gently but firmly explaining to Eli that he wasn't going to get his way while not pushing him to the point of a "mental meltdown" by keeping his beginning work very basic and simple. She made a huge effort to be very consistent and build a language between them one word at a time. Every slightly cooperative effort on his part was lavishly rewarded.

When Sue first asked me to help her with basic dressage, it was easy for me to tell from the ground when Eli was on the verge of one of his fits because I would see his eye roll around. This was not the sort of horse you'd want to challenge head on since he was used to fighting for his life. I suggested that Sue always work him a little below his pressure threshold; I wanted to keep him happy and Sue safe.

Over the course of those first four months, I watched Eli slowly change. He began to trust Sue. He knew he could count on her being absolutely consistent in her behavior: her aids were always given in the same way; he was always rewarded for trying and there were no surprises.

Within the year a wonderful partnership was born. Eli's eye always remained calm and confident. He had learned to trust Sue so much that if she pressured him, he took it and responded positively. As their relationship strengthened, Sue was able to go beyond the basic work very quickly. And the proof of Eli's emerging self-assurance was that at his first dressage competition not only did he behave like a paragon, but he also was the high score champion.

Here was a lovely animal that in someone else's hands would most likely have become increasingly dangerous to the point of having to be destroyed. But he found his niche, and under Sue's guidance he was able to fulfill his potential.

VARIETY IS THE SPICE OF LIFE

Ted Zajac from Bedford, Pennsylvania, (see photo 1.2) believes that a horse who is allowed to do lots of different activities is simply a happier animal. His horses do barrel racing, Western pleasure, saddle seat and hunter hack classes; they drive, jump, and trail ride; and they compete in dressage. They do it all and love the variety. He insists that a strong classical background enables him to produce such versatile animals. He doesn't drill his horses and as a result they don't get bored.

Dr. Zajac fancies horses of color; he's particularly partial to the Appaloosa because he feels it's one breed that is able to excel at doing a lot of jobs. But he's quick to add that any horse can do a good job if he's ridden consistently and given time to develop. He advises riders to evaluate each individual's strengths and weaknesses and make training a positive and pleasant experience.

He explains, "Dressage is just a good foundation for anything you want to do. The horse who does barrels has to be able to extend the canter and come back quietly and sensibly just like the dressage horse. It's really not so different. You're just doing it in different clothing." Zajac's champion mare Faith In Plaudit is living proof of his words. She can go out and compete at the Grand Prix level in dressage at one show and at another run "Barrels" and "Poles" and win.

My neighbor, Jan Floyd from Randolph Center, Vermont, also does it all (photo 2.9). She enjoys driving her horses as well as riding and jumping them in an English, Western or sidesaddle. When asked about her preference, she pauses and says, "I don't know. I love them all. If I had to pick just one, it would be very hard to choose." In fact, they're really very similar because a basic goal of each is a horse that's well-balanced, carries himself and is responsive.

Jan credits her versatility to a solid background in classical principles. Doris Eddy, her first instructor and major influence, based all of her training in dressage. Jan remembers with a chuckle, "Doris wanted me to learn to have a feeling, breathing contact with the horse's mouth. She'd always tell me to feel the horse at the end of the rein and ask him

2.9

Here, we see versatile Jan Floyd enjoying one of her many equestrian pursuits — riding sidesaddle on UVM Trophy. Photo: Paul Quinn.

to move up to the bit rather than pull him into a frame. At age eleven, I thought 'feeling the horse at the end of the rein' meant I was supposed to feel these little telegraph messages in my hands."

She believes that in any type of riding, you can cross-train with dressage to "strengthen and increase the agility of the weaker side in your quest for equality and strength of both sides. Balance, lightness, and total agility come when the front, back, and both sides are as nearly equally developed as possible."

Jan adds, "I've never owned a horse, but I've never been without one. Because of my classical background, I've been able to accept any horse that was offered to me regardless of his speciality."

The Horse as Therapist

Elsie Rodney's Orcland Supreme Echo, winner of the Single Horse Carriage Driving title at the Morgan Grand National, is a real jack of all trades (photo 2.10). In his lengthy career, Echo has shown saddle seat, hunter pleasure, Western pleasure, carriage driving, and dressage. He loves being a teacher and at age sixteen he still does twenty to thirty lessons a week as well as being a popular therapist in a handicapped riding program.

Elsie bases her training on classical dressage principles and has no doubt that this is why Echo is sound and going strong today. She believes that a straight horse that moves in a round frame with an engaged hind end (the hind legs coming well under the body) and a low head will go many more miles and be able to do a lot more than a horse that is "strung out." If a horse is strung out and crooked, with one side of the body working harder than the other, he can't be comfortable or happy.

Her primary incentive for schooling Echo in a "dressage frame" was keeping him sound and strong. Elsie explains that, "Echo has a long stride, and he likes to sprawl out. Plus, he has lazy stifles. If he doesn't use his hind end properly, he'll go lame. Every step he takes when he's not 'in frame' loosens the stifles. When he's pushing from behind with a

2.10

Elsie Rodney's Orland Supreme Echo showing his winning form. Because his muscles are loose and relaxed, the power generated by his active hind legs can flow unimpeded through his body. Photo: Bob Moseder.

full, complete step every stride, he's working those ligaments one hundred percent and getting stronger. Echo has gone a lot of miles, including competing in Three-Day Combined Driving Events at the Preliminary Level at Myopia Hunt Club in Massachusetts and at the United States Equestrian Team Headquarters in Gladstone, New Jersey. And I know he wouldn't have been sound enough if I hadn't schooled him classically."

What a great endorsement for dressage. Keep your horse sound and strong and prolong his useful life.

Echo is also a favorite in a handicapped riding program. You may be wondering how Echo's specialized dressage training can make him so useful as a "therapist." Debby Sabin of Lovelane Special Needs Horseback Riding Program in Weston, Massachusetts explains about her program and how Echo's contributes to it.

Many of the children and young adults have neurological problems such as cerebral palsy, stroke or head injuries. Because of messages coming from the brain, they have abnormal motor patterns. Debby explains that when a horse walks, the movement felt through the person's hips is almost identical to the human gait and provides the feeling of normal walking. This can inhibit abnormal patterns and give the child the feeling of normal movement which he can later try to mimic. It's important to feel what a normal gait is like before you can successfully try to assimilate it. Even if the children will never be able to walk, they'll be able to work on skills like head and trunk control, balance reactions, increasing strength, and normalizing muscle tone. This allows them to become more functional in daily life.

In Debby's words, "Echo is an athlete. Because of his balance, regularity of pace, and impulsion, he can replicate a feeling of normal walking to the rider. This cannot be done with older, stiffer horses who have uneven paces. Plus, his advanced education in lateral movements is particularly useful for stroke patients who can't put weight on one side of their bodies. Doing a leg-yield or shoulder-in while on the long lines helps to get them more symmetrical as the rider is encouraged to try to put more weight on the involved side."

"Echo is such a star. He has all the energy he needs in the show ring, but when the kids get on, he's very gentle and placid. All of Elsie's horses are like that. She has another Morgan that can really challenge an experienced rider, but knows it's his job to take care of these kids."

KEY POINTS

- Although not every horse can become a dressage specialist, every horse can benefit from dressage training.

- Cross-training with dressage increases communication and establishes a foundation from which a horse can excel in any other discipline.

- Dressage can help you improve a horse's physical problems, such as stiffness, soreness, and unathletic movement, as well as mental problems such as tension, disobedience and inattentiveness.

CHAPTER THREE

The Secret to Success

In the last chapter, you had a chance to hear how riders in many different disciplines have discovered the benefits of cross-training as therapy for their own horses. These people found out that by incorporating classical training into their systems, they could improve both their horses' physical and emotional well-being.

Now, let's have a look at how the experts cross-train with dressage in order to excel in their specialty.

If you think about it, it's pretty amazing that Dennis Reis, the cowboy; Rob Byers, saddlebred trainer; Anne Kursinski, champion show jumper; Lynn Palm Pittion-Rossillon, Quarter Horse trainer; Becky Hart, endurance rider; and Heike Bean, carriage driver all have similar training methods.

After all, these people train diverse breeds with very dissimilar conformation and temperaments to do totally different jobs. To see them in competition with their very distinctive clothing and tack, you'd never guess how much they have in common.

If you look beyond the obvious differences, however, you'll find that they all speak the same language. As a group they talk about the joy of communicating kindly with their equine partners. They train patiently and methodically to produce better balanced, supple, and obedient athletes. Although their terminology, attire and training environments are as varied as the experts' riding disciplines, they all credit cross-training with dressage as a major factor in their enormous successes.

There was a time when I thought that I couldn't possibly have anything in common with a rider wearing a cowboy hat and fringed chaps or satin and sequins. But then, I did some extensive research. I interviewed lots of highly successful trainers from many different fields of riding and discovered that they were all in agreement about two things. They all use basic dressage principles in their training and they're quick to credit much of their success to the strong foundation provided by it.

In what follows you'll see that these very successful trainers strive for obedience and harmony. They all ride their horses forward and straight as dictated by the principles of classical dressage. They recognize that to develop the animal as an athlete, their horses first must be connected so there is a bridge between the power of the hind legs and the front legs. Once connection is established, they improve balance and self-carriage through collection. And, above all, these experts abhor shortcuts and quick-fixes that are detrimental to both the mental and physical well-being of their animals.

Obedience

Every one of the experts I talked to mentioned dressage in the same breath with obedience. An obedient horse makes for a ridable horse. Take Robert Oliver. He's one of the United Kingdom's top producers of show horses. He trains and shows hunters, hacks, cobs and riding horses. Mr. Oliver stresses the importance of obedience. He says his mounts have to perform in a ring with anywhere from ten to thirty other horses, and they must be able to concentrate. Since his animals must be controllable in this electric setting, he places a heavy emphasis on dressage in his schooling. Through dressage he's able to develop a clear, nonverbal language with his horses, so that there's a constant yet quiet conversation going on. It is this communication and understanding between horse and rider that allows Oliver's show horses to focus on him fully despite all the activity and distractions of a competitive setting.

Rob Byers, another trainer of show horses in a completely different part of the world, will tell you with a chuckle that he's reluctant to watch riders at a dressage show for any length of time. He says that he's good for about two rides, but then it's time to get a Coke! However, he's the first to admit to the advantages of incorporating classical dressage into his training repertoire. He echoes Robert Oliver's sentiments. "Our horses are a 'Go forward, hot-blooded' show breed. We want power and speed when we show, and our horses often get very aggressive. It can get very exciting when twenty or thirty horses are charging around a ring flat out. So it's vital to have the horse responsive and adjustable. For example, you might need to take back in order to negotiate a turn. Or, if you're coming up on a group of horses, you can take back to turn across the ring and find an open spot."

Among her many accomplishments, Kelli McMullen Temple was a member of the Canadian Three-Day-Event team for the 1996 Olympics

3.1
Kelli McMullen Temple brings her dressage expertise to the cross-country phase of a combined training event. Her horse is keen, attentive, straight between her legs, and even in the reins. Photo: Christine Tchir.

in Atlanta (photo 3.1). She trains three-day event horses—equine all-around athletes, who must show their expertise in three different areas. The competition begins with the dressage test, showing the horse's obedience and suppleness. Next, comes the endurance phase where the horse is asked to go cross-country for many miles, jumping solid obstacles along the way. The final phase is show jumping, which is designed to test whether or not the horse can still perform over a technical jumping course after the extreme efforts of the endurance phase.

Kelli's combined training horses are imported from England and Ireland exclusively. She prefers these horses because they're bred specifically as sport horses by crossing thoroughbreds with quieter breeds such as Irish Draft or Cleveland Bays. With their greater physical substance and more tractable temperaments, she feels they're better able to stand up to the rigors of three-day eventing.

When I asked Kelli about the role of dressage in her training program, she stressed its importance not only as an end in itself but also as a means to an end. She said, "Of course, dressage helps me to do a good test during the first phase of competition. It enables me to develop obedience and the resulting ridability in these very fit horses. Many people feel that because event horses have to be so highly conditioned to do the jumping phases of a three-day event, they can't do a good dressage test. I believe that's a fallacy. In fact, I use dressage to teach my very fit horses how to relax. Dressage has enabled me to turn hot temperaments around because my horses know how to respond to the aids in a relaxed manner.

"But I'd like to add that the exact same schooling that allows me to influence and communicate with my horses in a dressage arena helps in the jumping phases as well. For instance, my horses are attentive and able to respond to me regardless of whether they're on a cross-country or show jumping course or performing in front of a big crowd.

"We event riders have to be extremely accurate on cross-country courses at a very fast speed. The same rules that apply in a dressage arena are used out on course. We need to keep the horses straight, between our legs, and even in the reins. It's essential to get an immediate response to an aid when you go to balance or collect so your horse can answer the jumping questions that are asked."

Harmony

In its description of the object of dressage, the American Horse Shows Association rule book says that "the horse gives the impression of doing of his own accord what is required of him. Confident and attentive, he submits generously to the control of his rider...."

That sounds very much like international and Olympic rider Anne Kursinski's training philosophy (photo 3.2). Ever watch her negotiate a course of fences? Absolute poetry in motion. In Anne's words, "My belief is to become one with the horse—like a pair of figure skaters working together, rather than against each other."

Anne believes in the benefits of dressage to build a better athlete. "It's somewhat like going to the gym or an aerobics class. When horses carry themselves, they feel better, stronger, look better, and are more of a pleasure to ride.

"As in dressage, a jumper must be able to extend and collect as well as turn left and right with a minimum of effort. Generally smoother is more efficient. I see my job as basic dressage and the jumps just happen to be in the way!"

But in the quest of two living beings functioning as one, the benefits of dressage extend toward the rider as well. Anne credits her dressage background with teaching her a lot about the mechanics of equine movement and how the rider can influence it. "Flatwork teaches students

Anne Kursinski and Eros, at the 1996 Olympic Games in Atlanta, showing the kind of harmony and "oneness" that Anne is known for. Photo: Mary Phelps.

to feel the entire horse. The exercises teach them to influence the horse front, back and laterally."

And, although master horseman, "horse whisperer" Ray Hunt from Idaho might not be found on any Grand Prix jumper courses, when this leathery-faced, blue-eyed cowboy sits on a horse, he's connected to that animal with the same kind of oneness that Anne feels (see photo 2.5). This Western rider successfully accomplishes every dressage rider's goal of physically and mentally merging two separate beings into one. He's connected to his horse and says his horse's feet become his feet. He describes this harmony succinctly by saying, "My horse's body is my body."

While practicing her skills on her own, polo player Pam Gleason discovers the serenity of oneness while hitting a white ball across a beautiful green field on a summer's evening. What a joy "to become one with the animal—to have the human brain direct the power and strength of a magnificent animal, to take for ourselves the ability to move and to run and dance like a horse. The pinnacle of horsemanship comes when horse and rider merge to think and act as one. There's nothing like the thrill of the moment when everything clicks, and the horse responds to your thoughts rather than your aids, and you have become, in effect, a single being."

Forward and Straight

There are two cornerstones of dressage—forward and straight. These qualities serve as a guide not only for dressage riders but also as the foundation for correct riding in every discipline. "Forward" means simply that the horse covers ground with energetic and free strides. "Straight" means more than the word implies: the straight horse's body corresponds to the line he's traveling on: straight when the line is straight, and *bent* when following the curves of corners, circles and the like.

All of the experts talked about forward and straight as being the basis for their work. Champion Quarter Horse trainer Lynn Palm Pittion-Rossillon says, "Before I ever teach a horse to slow down, I teach him about forward motion—to move on (see photos 3.5). By teaching forward motion, you build impulsion, which is necessary for collected movement." Lynn knows that forward motion is a vital ingredient for all the jobs her versatile horses are required to do, from reining spins to jumping fences to going through water while trail riding.

Pam Gleason, a trainer of polo ponies, echoes Lynn's sentiments. "I want my ponies to be very responsive and go forward from the lightest of leg aids."

Not only must Pam's polo ponies be forward, but as with all correct training, they must also be straight. Part of this means that they must remain straight on lines. And like many of us, Pam has been challenged with wiggly horses who have difficulty keeping their shoulders directly in front of their hindquarters.

But another aspect of straightness is the ability to bend equally in both directions. Pam has run into problems with many ex-racehorses who've only learned to gallop on one lead–the direction of the race course. This one-sidedness is complicated by the fact that although polo players want their horses to be equally comfortable on both leads, the riders themselves prefer the right lead, because most of the shots are made from that side. To encourage both horse and rider to become more ambidextrous, she incorporates the same type of work on circles that I use with my dressage horses.

World Champion endurance rider Becky Hart (see photo 2.6) also incorporates lots of bending and suppling exercises when she schools her horses. She points out that they not only need to travel on straight lines on the trail but also to bend around trees. For Becky, it's a matter of safety and comfort so she can get around what she calls those "knee-knockers."

Dennis Reis is the founder of Universal Horsemanship in Penngrove, California (photo 3.3). Dennis started his school with the understanding that the skills and techniques used by the best classical dressage rider, reiner, cutter, rancher, and backyard rider are the same. His techniques are based on understanding the true nature of the horse and communicating with that nature. His objective is to replace fear and confusion with confidence and understanding.

Dennis says,"I just can't overemphasize the importance of teaching your horse to go forward. Perhaps it would be better if I said 'the importance of fostering the natural forward urge in your horse' because your horse can't even back up properly unless that forward urge is there."

He uses a variety of dressage bending exercises to make his horses straight, supple, and strong, while laying a foundation for the right posture for spins and rollbacks. As you watch him, you might think this cowboy is warming up for a dressage test of moderate difficulty as he

3.3
Dennis Reis' horse demonstrates a fluid and soft leg-yield. His mount is light, easy to guide, and willingly responds to Dennis' request to move sideways. Photo: John Carlson

3.4

Heike Bean's pair reflect the results of a kind, systematic method of schooling. They are the picture of relaxation, suppleness, and harmony. Photo: Ronni Nienstedt.

works his mounts on circles and leg-yields, in extension and collection, as well as in all the classical lateral exercises such as shoulder-in, haunches-in, and half-pass.

You'll find Rob Byers doing a lot of bending work with his Saddlebreds on long lines. Rob feels this bending work is crucial in developing the horse's ability to be equally flexible in both directions. He'll ask his horses to bend, circle, leg-yield and do shoulder-in while always making sure that they have forward momentum and are seeking contact with the bridle.

Patience

It's the dressage trainer's creed that training be thought of in months and years rather than days and weeks. If there's one thing the experts are passionate about, it's that shortcuts are ruinous to both the physical and emotional well-being of their animals. As Ray Hunt says, "The way to make fast progress is slowly; and to those who have practiced, everything will be given—a gift."

Heike Bean, author of *Carriage Driving: A Logical Approach Through Dressage Training,* firmly believes that a systematic, progressive method of schooling is the only way to develop a relaxed, supple, responsive, and happy animal (photo 3.4). In Ms. Bean's words, "The horse would handle so much better if the dressage training were better. Plus he would be happy and relaxed in his work. All I care about is making my horses happy. And this is a reasonable goal for horses trained with basic dressage principles. If they're not happy, there has to be a good reason such as unsoundness, ill-fitting equipment, or lack of strength."

She laments, however, that very few people are willing to take the time to train classically. Many young driving horses are still put into harsh, unjointed "bar" bits. They are rushed along on an unreasonable timetable before they've even had a chance to develop the strength to easily move the vehicles.

She admits that maybe in the past the unjointed bit was a necessity. Back in the days when we relied on horses as a means of transportation, the better-trained animals were used for riding. The rest, many not so well trained, were used for driving. And sometimes harsh bits were necessary simply to control these driving horses because no one had taken the time to train them properly.

However, Ms. Bean feels strongly that tradition is not a good enough reason to continue using this bit. This is particularly true since nowadays we use horses predominantly for pleasure and sport rather than for transportation. She says, "The young horse schooled in a bar bit will not learn to give softly in the mouth. You can't get a lateral response in the jaw because the bar bit works in curb action, affecting the whole mouth at once. It's impossible for the horse to give on only one side of his mouth, and the jaw is tense. If the jaw is tense, nothing works. The result is a cranky, stiff animal who might look collected but is in total tension."

Lynn Palm Pittion-Rossillon is as passionate about the shortcut issue as Heike Bean. She is frustrated by riders trying to accomplish in six months or a year what should take years to train and develop. This immediate-gratification approach leads to the use of harsh devices or hand riding to get the desired "head-set." These techniques might seem effective, but she cautions riders that results are only for the short term.

3.5

The epitome of a true partnership—Lynn Palm Pittion-Rossillon and a bridleless Rugged Lark, wowing the crowd at one of their demonstrations. Photo: Mike Rastelli.

The same horse and rider competing in a trail class at the World Quarter Horse Show.

By taking shortcuts and focusing primarily on the "head-set," you create a horse who can't balance himself correctly. Specifically, the balance is on the forehand rather than on the hindquarters where it should be. A vicious cycle ensues: because the balance is incorrect, the rider resorts to abusive methods and force. She sadly cites examples of harsh spurs, severe bits, and gadgets to force the horse's head down.

"You might build a short term horse for competition, but these shortcuts lead to incorrect movement. When a horse is on the forehand, it's impossible for him to have the correct rhythm and cadence in his paces. Plus, use of force and harsh devices takes the expression and happiness out of the performance." There's that word "happy" again.

According to Diane Sept, her Tennessee Walkers are the ultimate pleasure horses (see photo 2.9). She says, "They have heavenly dispositions. By nature they're mild mannered and docile, and I wouldn't want to ride anything else on the trail."

However, Diane also competes her Walkers and she takes it as a compliment when she overhears her critics complain, "She's a good trainer and will get your horses into the blue ribbons...but it'll take her two years instead of two months."

That's just fine by Diane because those "two-month wonders" don't last long!

Athleticism

If you still need proof that dressage is a means to an end and not an end in itself, let's go back to Lynn Palm Pitition-Rossillon and her famous Quarter Horse, Rugged Lark, as they "wow" the crowd at the United States Dressage Federation's National Dressage Symposium in Orlando, Florida. Dressed in cowboy hat and chaps, using a Western saddle and curb bit, Lynn skillfully guides her partner through an exhibition as demanding and varied as any upper-level dressage test. Rugged Lark flows sideways in half-passes, clocks off flying changes, and pirouettes in response to invisible signals from a quiet and balanced rider (photos 3.5).

Then to show what real training is all about, Lynn becomes a quick-change artist. She removes her chaps to uncover English breeches and exchanges her cowboy hat for a hunt cap. Not to be upstaged, Rugged Lark does his own version of the quick change act. Not only is his Western saddle replaced by an English one, but his bridle is removed and not replaced at all. Lynn then rides her bridleless horse through a fabulous display of canter pirouettes, flying changes in a sequence, and collection and extension of the paces. And for good measure, they handily jump some fences.

3.6
Randy Konyot's jumper Entree, didn't think it was a big deal to switch careers at age twelve to become an upper-level dressage horse. After all, he had been "doing dressage" all his life as part of his basic education. Photo: J.S. Buck.

Joyfully communicating with your horse is what training is all about, and Lynn proves unequivocally that dressage is the foundation for any style of performance. According to Lynn, "Dressage is simply the training of the horse according to his anatomy and natural instincts and habits." A sound philosophy for any discipline. She also adds that, "Dressage is a discipline that, above all, requires a rider to have correct position, balance, and precise use of aids. This is what the art of riding is all about."

With renowned dressage trainer Alex Konyot for a father, it's inevitable that son Randy, who trains and shows jumpers, gives all his mounts a good solid base in dressage (photo 3.6).

So, it wasn't a big deal for Entree, a twelve-year-old Dutch Warmblood gelding who had been trained as a jumper since age three, to switch careers at midlife and specialize in dressage. It wasn't difficult because all the basics were already part of his education.

Part of the Konyot charm—on horses as well as people—is that training is always made to seem more like play than work. Let me give you an example. When I went to visit Randy at his winter base in Del Ray, Florida, it was one of those sultry ninety-five degree days. It was really much too oppressive to go out and work in the blistering heat. So, Randy's solution was simple—barn riding. Wearing jeans and sneakers, he hopped aboard Entree in the stable. He stood on the spot where he had tacked him up, and with a mischievous gleam in his eye said, "Watch this!" He gave some kind of verbal cue that was vaguely similar to a sound I'd make if I were stung by a bee. Entree confidently responded by doing a beautifully balanced levade, which is a movement where the horse sits on his hind legs and rears up with his forelegs.

Then he proceeded to do half-passes while walking back and forth across the barn aisle. Once his horse was "warmed up," he gave a demonstration of piaffe and passage that was worthy of any Grand Prix dressage test.

Not only did Entree think that all of this was fine and dandy, but he also took it in stride when Randy dismounted, told him to "Stay" and walked off. He stood like a rock until he heard Randy's voice behind him saying, "Entree, come." Entree bent his neck around one hundred and eighty degrees until he could see Randy behind him. Then he turned slowly and obediently walked up to him.

So, the consensus is in and the experts agree. No matter what riding discipline you prefer, cross-training using dressage techniques can help your horse become a willing partner and an able athlete. But, before I get started with the horse's actual primary education (what I call *Dressage 101*), I'd like to spend some time explaining how to longe your horse and how to improve your riding skills: in Chapter Four I'll discuss the purpose and basic technique of longeing, and in Chapter Five I'll look at you as the rider—the development of your seat and the right attitude towards training.

KEY POINTS

🐎 Many champions in other disciplines have discovered this secret—cross-training with dressage gives them the competitive edge.

🐎 The common threads that are woven through the fabric of all successful training systems include:

🐎 Obedience

🐎 Harmony

🐎 Rhythm

🐎 Forward and Straight

🐎 Patience

🐎 Athleticism

CHAPTER FOUR

Longeing—Riding from the Ground

To longe or not to longe? As with most training questions, there are different schools of thought as to whether the advantages of training on the longe outweigh the disadvantages of wear and tear on the horse's body. I agree that trotting endlessly around on small circles can be tough on legs and joints. However, I do think that longeing my horses for short periods (fifteen minutes or so) can be very useful for a variety of reasons that I'll get into shortly.

Think of longeing as riding from the ground. I longe a young horse to get some basic rules established. I teach him the simple voice commands like slow, whoa, walk, trot, and canter, which I'll also use when I start riding. I explain that the reins (the longe line) mean stop and that the driving aids (the whip) mean go forward. He becomes attentive and tunes into me for all his instructions—not only voice commands but also subtle changes in my body position and the way I use the longe whip. When it's finally time for mounted work, we have a way to communicate.

The horse experiences **contact**—the connection from the rider's hand to his mouth that will happen when being ridden—as he stretches into the side reins (reins that attach from the girth to the bit) and seeks contact with a long neck and a lowered head. Seeking the contact forward and down toward the ground will help him to come into a "round" frame (I introduced the word "round" on page 14)—a very desirable shape to work in to develop his muscles correctly (figs. 4.1 and 4.2).

He also discovers his balance on circles and develops regularity in his gaits without the burden of a rider. For example, let me tell you about Basil. Basil was a big-moving, young horse who managed just fine in walk and trot. When it was time to canter, however, pandemonium broke loose. Because he was gawky and unbalanced when his rider, Leslie, would ask for a depart, he'd leap forward, leaving his hind legs way out behind his body and just go faster and faster.

4.1

Don't be fooled by the arched shape of this horse's neck. It might look correct, but he's avoiding taking a contact with the side reins. If he does this when being longed in side reins, he'll most likely also avoid a contact with the reins when being ridden.

4.2

Because he's being sent more forward, this horse is now starting to stretch into and seek the contact forward and down towards the ground. Note how nicely his hind leg steps under his body. As a result his back is very round, his neck is long, and he takes a definite contact with the side reins. Ideally, his head should be positioned a bit more towards the inside of the circle.

We helped Basil learn to balance himself in the canter by first letting him canter on the largest circle possible while on the longe, without the additional burden of a rider. To set him up for the canter depart, Leslie drew him onto a slightly smaller circle. Next she pushed him back out to the larger circle by pointing the whip toward the girth, while she gave the voice command..."Aaannd canter!" Reducing the size of the circle improved his balance (something he was losing when asked to canter under saddle) while enlarging the circle during the transition ensured that he stayed bent to the inside and increased the likelihood of cantering on the correct lead. With the aid of comfortably adjusted side reins and no interference from a desperate rider, he soon learned how to balance himself.

There are a number of situations where longeing is just plain useful. You can longe a horse for fifteen or twenty minutes to keep him exercised when you're unable to ride or he can't wear a saddle for some reason. The stiff or tight horse often benefits from ten minutes of longeing prior to mounted work. Longeing allows him to loosen, stretch, and warm up before the added weight of the rider on his back. And, because I have a keen sense of self-preservation, I'll longe a fresh horse for a few minutes so he can get the bucks out of his system. Besides the fact that it's not going to do my aging body any good to be bucked off, I never want him to realize that he is, in fact, capable of depositing me in the dirt! Discretion is certainly the better part of valor.

4.3

To prevent the reins from hanging down, twist one rein around the other and feed the throatlatch of the bridle through one of the loops before you fasten it.

Equipment

I'm assuming that your horse is not an unbroken youngster and has already been under saddle. Prepare him for his longeing session by first tacking him up with a bridle and a saddle. Remove the bridle's reins or tie them up out of the way by twisting one rein around the other and feeding the throatlatch through one of the loops. Tie up the stirrups by winding the leathers around them and feeding the free end of the leather through the loop (figs. 4.3 to 4.5).

4.4

Place the longeing cavesson on your horse's head and secure the noseband first. The cavesson should fit snugly so it doesn't shift and rub your horse's eye.

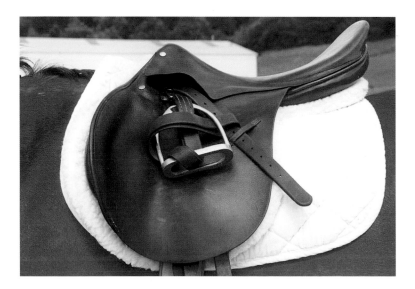

4.5

Tie the stirrups up out of the way so they don't bang against your horse's sides.

Basic equipment for longeing includes a longeing cavesson, two side reins, a longe line and a whip. It's important for the cavesson to fit securely so it doesn't move around and perhaps rub against his eye. Place the cavesson on his head and secure the noseband first. Then fasten the cavesson's throatlatch. A halter is a poor substitute for a cavesson, but if you opt to use one over the bridle, be sure to adjust it very snugly so it doesn't twist or slide around and rub your horse's outside eye. Never attach your longe line to the bit because it could hurt the bars of your horse's mouth.

I also recommend using gloves because it can be pretty painful to have a fresh horse pull a nylon or web longe line through your hands. Without gloves, rope burn might force you to let go so that your horse ends up running around with a thirty-foot longe line trailing along behind him. If that happens, he might panic and bolt or perhaps get himself tangled up in the line. At best, he'll scare himself, and at worst, he could be badly hurt.

I also like to put boots or bandages on my horse's legs to protect them from damage if they hit each other.

Both the longe line and the longe whip should be long—at least thirty feet long for the line and a minimum of twelve feet, including the lash, for the whip. The line should be long enough so that your horse can make a fairly large circle, yet not so long that you can't influence him with your body, voice and whip. The circle you should make with most horses is twenty meters in diameter (approximately sixty feet).

Hold the longe line in your leading hand (that is the left hand if the horse is tracking to the left), with the slack layered back and forth across the palm of your hand. Never wind the slack around your hand, because it can be dangerous if your horse decides to take off (fig. 4.6).

Hold the longe whip in the other hand. Ideally, the whip needs to be long enough for you to stand in the center of your circle and, if necessary, reach the horse's barrel with the lash. I've been known to put "extenders" like shoe laces on the end of whips to make the lash longer. You see, in order for a circle to be a good gymnastic shape in terms of teaching the horse something about balance, it must be round. You may say, "well a circle is always round," but it's nearly impossible to make a round circle if you're walking along with the horse because your whip is too short. You need to be able to stand almost still in one spot and just pivot around your leading leg. For example, when your horse is circling to the left, you pivot around your left leg, which remains in the same spot. Stand with your feet apart and your knees slightly bent so that you can absorb any sudden movement.

Side reins, which attach from the girth to the rings of the bit above the reins, can be made of all leather, leather and elastic, or with a round rubber doughnut insert. I personally prefer all leather because some horses feel the "give" in the elastic and test the contact by pulling or snatching at the reins. I don't want them to learn how to do this on the longe because I certainly don't want them doing it when I ride. The side reins with the rubber doughnut are a good compromise because they provide some give without being too "stretchy."

When I'm ready to use the side reins, I'll attach them to the back billet strap on the saddle. I don't place them around both billets or around the entire girth because I don't want them to slip down too low. As far as the height of the side reins is concerned, a good rule of thumb is that they should be placed at the height of the rider's knee (fig. 4.7).

However, I always lead the horse away from and back to the stable with the side reins unhooked. I do this prior to work because the horse's body is

4.6
Safety first. Layer the excess longe line back and forth across your hand. Never wind it around your hand or let it drag on the ground where you could get it wrapped around your foot.

4.7

Place the side reins around the back billet to prevent them from slipping down too low on the girth.

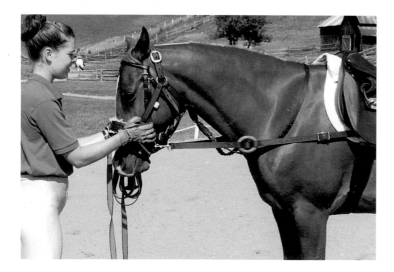

4.8

Make sure that the side reins are the same length. They should be short enough to establish a light contact with your horse's mouth but long enough so that he doesn't feel confined.

stiff and cold from standing in the stall. I don't want him suddenly to feel restricted or surprised by the side reins while walking out of the barn, because he could run backward or rear and hurt himself seriously. I unhook them after work as a reward.

When I'm in the arena ready to work, I attach the side reins loosely. I adjust them long enough so the horse doesn't feel stifled, restricted, or crammed into a frame, but short enough so that there is a light contact with his mouth and so that his outside shoulder doesn't pop out of the line of the circle (fig. 4.8).

I almost always keep the two side reins the same length. Some people like to have the inside side rein a couple of inches shorter because they believe this helps the horse bend to the inside of the circle. The danger here is that the hindquarters might swing to the outside of the circle in order to avoid the increased bend caused by the shorter inside side rein. If you discover that your horse's tendency is to escape to the outside with his hindquarters, it's best to keep the side reins the same length.

Both the shoulder popping out and the haunches swinging out mean that the horse is crooked. His entire body needs to overlap the line of the circle in order for him to be straight (fig. 4.9). We'll delve more into **straightness** in Chapter Six.

Stand in the center of the circle pivoting around your leading leg. Stand across from the saddle so there is a triangle formed by the horse's body, the longe line, and the whip (fig. 4.10). Then you can adjust the horse's speed by the position of your body as well as by the use of the longe whip and longe line. To ask him to slow down, stay equidistant from his body but step laterally more toward the front of his body and give

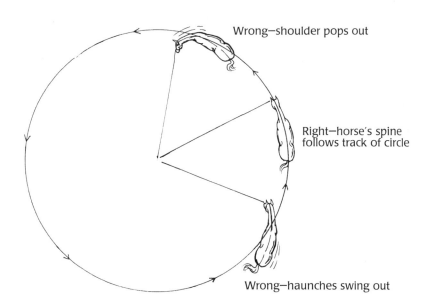

Wrong—shoulder pops out

Right—horse's spine follows track of circle

Wrong—haunches swing out

4.9

Unless the entire body of the horse overlaps the line, or arc, of the circle, the horse is crooked. Here, the horse is first swinging his haunches out, then going straight before his haunches fall in and his shoulders pop out.

4.10

The "triangle of control" formed by the horse's body, the longe line, and the longe whip.

Moving backward sends horse forward

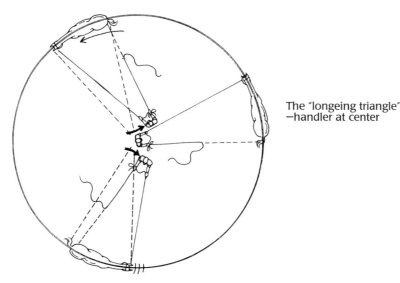

The "longeing triangle" —handler at center

Moving forward to slow horse down

4.11

You can adjust your horse's speed by making minor adjustments in the position of your body. Here, if you step to the left, you can slow him down. If you step to the right, you can send him more forward.

some little tugs on the longe line. To speed him up, stay the same distance away from the horse but step laterally toward the back of his body and raise the whip more toward the hindquarters (fig. 4.11).

Always combine these signals with a voice command so you can develop your horse's knowledge of your vocabulary. Your tone of voice is very important here. For instance, a soothing, quiet tone is appropriate as you say, "Slow" or "Whoa." While you'll want to be more animated as you ask for an upward transition or for more energy as you say something like, "Trot On."

Once he understands basic signals, you can begin to put his body in the desired round, connected frame by combining the aids in the same way that you do when you ride. In other words, at the same moment that you push him forward with the whip, take and give on the longe several times. Then be quiet for a few strides and see if he stretches into the contact. If not, repeat the taking and giving while sending him forward. Be sure to praise him each time you see him even begin to think about stretching toward the contact and becoming rounder in his frame.

Safe is fun. So use your work on the longe to establish obedience to your spoken aids. I remember watching dressage team rider Shelly Francis starting numerous babies on the longe. They knew when she said "Whoa!," they were to stop on a dime. There was no room for discussion. She would say it once, and if she didn't get an immediate response, they'd get several sharp tugs on the longe line. Before she ever set her foot in the stirrups, Shelly was confident from her groundwork that she'd have instant immobility when she said the word "Whoa!"

On the other hand, there are some horses that aren't forward thinkers. They'd rather stop, buck, rear, or wheel around than go forward. Three-day event and dressage trainer Deb Dean-Smith who is featured in many of the photographs in this book, was training a young stallion who would not go forward when under saddle. So she put him on the longe and laid down the "forward rules" over again while she was safely on the ground. She'd cluck once softly, and if the stallion didn't react immediately, she'd tap him with the whip. She was teaching him to *choose* to go forward. When he was attentive to the cluck and willing to go forward, Deb praised him with her voice. If he was at all "nappy" when she clucked, she used the whip. He soon decided that going forward was more fun than getting tapped by the whip. Then, if he started thinking backward while she was riding him, all Deb had to do was cluck once, and his automatic, conditioned response was to go forward.

Longeing is an important part of your horse's education. Done correctly, it's a very useful addition to the training and exercising of your horse. Done incorrectly, it can do more harm than good. I've only given you a brief account here in order to get you started on the right track. For those of you who want to delve deeper into longeing technique, you'll find clear, in-depth explanations in good books like Alois Podhajsky's, *The Complete Training of Horse and Rider* and Jennie Loriston-Clarke's *Lungeing And Long-Reining.*

In the next chapter, I'll discuss your position and your attitude toward riding and training.

KEY POINTS

🐎 Think of longeing as riding and training from the ground. The same guidelines that are used under saddle—moving forward in rhythm, straightness, contact, balance, communication, and obedience—apply on the longe as well.

🐎 Keep longeing sessions brief.

🐎 Basic equipment includes:

  🐎 HORSE
   Longeing cavesson
   Side reins
   Boots or bandages

  🐎 RIDER
   Gloves
   Longe whip
   Longe line

CHAPTER FIVE

Let's Get Personal

Before you begin to do dressage, either for cross-training or as an end in itself, you should take a moment to evaluate yourself as a rider. You need the physical skills that enable you to give commands from an independent seat that is balanced, not only over your center of gravity, but over the horse's center as well. The center of gravity of the horse and the rider is located between the diaphragm and the pelvis. An independent seat means that you can give an aid, or use one part of your body, without causing unwanted motion elsewhere in your body (fig. 5.1).

You'll also need to understand and appreciate your own disposition as well as the nature and character of your partner. This is important because it will enable you to adapt your approach to training to your personality as well as your horse's temperament. For instance, the program for a hot-tempered rider with a flighty horse will be vastly different from the one with the same rider and a phlegmatic horse. And that program will also need to be modified for a passive rider on a lazy horse.

So first we'll discuss your position, and then we'll do an attitude check.

Your Position

THE IMPORTANCE OF A GOOD SEAT

Picture this. Two riders are getting ready to ask for the canter from the trot. Rider A sits in balance with her feet and legs under her center of gravity, her legs resting quietly on her horse's barrel in a "ready" position. In addition, her center of gravity is directly over that of her horse. Rider B leans behind the motion of the horse, with her legs banging noisily on his sides. Because her center of gravity is behind that of the horse, she sits heavily on his back and hangs onto the reins for balance.

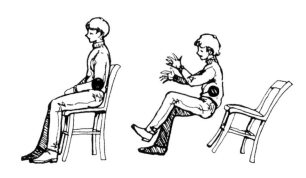

a) *Sitting in balance with feet under your center of gravity*

b) *Person in balance even when stool is removed*

c) *Sitting out of balance with feet ahead of your center of gravity*

d) *Person out of balance falls backward when chair is removed*

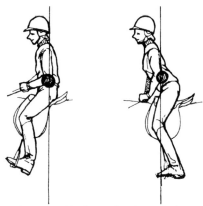

e) *Rider in balance, feet under her center of gravity—dressage seat*

f) *Rider in balance, feet under her center of gravity—jumping seat*

g) *Rider out of balance backward, feet ahead of her center of gravity*

h) *Rider out of balance forward, feet behind her center of gravity*

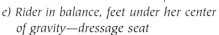

5.1 In order to sit in balance, your feet need to be under your center of gravity.

Both riders give the same signal for the canter depart. Rider A's horse obediently steps off into a comfortable canter. Rider B's horse feels those furiously flying legs and just trots off faster. The more he runs, the more his rider loses her balance, until eventually they are so out of sync that Rider B has to stop (if she can) to get reorganized.

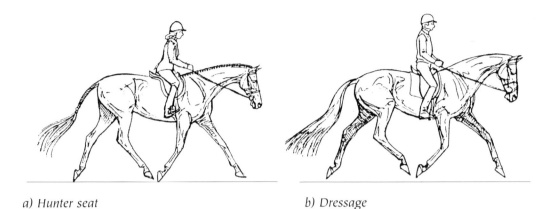

a) Hunter seat

b) Dressage

c) Saddle seat

d) Western

5.2 *Balanced seat positions*

Both riders gave the same aid to canter. Why did rider A succeed and rider B end up with jostled kidneys? A good seat. All other things being equal, the rider with the balanced, independent seat will be more effective in communicating her wishes to her horse. Giving signals from a poor or out-of-control position is a wasted effort. You need to sit correctly in order to be effective with your aids. (Which rider were you, by the way?)

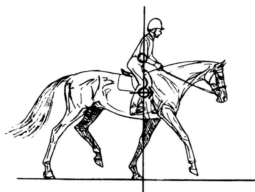

a) Posting with the motion

b) Posting behind the motion

c) Posting ahead of the motion

d) Falling behind the motion

e) Falling ahead of the motion

5.3

In addition to being balanced over your own center, you need to be balanced over your horse's center as well in order to give effective aids and move in harmony with him.

A balanced seat looks different in the various riding disciplines. The dressage, Western, and saddle seat riders, have long stirrups and sit with their shoulders, hips and heels in a plumb line. Because hunter seat, jumper, and combined training riders use shorter stirrups for jumping, they need to sit with the upper body more forward in order to be in balance. In all cases, however, the riders' shoulders are over their feet. So, good balance for you means balance for the particular type of riding you do. The one common requirement for effective riding in all disciplines, however, is having a balanced, independent seat (figs 5.2 and 5.3).

Let's look at how that can be accomplished.

DEVELOPING YOUR POSITION ON THE LONGE

As I explained earlier, an independent seat means that you can use one part of your body without affecting any other part. For example, you can use your right leg without jerking on your right rein. Or you can gently close your right hand without pulling backwards on the rein. Or you can find your balance without hanging on your horse's mouth.

And, since you can't purchase it in a tack store, you might ask how you go about acquiring one of these very desirable independent seats. One of the best ways I know of is for you to be longed on your horse. Now, I know the idea of giving up control of your animal to someone on the ground might not be your method of choice. But look at it this way. You actually get a break from having to control and guide your horse around while arguing with your uncooperative body at the same time. Make it your "quality time"—a golden opportunity to focus totally on yourself and your riding for a while.

The first thing you need is a suitable mount. If your horse is the type that gets hysterical when the tractor starts or takes advantage of you as soon as he feels you coming slightly unglued, it's probably a wise idea to borrow a quiet, generous horse. Find one with comfortable paces who'll go around and around without speeding up or slowing down and won't object to your gyrations.

Limit sessions to fifteen to twenty minutes because all that circling can be tiring for your horse. And, be sure to change direction halfway through.

Tack him up with a saddle, bridle, longeing cavesson, and side reins (see Chapter Four). Twist the bridle's reins around each other and feed the throatlatch through them so they are out of the way (see photo 4.3 on page 43). Yes, you're going to be riding without reins! Contrary to popular belief, the reins are not your lifelines. You're going to have to learn how to balance yourself without hanging on them.

Adjust the side reins so they are short enough to prevent your horse's shoulder from popping out. The side reins will also help keep him in a

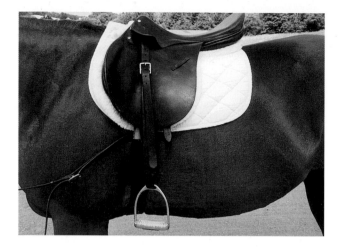

5.4

To prepare the saddle so that you can do exercises on the longe without stirrups, first pull the buckle on the stirrup leather down a bit so you don't get a bruise on your leg.

5.5

Then cross the stirrups in front of the saddle.

rounder frame so his back will be easier to sit on when you trot and canter.

I like to do two kinds of exercises on the longe. The first is designed to develop an independent seat: you move one part of your body while paying close attention that the rest of your body stays still and in the correct position. The second kind of exercise gives you practice sitting perfectly during transitions—both transitions from one pace to another as well as lengthenings and shortenings within the same pace.

EXERCISES TO DEVELOP AN INDEPENDENT SEAT

Keep in mind that you want to make slow, deliberate movements while maintaining control of the parts of your body not directly involved in the exercise.

All these exercises start at the walk. Let the person doing the longeing be responsible for keeping the horse going and making any adjustments. You concentrate solely on yourself.

1. Remove the stirrups from the saddle or cross them over the front of the saddle (figs. 5.4 and 5.5). Place your legs underneath you in correct riding position with your shoulders, hips and feet in a plumb line with a low heel. Place your arms in riding position with your elbows bent at your sides and your hands softly closed around imaginary reins. Now slowly circle your head a few times to the right and then a few times to the left (figs. 5.6 to 5.9). Do a body check. Did your hands stay steady? Did your legs rest quietly on your horse's sides? Did your upper body remain upright?

2. Arm circles: make slow, big circles with your arms. Always circle backwards so you open your chest. Alternate one arm and then the other, controlling the arm throughout the entire arc of the circle (figs. 5.10 to 5.12). While doing so, run through your checklist to see if the rest of your body stays quiet and controlled.

5.6

Start circling your head by letting your ear drop down toward one shoulder as Carole Ann Cahill (Pinky) is doing here. Note: the horse is being allowed to carry his head too low.

5.7

Continue circling your head slowly until your chin is pointed towards the sky. Do a position check. In this photo there's some tension in the rider's lower back. Also, her lower leg has slipped a bit forward. Her toe should stay directly under her knee.

5.8

As Pinky continues to circle her head, her back is more relaxed and her lower leg is back in a better position.

5.9

Her back remains relaxed, but her lower leg is slipping forward ever so slightly.

5.6 to 5.9 Head Circling

5.10

Circle one arm at a time while the other arm stays in riding position. Always circle backwards to open your chest and encourage your shoulders to stay down and back.

5.12

Her leg is better here, but there's tension in her outside shoulder. It is apparent because her outside hand is raised.

5.11

Here, Pinky has drawn her leg up slightly. She needs to keep it long and relaxed.

5.13 and 5.14 Shoulder Rolls

5.13

*Drop the fingers of one hand loosely behind your leg.
As you circle each shoulder, think "Up, Back, Down".*

5.14

*Pinky's upper body looks good here, but her lower leg has
moved slightly forward.*

3. Shoulder rolls: rotate each shoulder up, back and down in the same
   circling action that you did with your arms (figs. 5.13 and 5.14).
4. Waist twists: place both arms straight out to the sides and slowly
   twist your torso left and right. Keep your hips square and your legs
   still (figs. 5.15 to 5.17).
5. Windmills: stretch both arms straight up over your head, then
   lower them until they are straight out to the side. Then return to
   riding position as if holding the reins (figs. 5.18 to 5.20).
6. Scissors: stretch one leg straight forward and one straight back.
   Point your toes and lock your knees. Then very slowly alternate the
   position of your legs as if they were a pair of scissors. Keep your
   hips and torso square (figs. 5.21 to 5.23).

5.15

Starting position for the waist twist. Shoulder, hip, and heel in a straight line. Arms level and out to the side with palms facing down. In this photo and the next I would prefer the horse's head to be higher when being longed.

5.16

Twist from the waist and follow your back arm with your eyes.

5.17

Slowly twist in the other direction. Here Pinky's back arm has dropped slightly. Also her left toe is turned out showing that she's looking for balance by gripping with the back of her calf.

5.18 to 5.20 Windmills

5.18

Stretch both arms straight up over your head with palms facing each other. Keep your elbows beside your ears.

5.19

Slowly lower both arms straight out to the side.

5.20

Put your hands back in riding position. Her upper body looks good, but her lower leg has moved a little too far back.

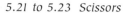

5.21 to 5.23 Scissors

5.21

Straighten your legs and point your toes like a ballet dancer. When your left leg is forward, your right leg is back.

5.22

Very slowly change the position of your legs. Make sure your hips and shoulders stay square.

5.23

If you feel your body twisting, hold on to the front of the saddle with your outside hand to steady yourself.

5.24

Sit squarely and symmetrically with equal weight on both seatbones.

5.24 to 5.25 Legs Away

5.25

Keep your legs in riding position but lift them away from the saddle so you're balanced on your seat bones.

7. Legs away: put your legs in riding position, then lift your legs off the saddle from your hips so that you're balanced on your seat bones. Be sure not to lean back or round your shoulders (figs. 5.24 and 5.25).

Once you're feeling pretty secure about the exercises, try them in trot and canter. Gulp!

5.26

If you feel like you're losing your balance during any of the exercises, hold on to the front of the saddle until you feel secure again. If the particular exercise you're doing gives you a choice, pull yourself close to the saddle with your outside hand. This will make it easier to sit with your inside shoulder back so that it is parallel with your horse's shoulder as he circles.

If you momentarily lose your balance, hold onto the front of the saddle and pull yourself down into it until you feel secure again. Then put your hands back in riding position and carry on (fig. 5.26).

MAINTAINING BALANCE DURING TRANSITIONS

Now that we've looked at exercises that will help you develop an independent seat, let's look at the second type of exercise I like to do on the longe: sitting quietly and in perfect balance while the horse is asked to do transitions. Practice transitions from one pace to another as well as lengthenings and shortenings within a pace. Ask the person longeing you for feedback during these transitions. Do your hands stay steady? Do your legs remain softly in contact with your horse's sides? Does your body stay centered or do you lean backward, forward, or sideways?

Transitions on the longe line will teach you to "go with" your horse rather than getting ahead of him or being left behind. You'll be developing some muscle memory for sitting quietly and elegantly, and then you can conjure up that feeling again when you're back in control.

DEVELOPING YOUR POSITION OFF THE LONGE

If being longed is not a viable option because you lack a suitable horse or someone to longe you, you can still pick away at your position faults on your own. It takes approximately three weeks to develop a habit. And that goes for a good habit as well as a bad one. So devote some time each day to working on the areas of your body that need attention.

Since I know I can only concentrate fully on one thing at a time, I work on my position during the first ten minutes of my ride as well as each time I give my horse a break during a training session. During those moments I focus totally on correcting my position. I don't concern myself at all with how the horse is going.

Often I do what I call "extremes." I exaggerate the correction for a few seconds at a time. Then I relax for a bit and repeat the exaggerated correction. Eventually, I let my body find the happy medium.

5.27 to 5.29 Extremes

5.27

Open your hip joints and stretch your legs as far back as possible.

5.28

Allow your legs to settle around your horse's barrel in this "too-far-back" position.

Let me explain. I had a very difficult time getting my legs underneath me when I started riding dressage. I rode with my legs too far forward, my heels jammed down, and my toes stuck out. In order to correct this, each day when I first got on I dropped my stirrups and alternately swung each leg as far back as possible from my hips–much too far back for a good position. Then, I let my legs settle around the horse's barrel several inches behind the perpendicular. When I got to the point that my legs wanted to stay too far back, I stopped working on the exercise and just let them settle into the correct position (figs. 5.27 to 5.29).

5.29

Let gravity take over so that your lower leg comes forward until your toe is directly under your knee.

One of my students, Joyce, is now a beautiful rider, but that wasn't always the case. She tried so hard to make her position look picture perfect that the effort made her body stiff and rigid. Joyce needed to go to "extremes" to loosen up. We started by focusing on her wrists. She spent time every day making circles with her wrists to unlock them. I'd even see her walking through the barn developing muscle memory by keeping her hands in riding position while softly bobbling her wrists.

Within a few weeks, it became natural for her to ride with relaxed wrists. We systematically worked on the tight parts of her body in this way until she was eventually able to sit in a gracefully controlled way rather than with tension.

So attack your position challenges one at a time by concentrating on "extremes" for several minutes each day. If you tend to lean too far forward, lean too far back. If your heels are up, push them down as far as you can. If your entire arm is too straight and rigid, bend your elbows and hold them back behind your torso. If you tend to be stiff, sit sloppily and loosely instead. If you hunch over, stretch up and try to make yourself four inches taller than you really are. Remember to hold your "extremes" for just a few seconds and then relax before repeating the exercise. Be creative and play with "extremes" and watch your position improve one piece at a time.

I'd like to mention one other thing at this point about the position of your upper body in the canter. This will be particularly relevant for those of you who want to pursue your dressage education a bit further into the material covered in Book Two.

It's vital that you learn to sit back in the canter. At the basic levels, if you rock your upper body back so that your seat comes forward with every stride, you'll encourage your horse's hind legs to come more under his body. Then later on, when you are working on self-carriage and the elevation of your horse's forehand, you'll need to sit like this so that your upper body doesn't weight his front end excessively.

To understand the correct placement of your upper body, first halt and imagine a plumb line dropping down from your ear. If you're sitting absolutely straight, that plumb line passes through your shoulder, hip, and heel. I want you to think that no matter where your horse is in his canter stride, your shoulders can never come in front of that plumb line. So during one bound of the canter, your upper body can only rock behind the vertical and then up to the vertical. It never comes in front of that plumb line (figs. 5.30 and 5.31).

5.30 and 5.31
Compare the upper body positions of these two riders at the canter. In the first photo my upper body is rocking back behind the vertical and as a result, my seat comes forward. In the second photo, the rider's upper body is coming in front of the vertical and her seat looks like it's pushing her horse's hind legs backward.

Your Attitude Determines Your Altitude

In order to invite your horse to dance with you, it's important to examine your attitude objectively. This includes your attitude toward yourself as well as toward your horse. Since I covered this extensively in my book, *That Winning Feeling! Program Your Mind for Peak Performance*, I'll just touch on some of the major points in this book.

As you analyze your attitude, ask yourself if you fall into that group of riders who beat themselves up everyday. If so, your internal dialogue might sound something like this. "I'm an idiot. When am I ever going to learn how to do this without pulling on my horse's mouth? I'm ruining my horse. I should give him to a professional to ride because he'll never amount to anything with me."

If this sounds like you, you'll need to make some major changes in your self-talk. Denis Waitley, a sports psychologist, says, "It's important for you to realize that the greatest conversation you have every day is the one you have with yourself. So be sure to do it with all due respect."

I know this positive self-talk will be quite a challenge for some of you because we're all raised to be humble. I'm not saying you have to walk around sounding arrogant, but it doesn't hurt to speak highly of yourself to yourself. Since your self-image is always listening to and believing what you say about yourself, all self-criticism is essentially a complete waste of time and counterproductive to training. What good is it going to do to berate yourself with negative comments that only destroy your confidence?

You may not think you see yourself as negative and self-critical. But let's try an experiment and see. For the next twenty-four hours speak to yourself in a positive way only. Keep a note pad handy so you can jot down any self-criticism that slips out, including so-called constructive criticism.

Don't make jokes about yourself such as, "I have a terrible memory. I'd probably forget my head if it weren't attached." The subconscious doesn't have a sense of humor, and if you make fun of yourself, your humorless subconscious mind will simply see what you say as your goal. It's a good idea to ask a friend to keep an eye on you, because chances are you're not even aware of how often you put yourself down. Are you surprised to see how critical you are of yourself?

Okay. You're convinced that sometimes you can be pretty hard on yourself, but you feel embarrassed and self-conscious tooting your own horn. Well, if that's an issue for you, you're just going to have to learn how to lie!

I started lying back in the 1970's when I was showing my crazy Thoroughbred. I used to run around telling everybody who'd listen, "I love to compete!" The truth was, however, that I was actually sick to my stomach. People would ask me if I ever got nervous and I'd proclaim, "No, I never get nervous. In fact, I get a little concerned if I don't have a little extra adrenalin because you need that edge to really do well." (Lie, lie, lie!)

My subconscious didn't know or care that I was lying. It simply did what it could to help validate my statements. And, amazingly, I eventually loved to compete. My new attitude toward competition became as much a part of my life as my old show nerves had been.

BUILDING SELF-ESTEEM IN HORSE AND RIDER

Years ago I remember bringing a very insecure Zapatero, my Olympic candidate, to Robert Dover for training. Robert Dover, World and Olympic Games Bronze medalist in dressage, is one of our country's most successful and illustrious trainers. Robert rode "Z" and immediately felt how sensitive he was. His comment was, "You need to build this horse's self-esteem. You want him to believe that he can do absolutely everything fabulously." (fig. 5.32.)

5.32
You need to build the horse's self-esteem. You want him to believe that he can do absolutely everything fabulously!

This attitude goes for riders as well. Now, I realize that sometimes it's a real challenge to stay confident and poised in the face of screaming instructors who belittle and undermine your efforts. I'm not sure why this has become an accepted method of instruction. I've never known sarcasm and shouting at a student to promote understanding. Yet sometimes this is what we're exposed to in the quest for knowledge.

So be sure to take good care of yourself. Ideally, you should find an instructor who will work with you in an atmosphere of mutual respect. If this is impossible, protect yourself emotionally by not taking the criticism personally. Ignore the rudeness (which is actually a reflection of the teacher not the student) and salvage the information.

Build your self-esteem and your confidence in your abilities. The way to do this is to practice being positive about yourself. Create a mental image of yourself as a patient, capable, brave rider.

If you're obsessing about a potential disaster, visualize the scenario in great detail. But then do some "coping rehearsals" by continuing to play your mental videotape until you see a successful resolution to the situation. Believe that you can handle whatever comes up. Let's look at an example of how this would work.

5.33

Don't panic when you hear the weather forecast. Instead, "see" yourself entering the arena and having the performance of your life!

It's early spring and you're getting ready to take your four-year-old Thoroughbred to his first show. You're really excited all the way up until the time that you hear the weather forecast the day before the show. There's a cold front coming in overnight. The temperature is going to drop twenty-five degrees, the wind will gust up to thirty miles per hour AND your first class is at 7:45 A.M. You think to yourself, "I'm gonna get killed!"

Instead, do "coping rehearsals" several times the night before (fig. 5.33). "See" the scene unfolding in your mind's eye, but be sure it ends on a positive note. You arrive at the showgrounds. The atmosphere is electric. Your horse is very fresh, and his tail is stuck straight up in the air as you head to the warm-up area. He's pretty tight and you feel like you're sitting on a time bomb. He lets out a few bucks, and you see yourself confidently remaining in perfect balance. You're not the least bit unseated by his antics. Your heart rate stays slow and your breathing is deep and regular. After working him for ten minutes, he begins to settle down and becomes attentive and obedient. You see yourself entering the ring and having the performance of your life!

Do you think this is easier said than done? Then start today to re-program your mind so the new, confident you emerges automatically. But you can't use willpower or iron-jawed determination to achieve this, because the part of your mind that really controls your actions is the subconscious, and in a struggle between the conscious and subconscious mind, the subconscious always prevails. So we are going to direct our efforts toward the subconscious.

Here's your assignment. First, on the left side of a piece of paper, write down a list of all the negative things you believe to be true about your riding, but that you'd like to change. For instance, "I get nervous riding in front of others," "I can't sit the trot," "I always lean to the right," or "My horse takes advantage of me by wheeling around when he sees something scary."

Next, on the right side of the paper, write a replacement for each statement. Word your substitute sentences in the present tense as if you already possess the quality you desire. And use a positive rather than a negative statement. Your paper might look something like this:

I get nervous riding.	I am very focused and relaxed when I ride in front of others.
I can't sit the trot.	I sit deeply and in harmony with my horse in the trot.
I always lean to the right.	I always sit centered and in balance.
My horse takes advantage of me by wheeling around when he sees something different.	My horse is confident, obedient, and submissive even when he sees something that scares him.

Once your list is complete, set aside time at least once a day where you can sit quietly and be uninterrupted for fifteen minutes. Close your eyes and take a few deep breaths. With each breath feel yourself floating deeper and deeper into relaxation.

Now visualize a computer screen in your mind's eye. You'll be reprogramming yourself by replacing one negative statement at a time with a new, positive affirmation about yourself and your riding skills. Type in one of your negative statements. See the letters as they appear one by one on the screen. For instance, type in "I am a timid rider." Now look at the words and see yourself pressing the button that says "Delete." As you touch the button, the words vanish forever, not only from the screen, but also from your memory. They are no longer a part of you.

Now you are ready for reprogramming. Type in your replacement statement in capital letters. For instance, "I AM CONFIDENT AND BRAVE." Look at the words, and then see yourself pressing the button marked "Save." These are your new instructions to yourself, and they're now stored in your subconscious mind (fig. 5.34).

5.34

Reprogram your "mental computer". Replace your negative thoughts with positive ones.

YOUR ATTITUDE TOWARD YOUR HORSE

By the way, how's your attitude toward your horse? Are you one of those riders who blames the horse when things go wrong?

For example, recently I worked with a green horse and green rider combination. Both of them were struggling with their own lack of balance so neither one could help the other. The woman hadn't ridden for several years and was out of practice as well as out of shape. The horse was a sensitive four-year-old mare who was just barely learning how to balance herself with a rider's weight on her back. All went well in the walk, but every time she was asked to trot, the mare would hop into the canter. The woman's frustrated comment was, "She keeps doing that to me."

I explained that the horse wasn't doing anything to her. The poor horse couldn't trot in a regular rhythm because the rider didn't have an independent seat. During the posting trot, she was using the reins to pull herself up out of the saddle. Since the mare's rhythm and freedom of movement in the trot were being restricted during every stride, she found it easier to hop into the canter.

Another rider I know was upset because her horse was running in the canter and pulling her arms out of their sockets. I had to explain to her that it takes two to pull—so who's hanging on to whom? It took me some time to convince her that she was compounding his balance problem because she was leaning too far forward and hanging on his mouth. Because his hind legs were so far out behind him, it was impossible for him to balance himself. This horse was simply not in a position to slow down. Despite what his rider thought, he was not being disobedient. It's not that he "wouldn't" but that he "couldn't."

There's also the rider who is looking for the quick fix—the magic formula. You probably know the type. She jumps from instructor to instructor and from clinic to clinic looking for the "key." Sometimes she thinks the "key" might be a special exercise. Sometimes it's a different bit, bigger spurs, or some sort of training gadget. Or perhaps the answer is to longe her horse for an hour until he's so exhausted that he's tractable.

This instant gratification approach to training is unrealistic and always leads to frustration. This rider needs to follow a systematic program and be content with a little bit of progress each day. She'll actually be better off and will enjoy the process a whole lot more by thinking of training in terms of months and years rather than days and weeks.

Most distressing to me is the rider who vents her emotional problems on her horse. Years ago at a clinic I taught a woman who was riding an extremely sensitive ex-racehorse. This mare was very tense and the rider was using this as an excuse to abuse and bully her. I tried to appeal to this rider with logic, saying that since the mare was so nervous to begin with, any strong punishment would only make her worse. To that she replied, "....but it makes me feel better." I have to say it's the one and only time I gave up on a student. My comment was, "Then I can't help you," and I left.

Most riders, on the other hand, fall into the category of true horsemen—the compassionate riders who really love their animals. A good example of the right attitude is the following story about Marcia Kulak, a three-day event rider who is featured on the cover of this book. Marcia had grown up dreaming of one day being able to represent her country in international competition, and she had worked diligently for a lifetime to make her dream a reality.

Just prior to the 1992 Olympics in Barcelona, Marcia and her horse Chagall were short-listed for the United States team. The final selection of the team members was to be made at the Savernake Forest Horse Trials in England. Earlier in the week before the competition, Marcia noticed that Chagall's left front leg was slightly filled. Although he was sound and would have most probably passed the veterinary inspection before competition, she decided to withdraw. She wouldn't let ambition color her judgment when it came to her horse's health. She might have achieved her personal goal of riding in the Olympics, but there was no way she'd even consider doing that if there were a risk that she'd return home without her best friend intact.

We also have my friend, dressage team member Sue Blinks, whose love and concern for the welfare of her horses precedes all else. I've always said if I died and were reincarnated as a horse, I'd want to be in Sue's barn. Sue, like Marcia, is also very competitive, with high goals, and is very protective of her animals. She never lets ego or ambition affect her training decisions.

Sue found her young horse, Flim Flam, in Germany as a three-year-old. Flim is a real talent and as they have progressed through the dressage levels, they often have been seen in the winner's circle with record-breaking high scores. Because of Flim's incredible talent and athleticism, ambitious trainers have often tried to persuade Sue to push his training along at a faster rate.

Despite substantial outside pressure and the lure of gold medals, Sue sticks to her conviction that dressage is a process and takes time. She believes that it's both physically and mentally detrimental to demand more of a horse than he's been prepared for systematically, and she just won't sacrifice her animals. As I'm sure you can imagine, her horses adore her and turn themselves inside out to please her.

5.35

Patient, creative trainers often see schooling as a big jigsaw puzzle. They fill in the blanks one piece at a time.

ATTITUDE TOWARD TRAINING

By the way, how do you stack up as a trainer? Patient, creative trainers often see schooling as a big jigsaw puzzle. They first look on the cover of the puzzle box to see what the final picture should look like. And then they content themselves with filling in the blanks one piece at a time. In the beginning the final picture isn't even recognizable. But piece by piece it begins to take shape (fig. 5.35).

For instance, let's say you get a thoroughbred off the track to reschool as a potential combined training horse. Thoroughbreds are born to gallop and this particular horse is very bold. So the training for the cross-country and stadium jumping phases comes easily to him and progresses relatively smoothly.

His performance in the dressage phase of a combined training event, however, is sadly lacking. Because of his background as a racehorse, his body is tense and his back is stiff. One of the consequences is that the quality of his trot suffers by becoming ground bound. He hurries along, lifting one diagonal pair of legs and putting them back down on the ground before lifting the other diagonal pair. Consequently, there is little, if any, period of suspension. And it's the period of suspension that makes a trot expressive and pretty to watch.

So you need to work on this one piece of the puzzle before tackling anything else. In Chapter Thirteen on troubleshooting, I'll explain how to do this in depth. But for now, in a nutshell, the process of improving his trot, which can take anywhere from several weeks to several months, looks something like this:

1. Slow the speed of the trot to reduce tension.
2. Relax your horse's body by asking him to stretch his head and neck forward and down.
3. Add energy back into the trot with the goal of longer, rather than faster steps.
4. If tension builds or the strides get quick, slow down again.

How long does it take to complete the puzzle? It all depends on your horse. Horses hardly ever progress according to human timetables. They develop at their own rate and will excel at some movements but need more time for others.

The whole jigsaw puzzle process should be fun and rewarding. Since you've made a conscious decision to be patient, there's less anxiety than if you felt pressured to fix everything in one day. Training progresses more or less smoothly because you are allowing yourself the luxury of time to develop your horse's understanding of a movement as well as his strength so he can perform it easily.

Remember that no matter how hard you try to get everything right, you're going to make mistakes. Rather than berating yourself, think of these mistakes as opportunities to develop your abilities as a rider and trainer. If everything always went smoothly, you'd never have a chance to refine your skills. So rather than getting frustrated when your horse keeps picking up the wrong canter lead, think how lucky you are that his mistakes give you the chance to learn how to prepare him better for the transitions.

In addition, you have a built-in instructor. Your horse gives you direct and immediate feedback of your progress as a trainer. His resistance decreases proportionately as your skill develops.

Enjoy the process of figuring out how to explain to your horse that you'd like him to do things differently. See your stumbling blocks as stepping stones and you'll have fun with all phases of his development. Each small change in your horse's behavior is proof that you're progressing with him both mentally and physically. You experience not only greater communication and cooperation but also improved strength and athletic ability.

KEY POINTS

- In order to effectively communicate with your horse, you need a balanced, independent seat.

- Riding on the longe line is the best way to develop an independent seat.

- Your attitude toward yourself and your horse will determine not only how far you go but how much you enjoy the journey.

- Mental training exercises can have a tremendous impact on your riding skills.

- No one will ever care about your horse's welfare as much as you do. He depends on you to make the right choices for his well-being.

- You'll never be discouraged or bored if you see training as an intriguing puzzle and yourself as the problem solver.

DRESSAGE 101

Now that you have started your horse on the longe line, it's time to address his basic education under saddle. I'm assuming your horse is either young, green, or uneducated in dressage, but that he's at least able to be ridden quietly in the walk, trot and canter. The material that follows is not for the totally green horse, although many of these things do apply to him.

In Stage One: Dressage 101, (Chapters Six, Seven, and Eight), I'll be explaining the work that is the foundation for everything you do with your horse. This includes the concepts of **Forward, Straight, and Rhythm (the Basics), the Paces and Gaits,** as well as **Contact**. As you progress to later stages of training, you'll discover that if you're having difficulty with a particular movement or exercise, the cause of the problem is almost always found as a fault in the Basics. So that is where you need to search for the answers to your training dilemmas.

Once you've mastered the Basics plus the movements in Stage Two: Nuts and Bolts (Chapters Nine, Ten, Eleven, Twelve and Thirteen), you'll have an obedient horse who is fun to ride. You might decide that Stages One and Two are all you need in order to allow you to cross-train with dressage. But if you do decide to go on to Stage Three: The Professional's Secret and Stage Four: Fancy Stuff (all in Book Two), it will be an easy progression because you already will have laid the proper groundwork for more advanced schooling.

CHAPTER SIX

The ABC's of Dressage —Forward and Straight

N o matter what style of riding you prefer, your horse needs to move in a **forward** and **straight** manner. These two basic rules, together with **rhythm**, are the foundation for all correct work in every riding discipline. (I'll discuss rhythm at length, in Chapter Seven).

All riders need to be concerned with straightness. When a horse isn't moving straight, one hind leg continually carries a greater share of the weight. As a result he can become sore. This soreness can be expressed in a variety of ways including a painful back, lameness, resistance such as throwing his head up in the air, or even behavior problems like bucking and rearing.

You should place just as high a priority on teaching your horse to go forward as you do on making him straight. In this chapter I'm going to discuss two aspects of "forward riding." The first is that your horse *physically* goes forward over the ground and the second is that he *mentally* goes forward in response to refined driving aids.

This is where your horse's education must begin.

Forward

In dressage the word "forward" refers to the direction the horse moves over the ground. In other words, your horse moves forward as opposed to moving sideways. Forward designates where the horse goes, not how he gets there. Expressions such as "needs energy," "needs a livelier tempo," "needs longer strides," and "needs to cover more ground" explain *how* the horse should proceed in a forward direction.

Although physically moving forward over the ground is part of going forward, I also want you to consider the mental aspect of going forward.

> "One of the most fundamental rules of equitation is: straighten your horse and ride him forward."

So says Alois Podhajsky, former Director of the Spanish Riding School in Vienna, in his book *The Complete Training of Horse and Rider*

6.1

If your thick-skinned friend is sensitive enough to feel a fly on his side, then he ought to be able to feel subtle leg aids...!

Specifically, it is equally important that your horse *thinks* forward. If your horse is "thinking forward," he will react immediately to the lightest of leg aids. In "rider speak" we call it "hot off" or "in front of" your leg.

Keep in mind that a horse can actually go forward over the ground quite well and still not be thinking forward. I've ridden many Thoroughbreds who appear to an observer to be going forward with energy but are, in fact, rather dull to the driving aids.

To check to see if your horse is thinking forward, lightly close your legs. If he reacts immediately and enthusiastically to a feather-light squeeze, you're in business. If he doesn't, don't adjust your aid by repeating it or making it stronger to get a response. Instead, go through the process described in the next few pages of putting him in front of your leg.

Maybe you're skeptical that your horse will ever be hot off your leg. After all, you've had him a long time, and he's a pretty lazy fellow. You've always had to work hard to get him going. But believe me, it is not only possible, but it is also essential that you train him to do this. To prove to yourself that you can train your horse to respond to light leg aids, just watch what he does on a summer's day when the flies are out.

At the mere touch of a bug on your horse's side, he flicks it off with his tail. Now, if your "thick-skinned" friend is sensitive enough to feel a fly on his side, then he ought to be able to feel subtle leg aids if you take the time to school him to react to them (fig. 6.1).

PUTTING YOUR HORSE IN FRONT OF YOUR LEG

To put the horse in front of your leg, follow this simple guide. If you give a light leg aid and your horse eagerly responds by going forward, reward him. The reward encourages him to react the same way the next time you give a leg aid. On the other hand, if you give a leg aid and your horse doesn't answer at all, or responds in a sluggish way, punish him. (I'll discuss how in a moment.) The punishment will motivate him to change his response the next time you give an aid.

First, ask your horse to go forward in a transition from walk to trot by closing both of your legs *very* lightly on his sides. If he doesn't respond (and he probably won't if you're used to giving strong leg aids), punish him by sharply sending him forward. Don't worry if your horse breaks into the canter when you punish him. The point is that he must go *forward* even if he overreacts.

Before you actually punish your horse, take a moment to consider his temperament. The easy-going fellow might need a few taps with the whip or several sharp kicks to send him forward, but you should modify the severity of the punishment for the sensitive soul. The point is not to terrorize the animal but to get a clearly forward, hot-off-the-leg reaction.

6.2

What I want you to do, is whisper with your aids and have your horse shout his answer—not the other way around.

Also, if your horse is the type that bucks when you use the whip, it's better to kick him instead. First of all, you don't want to get bucked off. And secondly, if he's bucking, he's obviously not going forward and he's missed the point of the punishment.

Once you've chased him forward, it's vital that you go back to what you were doing and retest with a light leg aid. If he responds electrically by immediately going forward into an energetic trot when you retest, praise generously. At this point it's still okay if he breaks into the canter when you do the retest—later on you can refine the aid and explain to him that you want him just to trot. But for the moment *any* forward reaction is desirable. If his reaction to your legs is "better," but not a hundred percent wholeheartedly forward, repeat the whole process from the beginning until he does it right.

I can't emphasize enough that if you forget to do the retest, he'll only become more dull to the aids than he already is because you will have taught him to go forward only when he feels the whip or a good kick, rather than when he feels a light aid.

MAINTAINING HIS ENERGY BY HIMSELF

Make sure you don't fall into the trap of "helping" your horse to go forward by using your legs every stride. Unless you're giving a specific aid, your legs should lie quietly on the horse's sides. If you use your legs constantly, you dull the horse's reaction to your legs. You end up doing all the work, and your horse pays little attention to your efforts. What I want you to do is *whisper* with your aids and have your horse *shout* his answer rather than the other way around (fig. 6.2).

Many riders are not even aware how much they "help" their horses to go forward. Others erroneously think that it's their job to keep their

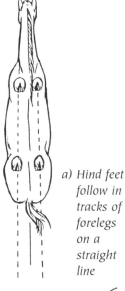

a) Hind feet follow in tracks of forelegs on a straight line

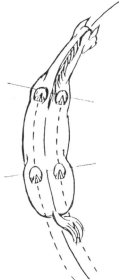

b) Hind feet follow in tracks of forelegs on a curve—this requires bending

6.4 *Straightness*

horses active. In the walk, these riders use alternate leg aids. In the posting trot, they squeeze each time they sit. And in the canter, they squeeze once during each stride. This is wrong. Your horse needs to maintain the momentum and liveliness of his gait all by himself.

Using your legs a lot really backfires on you. As I said earlier, if you use your legs repetitively to keep your horse going, you use yourself up and have no strength left to give other signals to your horse. Plus, constant leg aids are annoying to your horse, and he either becomes cranky or tunes you out altogether (fig. 6.3).

6.3

Constant leg aids are annoying to your horse. He will either become cranky or tune you out altogether.

Here's a simple test you can do to see if you're "helping" your horse too much. First, ask your horse to walk forward energetically. Then, take your legs completely away from his sides so you don't accidentally "cheat" and give a little nudge with your legs here and there. Now notice how long it takes before your horse starts to slow down. And, how long does it take before he stops completely? The length of time it takes for either of these things to happen gives you a pretty good idea of just how hard you're working to keep him going.

Make up your mind that your horse must maintain his activity in each gait on his own. Then do the following to explain the new rules to him.

After asking your horse to go forward in the walk, don't use your legs at all. The moment your horse slows down, chase him forward by kicking or tapping him with the whip as you did when you were putting him in front of your leg earlier. Re-establish the walk, and repeat the whole process. As long as your horse continues to march forward energetically on his own, praise him with your voice enthusiastically while he's walking. As soon as he slows down even a fraction, chase him forward again.

Go through the exact same procedure in the trot and in the canter.

I realize that the punishment might seem severe both in this exercise and when you're putting your horse in front of your leg. But the bottom line is that eventually you will have a happier horse. It's a lot more pleasant for both of you when you can use your legs lightly to give signals rather than grinding, pushing and squeezing every stride.

Straightness

Straightness refers to both the position of the horse's legs and the alignment of his spine. When a horse's legs are straight (I'll refer to this as **leg-straightness**), his hind feet follow in the exact same tracks as those made by the front feet. This is true whether he's on a straight line or a curved line.

When his spine is straight (I'll refer to this as **axis-straightness**), it overlaps his line of travel. His spine corresponds to whatever line he's on, whether it's straight or curving. Axis-straightness on lines such as the long side of an arena, the trail, or the approach to a jump means that the horse's shoulders are directly in front of his hindquarters, while axis-straightness on circles, corners, and curved lines means the horse's spine is bent accordingly (fig. 6.4).

If you look at a straight horse coming toward you while you're on the ground, you see only the two front legs, the base of his neck is centered in the middle of level shoulders, and his nose is in the middle of his chest. If you look at the same horse going away from you, you see only the two hind legs and the top of his tail in the middle of his hips. In either case, if you see more than two legs, the horse is crooked (fig. 6.5).

Some people believe that a horse's inherent crookedness is a result of his position in the womb. Others feel that carrying the rider's weight causes a horse to struggle with his balance and become crooked. And there's always the issue of an asymmetrical rider contributing to crookedness.

Whatever the reason for the crookedness, you will have to work on making your horse straight every single day in training. This holds true regardless of whether you're just starting out or whether your horse has reached the highest levels of dressage schooling. Striving for straightness is a continuous, on-going process. Your horse will always want to become crooked and you'll constantly need to take measures to keep him straight, or correct him when he does become crooked.

Making and keeping your horse straight is a priority. Your horse needs to use both of his hind legs equally so the energy that starts in his hindquarters can be transmitted over his back to his forehand–this is the **connection** our experts spoke about in Chapter Two. When your horse is straight and connected, the energy is automatically recycled back to his hind legs. It ends up being self-perpetuating, like a flywheel turning by itself. However, if your horse is crooked, the energy leaks out, and you constantly have to work at keeping the "rpms" up.

The fact that we as riders are not symmetrical either complicates the task of making our horses straight. Most of us have one hand that is stronger than the other. If you ask your horse to halt and you use your

a) Axis straight and leg straight, front view

b) Rear view

6.5 *Straightness*

6.6

Sitting in balance: a vertical line though head, hip, and foot; pelvis vertical.

right hand more strongly than your left hand, you'll make his hindquarters move over to the left and he'll become crooked.

We also don't always sit absolutely straight and centered over the middle of a horse's back (fig. 6.6). To check if you're sitting straight and centered, draw an imaginary line down the midline of your saddle from the pommel in the front to the cantle at the back. Is half of your body on either side of the line? If you lean to the right, let's say, your horse will feel this and try to compensate for your crookedness by stepping in that direction with his right hind leg (fig. 6.7).

RIDER-CREATED CROOKEDNESS

Often, riders make horses crooked by bending the animals' necks too much to the inside or the outside of the line they're following. The photos on the next page illustrate the differences between straight and crooked on both lines and circles.

In the first photo, (fig. 6.8) Deb Dean-Smith is bending Rapunzel's neck too much to the **inside** (left) while riding on a straight line. The horse's neck is bent too much to the inside because Deb is using too much inside left rein without supporting enough with the outside right rein.

The result is that the horse's spine doesn't correspond to the line she's on—her shoulders are falling out toward the rail, her haunches are drifting in toward the center of the ring, and her hind feet can't follow the tracks of her front feet.

Photo 6.9 shows Deb bending Rapunzel's neck too much to the **outside** (right) while on a straight line. As a result, the mare's shoulders fall in toward the center of the ring and her hindquarters drift out toward the rail. Once again, the horse's spine doesn't correspond to the line she's on and her hind feet don't follow the tracks of her front feet.

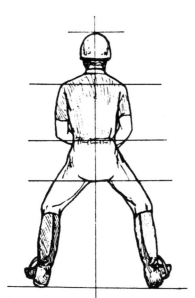

a) Straight and even rider; hips even, shoulders level, and head balanced

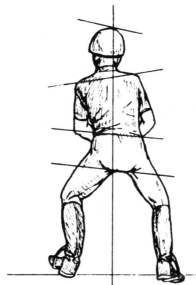

b) Crooked rider; hips to the right, shoulders to the left

6.7

Draw an imaginary line down the midline of your saddle from the pommel in the front to the cantle at the back. Is your body equally on both sides of the line?

<u>6.8</u>
This horse, Rapunzel, is not axis-straight because her spine does not overlap her line of travel. Her neck is bent too much towards the inside of the ring because Deb is using too much inside rein without an equally supporting outside rein.

<u>6.9</u>
Once again the horse's spine isn't overlapping the track. But, this time Deb has used too much outside rein without a complementary influence of the inside rein.

6.10
The horse's entire spine from poll to tail is absolutely straight and her neck is lined up directly in front of the rest of her spine.

6.11
Rapunzel is straight in every sense of the word! She is leg-straight, as well as axis-straight.

In the next photos, 6.10 and 6.11, the rider is keeping her horse straight by having an equal and complementary influence of the two reins. To correct the mistake in photo 6.8, which shows too much bend in the horse's neck to the inside (left), she takes a firmer feel on the outside (right) rein and softens the contact on the inside (left) rein.

To correct the mistake in photo 6.9, which shows too much bend in the neck to the outside, Deb relaxes the outside (right) rein and gives some soft squeezes on the inside (left) rein to reposition the horse's head so that it is in the middle of her chest.

6.12

Circling to the left: Rapunzel's spine doesn't overlap and correspond to the arc of the circle because Deb is bending the horse's neck too much to the inside.

Photo 6.12 shows the same fault as photo 6.8, but here the mare is going left on a circle. Her neck is bent too much to the inside (left) of the circle because the rider is not coordinating her reins correctly. Consequently, the horse's spine doesn't correspond to the arc of the circle—her shoulders and front feet fall to the right. Because the horse's hindquarters remain on the original track of the circle, her hind feet cannot possibly follow the tracks made by her front feet: she's no longer "straight."

Photo 6.13 shows the same fault as photo 6.9, but now we see it on a circle. The neck is bent too much to the outside (right), the shoulders fall in toward the center of the circle. As a result the hind feet can't follow the tracks made by the front feet and the horse is not straight.

6.13

Circling to the left: she's crooked here as well because her neck is bent to the outside of the arc of the circle. Deb is using her outside rein, but she has let her inside hand go forward so it has lost its influence.

6.14

Circling to the left: on a circle, "straight" means "bent"! Rapunzel is straight because her body is evenly curved from poll to tail so that it overlaps the arc of the circle exactly.

In photo 6.14 we see the horse being ridden "straight" on a circle. Deb is asking Rapunzel to look to the inside (left) by vibrating the inside (left) rein, while supporting with the outside (right) rein so the mare doesn't bend too much to the inside (left). She bends her horse in her rib cage by placing her inside (left) leg on the girth and her outside (right) leg behind the girth. Positioning her outside leg behind the girth not only helps bend the horse around her inside (left) leg, but also prevents her hindquarters from swinging out and off the line of the circle.

To maintain straightness, you need to ride with both legs and both hands. Depending on what you're doing, some of your aids will be active and some will be passive. On the circle that I just described, the inside aids are active and the outside aids are passive. There should always be a marriage of inside and outside aids—don't use one set of aids and abandon the horse by not using the other set of aids.

Perhaps your horse doesn't want to stay straight between your legs and hands. He feels very "wormy" as he bounces from side to side, becoming crooked by falling in and out from the line or curve with his shoulders, hindquarters, or both. Rather than correcting these losses of balance each time they occur, try instead to maintain the straightness. Make a corridor with your legs and reins, and let your horse bounce against the aids like a ping-pong ball until he finally stays straight.

CROOKEDNESS—HINDQUARTERS TO THE INSIDE

Earlier I said that when a horse is leg-straight, his hind feet are lined up directly behind his front feet. The rider must keep in mind, however, that the hips of the horse are wider than the shoulders. If you ride along a fence line and place the forehand too close to the rail, the horse will have no option but to drift inward with his hindquarters, because he doesn't have room for them. In this case the rider is causing the crookedness.

Another reason that a horse drifts inward with his hindquarters is to avoid bearing weight on his inside hind leg. In order to cope with the demands of curves in good balance this hind leg has to bend more and do more work than the outside hind leg (fig. 6.15).

In both cases, do not push the hindquarters back out. But straighten the horse by placing the forehand in front of the haunches. You should straighten the horse in this way because even though the hindquarters are deviating to the inside, you want to use your inside leg on the girth to send your horse *forward* not to push him sideways.

Riding in the shoulder-fore position is also an excellent exercise to make your horse straight. I explain this in great detail in Chapter Ten.

6.15
Crookedness: this horse is neither leg-straight, nor axis-straight.

KEY POINTS

Forward

- Riding your horse forward and straight is the foundation from which all correct training starts.

- Think of the word "forward" not only as moving over the ground in a forward direction, but also as your horse "thinking forward." That is, when you use the lightest of driving aids, your horse reacts immediately and enthusiastically.

- You're traveling down the wrong (and exhausting) road if you're from the "more leg, stronger leg" school of thought. Instead, teach your horse to be in front of your leg so you can do less and he can do more.

Straightness

- By nature all horses are crooked. It is our responsibility to make them straight so they can develop evenly.

- When a horse is straight, his spine overlaps the line he's traveling on and his hind feet follow in the tracks of his front feet. Therefore, a "straight" horse is straight on lines and bent when on the arc of a circle or corner.

CHAPTER SEVEN

Shall We Dance?
Paces, Gaits and Rhythm

A primary aim for all riders interested in improving their horses through dressage training is the development of their horses' basic paces. All the movements and exercises that I'll be discussing shortly are not an end in themselves. They are a means to an end. They're designed to make the horse more athletic so he can move with grace and beauty.

In common usage, you'll often hear the words "**paces**" and "**gaits**" used randomly and interchangeably. And the fact is that the various organizations that define and describe them are not always in agreement as to which word to use in certain cases. I don't want you to be confused by the inconsistent use of these words. So for the sake of clarity and consistency, in this book I'll call the walk, trot, and canter, when discussing them generically, the paces. I'll refer to the "gears," or variations of length of stride and balance within each pace, as the gaits—specifically: the working, collected, medium, and extended gaits of all three paces.

To reap the benefits of classical training, your horse does not necessarily have to be blessed with lofty, expressive paces. Dressage can take the most common animal as well as the truly gifted athlete and help both of them to move more expressively.

When training is correct, the basic paces always improve. When the training is incorrect for whatever reason—harsh gadgets, "front to back" riding that focuses on the position of the horse's head and neck and ignores the hindquarters, shortcuts—the quality of the paces degenerates (fig. 7.1).

In this chapter, I'll look at the halt, the medium walk, the working trot, and the working canter, because that is what you'll be concerned with at this stage of your horse's education. In Book Two, I'll discuss the collected and the extended gaits that will be used when you and your horse are more advanced.

a) Well-balanced Western horse whose gaits show results of dressage training

b) Poorly-balanced turn

c) A light-in-hand Saddle seat horse—a perfect picture!

7.1 Good and bad balance

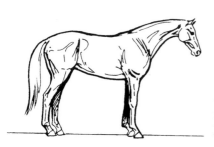

7.2

A halt in good balance.

The Halt

In a good halt, your horse should stand absolutely motionless, yet he should be alert and attentive enough to move off instantly from the lightest of aids. To be immobile, he must be in good balance. Good balance in the halt means that your horse's body is straight and his weight is evenly distributed over his four legs. This is what we call having "a leg in each corner." His front legs are side by side and so are his hind legs. He should maintain a soft contact with your hands, and he can chomp quietly on the bit (fig. 7.2).

In the first stages of training, school the halt as an obedience exercise. Later on, you'll use the halt to increase the engagement of the hind legs so you can improve your horse's balance.

The Aids for the Halt

When stepping into the halt, your horse should always look like he's closing himself up from the back to the front. This means you'll use your driving aids first and send him forward up to restraining hands. Never drag your horse into the halt by pulling on the reins. This results in a poorly balanced halt where the hind legs are left trailing out behind his body. In that position they can't support his weight. When this happens your horse has no option but to fall on his forehand and lean on your hands for support. Then, with his hind legs out behind his body in the halt, he's not in a "ready" position to react immediately to your light leg aids for an upward transition. So what you may perceive as a disobedience—a feeling that he is "behind the leg"—in reality might be that he is physically unable to respond to your command to go forward (figs. 7.3 to 7.5).

The aids for the halt are as follows:

Legs: close both calves to drive the hind legs under your horse's body.

Hands: close both hands in fists to resist the driving aids. Relax your hands as soon as your horse stops.

Seat: stretch up and brace your back by tightening your stomach muscles. "Still" your seat so that your hips no longer follow the motion of your horse's body.

7.3 to 7.5
Trot to Halt Transition

7.3

Preparing to halt from an energetic working trot at the spot marked by the letter M.

7.4

A few strides before M, Amy Foss drives Special Effects' hind legs further underneath his body by closing both of her legs and pushing with her seat. Note the lowering of his hindquarters as they are driven under his body. She then captures and contains this energy by closing her hands in fists.

7.5

As her horse steps into a completely balanced halt, Amy relaxes all of her aids without taking them off. Instead, she maintains a soft contact with her legs on his barrel and her hands with his mouth.

IMMOBILITY—THE BEGINNING OF DISCIPLINE

The first time you ask your horse to submit obediently to your requests is when you teach him to stand still while being mounted. Too often, I see riders neglect this very basic opportunity to establish the ground rules about who makes the decisions in this partnership. Riders will be "mid-mount" and their horses walk forward. Or, they manage to get completely aboard, and then the horses decide to walk off on their own.

Your horse should stand absolutely immobile while you mount, and he should wait until he receives a specific aid from your legs before he moves off. If you let your horse take over simply because you haven't paid enough attention to this aspect of obedience, you might find him starting to make his own decisions in other areas.

Insisting that your horse stand still while being mounted is your first chance to establish your role in the relationship. You must firmly, but quietly, establish your authority. What I do with horses that don't stand still is, as I begin to mount, I say the word, "whoa." My horse already knows what "whoa" means from our work on the longe line. If he takes even one step forward as I start to get on, I immediately get off, make him stand, and say "whoa" again. I might have to do this several times. But, as soon as he stands absolutely still, both while I'm mounting and while I'm sitting in the saddle, I make a big fuss over him. I'll pat him and tell him he's good or even reach over and give him some sugar. Then, when I'm ready, I'll close my legs in a definite signal for him to walk forward. I'll praise him again for waiting and then for reacting attentively to the aid to move off.

TRANSITIONS TO AND FROM THE HALT

It's important for you to think about the transitions in and out of the halt. The downward transition to the halt should be crisp but not abrupt. By crisp, I mean that your horse shouldn't do any "dribbly" trot or walk steps that get progressively shorter and shorter until he finally stalls out and stops. His last step of trot or walk before the halt should look just as active as the strides that he takes when he's motoring along with lots of energy.

If the downward transition looks abrupt, it's a good indication that you used your hands too much or too sharply, or, that you suddenly and harshly applied all of the aids.

In an upward transition, your horse should respond immediately to your aids with a deliberate step from the hind legs. In other words, your horse shouldn't shuffle with short, lazy steps until he finally accelerates into his first full stride of the walk, the trot, or the canter. If he does this because he's "behind your leg," you need to put him "in front of your leg" as I described on page 80. If he shuffles off because his hind legs are out behind his body, you need to pay more attention to getting his hind legs underneath him during the next downward transition to the halt. Make sure that you use your driving aids and "close him up" from back to front so that he's in a better balance to do whatever comes next.

Evaluating the Basic Paces

At this stage in your horse's career you will be concerned with the medium walk, the working trot and the working canter if you compete at the lower levels of dressage or are riding in another discipline and cross-training your horse with dressage. Even more advanced dressage horses being schooled in the collected, medium, and extended gaits, are still ridden in the working trot and canter during their warm-up and cool-down phases of a training session.

As you ride the walk, trot, and canter, some excellent images to hold in your mind are that the walk marches, the trot swings, and the canter springs. But, every horse's paces are unique to him. If you get frequent instruction, your teacher may say, "There. That's a good working trot." or "He needs to be more energetic for working canter."

For those of you whose lessons are few and far between, I'll give you three specific criteria to help you identify high quality paces on your own. Then, I'll also delve into them more fully under the individual headings of Walk, Trot, and Canter that follow.

The three criteria are:

- Rhythm
- Energy
- Hind Leg Placement

RHYTHM

In order to lay a solid foundation for training in any riding discipline, maintenance of a regular **rhythm** in all paces should always be a priority. Each horse's rhythm is individual to him, but a good rhythm is steady and regular with equal spacing between the steps of each stride of each pace.

The **tempo**, on the other hand, is the rate of repetition of the rhythm. To further understand the difference between rhythm and tempo, think of a dance like a waltz. The rhythm is always the same in a waltz—it's always done in a three-beat time. But the tempo can change, depending on whether the waltz is played faster or slower.

Your seat is the primary aid for influencing rhythm and tempo. You can steady rhythm, and slow tempo, by **"stilling" your seat**. When you "still" your seat, you stretch up, tighten your stomach muscles, and stop following the motion of the horse. (For more on this see page 139). Al-

a) Free walk

b) Medium walk

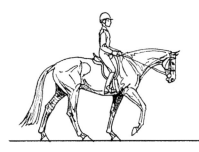

c) Collected walk

d) Extended walk

7.7 *Types of walk*

ternatively, you can use a **"driving"** **seat** to quicken the rhythm and speed up the tempo. To "drive" with your seat, you also sit up tall, but you push with your seat as if you're trying to move the back of the saddle toward the front of the saddle.

I will discuss how you can tell if your horse's rhythm is regular in the description of each pace that follows.

ENERGY

The second criterion for high quality paces is energy. Energy refers to vigor, activity, and liveliness—especially from the haunches. In dressage we often use the word **impulsion** when we speak of power in the trot and the canter. (We use the word "activity" when discussing the walk.) Impulsion refers to the "thrust" coming from the hindquarters. When moving with impulsion, the horse gives the impression of a desire to carry himself forward and spring off the ground (fig. 7.6).

A good working gait always has some degree of energy. But, how can you tell if your horse has enough energy? Simple. Ask for any upward transition—such as going from the trot into the canter or from a working trot into a lengthening of that trot. If you have to add energy in order to do the transition, there isn't enough activity in the gait to begin with. For instance, you should be able to do the trot to canter transition without first revving your horse up. All the energy you need for the transition to the canter should already be in the trot you are doing.

HIND LEG PLACEMENT

The third characteristic to look at when evaluating the basic paces is where the horse puts his hind feet in relation to his front feet.

Although you can lean over while riding and look at the footfalls in the walk, you'll have to ask someone to give you feedback on where the horse is stepping in the trot and the canter. Alternatively, have someone take a video of you riding. While being videotaped, adjust your working gait by slowing down and then speeding up the tempo or by adding energy, and announce what you're doing loud enough to be heard on camera. Make a verbal note on the tape of what you're doing as well as what you're feeling. Then when you study the tape later, you can easily compare what you felt when you were riding with what you see on the tape.

7.6

Impulsion refers to the "thrust" coming from the horse's hindquarters, giving power and energy to the horse's trot or canter.

The Walk

Four different types of walk are recognized by the governing body of dressage. The two that you'll be concerned with for the time being are the **medium walk** and the **free walk**. In Book Two we'll look at the other two—the **collected** and the **extended** walks, which are more advanced movements (fig. 7.7).

As the primary gait in the walk, the *medium* walk used to be called the *working* walk—corresponding to the working trot and the working canter. However, the new description, medium walk, is preferred over working walk because it has a connotation of marching more freely forward. Previously, in an effort to ride what they considered to be a *working* walk, riders ended up shortening their horses too much and restricting them with the reins. This can be disastrous because it's very easy to ruin a horse's natural walk if he feels confined. When he feels restricted, his rhythm can degenerate and become **lateral**—a rhythm fault that I'll describe shortly.

To avoid this hazard, we now work young or uneducated horses in what is called the medium walk. This walk is a free, regular and unconstrained walk of moderate lengthening. The horse walks energetically but calmly with even and determined steps, the hind feet touching the ground in front of the hoof prints of the forefeet (fig. 7.8).

7.8

The medium walk "marches." It is an active, ground-covering walk. The inside hind leg is just coming to the ground as Moxie finishes the third step of a walk with four clear beats. Note that her inside hind leg "overtracks" —it comes to the ground beyond the point where her inside front foot left the ground.

The free walk is a gait of relaxation. Here, Kelly Weiss allows Kousteau complete freedom to lower and stretch out his head and neck.

The free walk is a pace of relaxation in which the horse is allowed complete freedom to lower and stretch out his head and neck (fig. 7.9). The reins are totally loose so that the walk can be as unencumbered as possible. You'll do a free walk with your horse at the beginning and end of your ride as well as any time you give your horse a break.

RHYTHM IN THE WALK

Let's begin by looking at the sequence of legs and rhythm of the walk (fig. 7.10).

Starting with the outside hind leg, the sequence of legs in one walk stride is: outside hind, outside fore, inside hind, inside fore. Assess the rhythm of your horse's walk by counting with each leg movement. Start counting the rhythm out loud when the outside hind leg strikes the ground. You should develop a feel for this in all three paces, so beginning at the walk is a good idea since you'll have more time to think. Close your eyes so you can really feel when that outside hind foot is

a) First beat: outside hind

b) Second beat: outside fore

c) Third beat: inside hind

d) Fourth beat: inside fore

7.10 The sequence of legs in one walk stride

on the ground bearing weight. When the outside hind leg is on the ground, the horse's outside hip is higher, so you should also feel your outside seat bone or hip being raised slightly or pushed forward.

Each time you feel this, say "One." You'll say "One.., One.., One.., One..," each time the outside hind leg is on the ground. Then add in the other legs as they move. The sequence of your counting should sound like an even "One, two, three, four; one, two, three, four; one, two, three, four." This is a regular four-beat walk.

If you hear something like "One, two,...three, four" instead, your horse's rhythm is not regular. When the legs on the same side move too close together like this, we say the walk is becoming **lateral** (fig. 7.11). If the rhythm degenerates further and the legs on the same side move together completely so that you count only two beats, the horse is pacing not walking.

7.11

Lateral (or, "pacey") walk

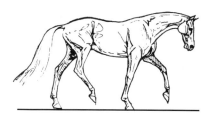

a) Working trot

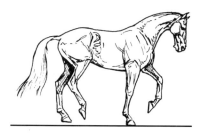

b) Collected trot

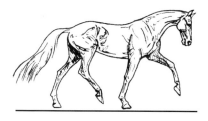

c) Medium trot

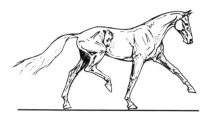

d) Extended trot

7.12 Types of trot

Both a "lateral walk" and a "pacing walk" are caused by tension and stiffness, especially in the back and neck. Neither is correct for basic training in dressage, so make sure that the purity of the walk—the regular four-beat rhythm—is always a priority.

There are different reasons that horses lose regularity in the walk. Some horses are born with walks that aren't one hundred percent "pure," or "regular." Other horses are born with pure walks, but they can momentarily lose their regular rhythm if they are tense in their backs or feel restricted by the rider's hands.

The following are some suggestions to help you make and keep the walk rhythm regular. You should experiment and do whatever it takes to maintain regularity. It's a requirement for all correct gaits and imperative if you want to correctly develop your horse.

If your horse's walk loses regularity, try either slowing him down or speeding him up. For most horses, slowing down encourages them to become more even in their steps, so that they have a four-beat walk. Some horses, however, are helped by riding them in a faster tempo than they are inclined to go. (For an additional tip to help the rhythm in the walk, see the shoulder-fore exercise in Chapter Ten).

Many horses have a regular rhythm in the walk when ridden on a loose rein. But as soon as the rider picks up a contact, the rhythm changes. Usually this irregularity is rider-created because the horse feels restricted by the reins. The rider's contact with the horse's mouth must be gentle and elastic so that the horse doesn't feel "claustrophobic."

A good practice exercise for horse and rider is to do many transitions from a free walk on a loose rein to taking up a contact for the medium walk. As you pick up the reins to establish contact, visualize your horse's legs continuing to move with the same long, full, regular steps of the free walk. Your goal is to keep the rhythm exactly the same by giving the horse the same feeling of freedom, whether he's on contact or on a loose rein.

ENERGY IN THE WALK

Now let's go on to our second criterion for a correct basic gait—energy. In a good medium walk your horse should march with active, determined steps. Check that your horse has enough energy in the walk by asking him to step into the trot. Ask for the trot by lightly closing both of your calves on his sides. Does he eagerly step into the trot or does he shuffle lazily through the transition? If he has enough energy in the walk, the transition is crisp and distinct.

HIND LEG PLACEMENT IN THE WALK

The third criterion for evaluating the walk is where the horse puts his hind feet. In the medium walk, your horse should overtrack to some de-

7.13 The trot swings.

In the working trot, Rapunzel's legs move together in diagonal pairs. The horse clearly "tracks up" as her hind foot steps into the spot where her front foot left the ground.

gree—that is, his hind feet should step in front of the hoof prints made by the forefeet. The amount of overtrack depends on many factors, including conformation and breed. I like a moderate overtrack of four to six inches. I find that when horses have huge overstrides, you can sometimes run into difficulties later in schooling when you go to collect or shorten the gait, because it tends to become lateral rather than remaining a pure, regular, four-beat walk.

The Working Trot

The **working trot** is the trot in which the young or uneducated horse presents himself in the best balance. One of your primary aims when schooling your inexperienced horse in dressage is to maintain the quality of the working gaits during all the exercises and movements.

Four different trots are recognized, but for the time being you should be concerned only with the working trot. Later on, if you decide to take your horse to more advanced levels, you will be schooling him in the collected, medium and extended trots (fig. 7.12).

In the working trot, the horse goes forward in balance with even, powerful, elastic steps. He should show good hock action, (bending of the hock joints) which is only possible when he moves with impulsion (fig. 7.13).

a) First beat: inside hind and outside fore

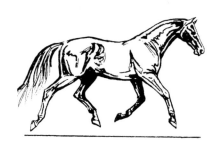

b) Suspension

c) Second beat: outside hind and inside fore

7.14
The sequence of legs in one trot stride

Now let's look at the sequence of legs and rhythm of the trot (fig. 7.14).

RHYTHM IN THE TROT

In one stride of the trot, the sequence of legs is: one diagonal pair of inside hind and outside fore, followed by a period of suspension during which all four legs are off the ground, then the diagonal pair of outside hind and inside fore.

You should hear yourself counting an evenly-spaced "One...two... one...two...one...two...."

If you're in posting trot and you're on the correct diagonal, you'll be rising out of the saddle at the same time that you see the horse's outside front leg coming off the ground and going forward. Therefore, since the horse's legs move in diagonal pairs in the trot, you are in the air when the outside hind leg is on the ground and you are sitting in the saddle when the inside hind leg is on the ground (fig. 7.15).

In fact, this is one of the reasons that we have posting diagonals. It's easier to use your leg and, therefore, influence a hind leg when you're sitting in the saddle rather than rising in the air. Since your horse's inside hind leg is the leg you want to energize on circles and turns, you'll feel more coordinated about activating that leg when you're sitting rather than posting.

I don't mean to give you the impression that you use your inside leg every time you sit. Doing that would make your horse dull to your aids very quickly. Unless you're specifically giving an aid to ask your horse for more activity, your legs rest quietly on your horse's sides.

If you're in sitting trot, you can do the same exercise that you did in the walk. Decide when the outside hind leg is on the ground by closing your eyes and feeling the moment your outside seat bone is raised slightly or pushed forward. Count "One...one...one...one...," each time you feel this. This is the moment that the diagonal pair of outside hind and inside fore are on the ground. Then add in the second beat. Do your "One...two's" sound evenly spaced?

If the trot rhythm is not regular, you first need to be sure that the horse isn't uneven because he's lame. Check with your veterinarian to eliminate this possibility.

FAULTS IN THE TROT

A common fault in the trot is when the horse hurries his steps so that the foreleg comes to the ground before the diagonal hind leg does, so that two separate hoof beats are heard instead of one (fig. 7.16a). This horse is carrying most of his weight and that of his rider on his shoulders. The solution is to shift the horse's center of gravity back toward the hind legs so that his shoulders can be lighter and freer. Transitions

7.15
Posting on the correct diagonal. Rider rises when the outside foreleg and inside hind leg are in the air.

going from the trot to the halt and back to the trot are particularly useful in this situation. (You can also do a shoulder-fore exercise. More on this under the section on shoulder-fore in Chapter Ten).

Another common fault is when the hind leg is put down before the diagonal foreleg. Again two hoof beats will be heard (fig. 7.16b). This occurs when the horse is lazy with his hind legs and drags his feet along the ground. To help activate his hind legs try the following frequent transitions:

1. Alternate lengthening and shortening the stride. To adjust the length of stride, close both of your legs and ask your horse to cover more ground for several strides. Then steady him back to the shorter strides or a few moments by stilling your seat and using your outside rein. Repeat this several times to freshen the trot.

2. Quickly go from trot to walk or canter. First go forward in the trot, do a transition to the walk or the canter for only three or four strides, then go right back into the trot again. (In Chapter Nine I'll discuss the aids for all of these transitions more thoroughly.)

The trot also becomes irregular when one hind leg doesn't reach as far under the body as the other, so that the steps look uneven. You may be able to feel this yourself because there will be an emphasis on one of the beats of the trot, and you will find yourself counting, "One, *two,* one, *two.* It's a good idea to ask an observer to watch the hind legs and visually check that each one steps equally under your horse's body.

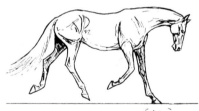

a) Irregular trot: diagonal breaking up, foreleg first; on the forehand

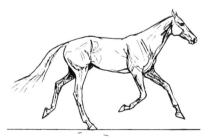

b) Irregular trot: diagonal breaking up, hind leg first; running

7.16 *Faulty trots*

a) Working canter

b) Collected canter

c) Extended canter

7.17 Types of canter

STRENGTHENING EXERCISES TO IMPROVE THE TROT

Some horses will take a shorter stride with one hind leg because they're either lazy, or weak behind. If your horse's left hind leg is lazy, close your left leg to ask the left hind leg to step more under the body. Do some exercises in the trot such as those described below to strengthen the weak hind leg and encourage it to take long strides and carry weight.

Ride to the right, (clockwise) around your arena. This will put your horse's left hind leg on the outside of the ring, next to the rail. Position your horse's head to the left so that it is towards the rail. Then use your left leg a couple of inches behind the girth to push his hindquarters to the right for a few strides. As you push his quarters to the right, you'll be driving his left hind leg deeper under his body. Then straighten the horse and close both of your legs to ask him to go more forward with longer steps for a few strides. As you settle back to the working trot, repeat the exercise by sending his left hind leg sideways under his body again.

Another strengthening exercise is to move the horse's hindquarters an inch or two sideways and keep them there as you ride all the way around the ring. Push his hindquarters slightly to the right no matter which direction you're riding. Your goal is to put your horse's left hind leg under his body so that it must always carry both his weight and your weight. As with all "weight-lifting," the muscles doing the work eventually get stronger. As the muscles get stronger, both hind legs can step under the horse's body with equal power.

ENERGY IN THE TROT

Once you know you have a regular rhythm, go on to the second criterion and check the energy level of the trot. Remember that the ease with which you can do a crisp transition will give you information about energy. In the walk example I asked you to do a transition from walk to trot. For variety's sake, check your energy level in the trot by doing a different kind of transition—a lengthening in the trot. Close both of your calves on your horse's sides and see if he reacts immediately by covering ground with longer strides. If he has lots of energy in the working trot, the transition will be dramatic.

HOOF PLACEMENT IN THE TROT

Ask someone to watch where your horse's hind feet land. In the working trot the horse should "track-up"—his hind feet stepping into the hoof prints of his forefeet. (See fig. 7.13 on page 101).

a) First beat: outside hind

b) Second beat: diagonal pair—
   inside hind and outside fore

c) Third beat: inside fore (leading
   foreleg)

d) Pushing off

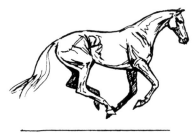

e) Suspension

7.18 The canter with horse on left lead

The Working Canter

Like the working trot, the working canter is the canter in which the young or uneducated horse presents himself in the best balance.

Four different canters are recognized in dressage, but for your purposes the working canter is the gait you will be riding. In Book Two, I'll introduce the collected, medium, and extended canters (fig. 7.17).

RHYTHM IN THE CANTER

Now let's look at the sequence of legs and rhythm of the canter. The canter has three beats. In one canter stride, the sequence of legs is: first the outside hind, next the diagonal pair of inside hind and outside fore, and finally the inside fore followed by a period of suspension during which all of the legs are off the ground (fig. 7.18).

a) Correct (inside) lead: left lead on left turn

b) Incorrect (outside) lead: right lead on left turn

7.19 Correct and incorrect lead when cantering to the left

Your horse has two leads in the canter. When he's cantering on the correct lead, he moves with his inside foreleg leading. In other words, when going to the left (counterclockwise), he strikes off first with his right hind leg, then comes the diagonal pair of the left hind leg and the right foreleg, and lastly his left foreleg "leads" or steps out further in front of his body than the right foreleg (fig. 7.19a). When going to the right (clockwise), he should canter on the right lead. He starts with the left hind leg, then comes the diagonal pair of the right hind leg and left foreleg, and finally the right foreleg reaches in front of his body.

You should be able to hear yourself count an even rhythm "One...two...three...one...two...three..." During the second beat of the canter, your seat moves from the back of the saddle toward the front of the saddle. You can also check that you're counting correctly by looking at your horse's mane. You'll see that his mane lifts up on the second beat while you're saying "two."

Rhythm faults occur when the canter becomes four-beat and the horse moves along awkwardly rather than covering the ground in a series of graceful bounds. There are three ways the rhythm can become irregular so that the canter degenerates into four beats.

First, when the horse canters too much on the forehand, the diagonal pair of legs can split and the foreleg comes to the ground before the opposite hind leg (fig. 7.20a).

Second, when a horse is crammed together and forced to go with a shorter stride than he can manage for his degree of training, it's possible that the diagonal pair will split and the hind leg will come to the ground before the opposite front leg (fig. 7.20b).

Lastly, when a horse is very stiff in his neck and back, the rhythm of the canter can become almost "lateral." It will appear that the left fore and hind legs and the right fore and hind legs move almost together (fig. 20c).

Often a horse's canter becomes faulty when there's a lack of energy. To freshen a canter that is losing regularity, ask your horse to canter more forward over the ground with brisk, energetic strides.

Check for a good working canter by closing both calves and asking for a transition to a lengthening in the canter. Is it easy? Or do you have to wake your horse up first before he'll give you more effort?

HIND LEG PLACEMENT IN THE CANTER

For the third criterion of working canter, have someone watch your horse's inside hind leg. In a good working canter, it reaches well under the body. To check this, have your person on the ground look from the side at the distance between your horse's hind legs during that second beat of the canter. In a good working canter, the inside hind steps well under the horse's body: your ground person will see a wide space between his hind legs (fig. 7.21).

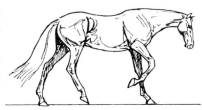

a) Irregular four-beat canter: diagonal breaking up, foreleg first; on the forehand

b) Irregular four-beat canter; diagonal breaking up, hind leg first

c) Lateral four-beat canter: approaching a pace

7.20 *Faulty canters*

7.21

The canter "springs." An active, bounding, working canter: note how Moxie's inside hind leg reaches well underneath her body.

KEY POINTS

✦ When training methods are correct, the horse's paces always improve.

✦ Your goal is to teach a horse under saddle to move as gracefully and expressively as he does when he's at liberty.

✦ Initially, you'll school the halt as an obedience exercise. Later on, you'll use transitions in and out of the halt to improve your horse's balance.

✦ Three elements of high-quality paces are regularity of rhythm, good energy, and hind legs that step well under the body:

1. Regular rhythm refers to the even spacing between each of the steps within a stride.

2. When a horse has sufficient energy in his paces, he finds it easy to do transitions either within the pace or from one pace to another.

3. In the walk, the horse's hind feet should step in front of the tracks made by his front feet. In the trot, the hind feet should step into the tracks of the front feet. In the canter, the horse's inside hind leg should step well underneath his body.

CHAPTER EIGHT

Contact—Your Communication Center

No matter which riding discipline you prefer, all of you reading this book will benefit from learning how to establish a sympathetic **contact** with your horse's mouth. Your reins serve as transmitters from your brain, through your hands, to your horse's mouth. Establishing this contact with his mouth allows you to communicate with his hindquarters—his engine. Even those of you who just want an obedient, well-schooled partner need to know about contact so you can stop and steer.

For those of you who decide to go on to Stages Three and Four you'll see that contact is essential to establishing a **connection** from your horse's hindquarters to the bit. In order for the energy that originates in the hindquarters to be fully used, it must travel over your horse's back, through his neck, and be received by your hands. When this occurs, your horse will be connected, also known as **"on the bit."** We'll explore this in Book Two.

In this chapter I am going to describe five properties that are necessary in order for you to establish an inviting contact with your horse's mouth. The late Colonel Bengt Ljungquist, former coach of the United States Dressage Team, described this contact as follows: "If you take a flat piece of wood, close your fingers around it and put it in a running stream of water, you will feel a gentle and steady tug on your hand from the current. That is the feel you should strive to have when you ride: a live but comfortable link with the horse's mouth and the sensation that he wants to take you forward while staying in constant communication." (See fig. 8.1).

Later, I will also explain some of the basic ways to use the reins to communicate with, and influence, your horse. These subtle variations of the use of the reins are called the **rein effects**.

> **"If God had given us conformation for riding, our forearms would reach from elbow to bit."**
>
> Charles de Kunffy, author of *Training Strategies for Dressage Riders*

8.1

Take a flat piece of wood and put it in a stream. This sensation is like the gentle tug you should feel when you have a comfortable link to your horse's mouth.

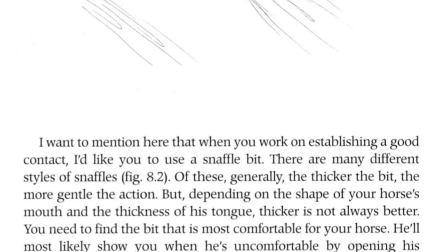

8.2 Appropriate snaffle bits

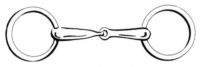

a) Hollow-mouth loose ring

b) Eggbutt

c) Full-cheek (Fulmer)

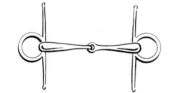

d) Dee ring

e) French link

f) Straight bar

I want to mention here that when you work on establishing a good contact, I'd like you to use a snaffle bit. There are many different styles of snaffles (fig. 8.2). Of these, generally, the thicker the bit, the more gentle the action. But, depending on the shape of your horse's mouth and the thickness of his tongue, thicker is not always better. You need to find the bit that is most comfortable for your horse. He'll most likely show you when he's uncomfortable by opening his mouth, twisting or tossing his head, or showing a reluctance to be bridled. If you are not sure if your bit is appropriate, it's best to ask a professional to advise you.

Qualities of Contact

The five qualities of contact that make an inviting link are:

- Straight line from bit to hand to elbow
- Firmness
- Consistency
- Elasticity
- Symmetrical hands

STRAIGHT LINE

Always maintain a straight line contact from the bit through your hands to the elbows so that your arms seem like they are simply an extension of the reins (figs. 8.3 and 8.4). When you pick up contact, imagine that your arms no longer belong to you—they are part of the reins and they belong to the horse.

A classical straight line contact from the bit through Deb's hand to her elbow in the walk. It's hard to tell where the rein leaves off and her arm begins.

8.4
In the rising trot the rein looks like an extension of Deb's forearm.

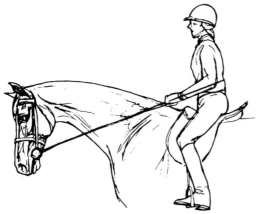

*a) Straight line from bit to elbow—
bit acts neutrally*

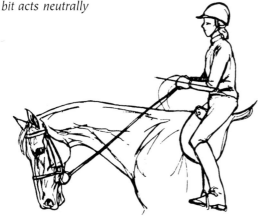

*b) Line broken upward—bit acts
upward in corners of lips*

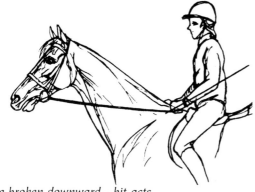

*c) Line broken downward—bit acts
downward against bars of mouth*

8.5 Bit and rein angles

The straight line allows the action of the reins to pass through your hands, shoulders, and back so that it can influence the horse's back. If your hands are carried too low or too high, that straight line will be broken and the action of the reins will stop at your hands. Any time there is an angle at the point where the reins meet your hands, the signals you try to transmit to your horse will be interrupted as though they were being sent on a cut telephone line (fig. 8.5).

FIRMNESS

Although your hands should always be quiet and sensitive, in the initial stages of training contact should also be firm. Provided that you're using a snaffle bit, take a good solid one or two pounds in each hand. If the contact is too light, there's no connection from the hind legs into the hands. If your horse doesn't seek the contact from you, take it from him. But do this only by riding him forward from your legs into a firm contact (figs 8.6 and 8.7).

A lot of riders don't feel comfortable with the idea of having one or two pounds of weight in their hands. They think that contact should always be feather light. The lightness they want is the result of a horse being in self-carriage. But, in the beginning stages of training which is what we are concerned with now, self-carriage isn't relevant.

Self-carriage becomes an issue when I begin to discuss **collection** (the shifting of the horse's center of gravity toward the hind legs) during Stage Four in Book Two. Prior to collection, a contact that is too light merely indicates a lack of connection. At this stage, if the contact is too light, it is probably because the rider is either leaving a loop in the reins and allowing the horse to go along with his nose poked forward (fig. 8.8), or because she is riding the horse behind the bit (see fig. 13.11).

So, don't be afraid of firm contact. It's a necessary but temporary stage. The horse must first be taking a solid contact with your hands before he becomes light in the correct way.

8.6
Figaro's Boy avoids taking a contact with Deb's hand by dropping "behind the bit."

a) Correct contact: firm and consistent

b) Contact too light: horse going above bit

8.8 Contact firm and too light

8.7
Deb rides him actively forward from her legs to make the contact more firm. As a result, she's created a solid connection from his hind legs into her hands.

8.10
"Home Position" for the elbows in the walk and canter. My elbows are softly bent. However, it's not a perfect picture; there is some tension in my wrist as seen from the way my inside hand is tipped down.

On the other hand, it isn't desirable to have a "death grip" on the horse's mouth. If you know you are the type of rider who tends to hang on with too strong a contact, try this image to help you become more sensitive. Visualize that the reins are delicate threads and you'll break them unless you maintain a really delicate contact with your horse's mouth (fig. 8.9).

8.9
If you tend to hold your horse's mouth in a "death" grip, visualize your reins as fragile threads that can easily break.

CONSISTENCY

Consistent contact means that you don't allow the reins to go slack and then tight and then slack again, and so on. This inconsistent contact punishes the horse in the mouth with every step he takes. A steady contact, even if it's a bit too firm, is preferable to the contact that repeatedly touches the horse's mouth and then gets loose.

8.11
I'm following forward with my arms so that Woody can use the full range of motion of his neck.

ELASTICITY

Elastic contact refers to the action of your elbows. In all three paces, your elbows should move. However, the action of the arms is different in walk and canter than it is in the posting trot.

In the walk and canter the horse uses his head and neck in a forward and back motion, so your elastic elbows should open and close forward and back as well. Your hands go toward the horse's mouth during each stride, maintaining the exact same contact all the time. It may help you to think of starting with your arms bent at right angles and your elbows at your sides. Let's call this "home" position. During each walk or canter stride, extend your arms forward toward your horse's mouth while maintaining a consistent contact, and then let your elbows return to "home" position (figs. 8.10 to 8.13).

8.12

I'm starting to bend the elbows again in order to stay in contact with Woody's mouth as he shortens his neck.

8.13

"Home Position" again. I'm ready to start another sequence of following forward and back.

To help you understand how important this elastic contact is to your horse, follow the motion of his head and neck with elastic elbows for several strides, and then lock your elbows at your sides. If you're in the walk, your horse will slow down or stop altogether. If you're cantering, eventually your horse will break to the trot.

I see many people who have ridden with locked elbows for some time—even years. The horses they ride usually have shortened strides because they feel that they can't move their heads and necks for balance. If you have this tendency to lock your arms, exaggerate following the motion of your horse's head, even at the expense of temporarily losing the contact. Once he develops some confidence that he's not going to run into stiff arms, you'll find that he starts to stretch his neck and his strides become longer.

In the trot the horse's neck stays still. So when you sit to the trot, your arms don't move either. But when you post up and down, your elbows need to allow for your movement so that the contact can remain consistent. The opening and closing of the elbows is comparable to the amount you open and close your knees in posting trot. If your elbows are locked, your hands go up and down and the contact is disturbed because there's a jerky motion on the horse's mouth (figs. 8.14 to 8.17).

Sally Swift, creator of *Centered Riding,* explains how she demonstrates to riders that a rigid contact is distracting and uncomfortable for the horse. "While standing still, I offer the rider one finger just above the withers where the hands would normally hold the reins. I then ask the rider to hold onto my finger and rise up and down as if posting to the trot. As the rider rises up and pulls on my finger, I immediately say, "Ouch!" The student invariably looks surprised, not having noticed that as he rose, he tried to take his hand up too. Because he was holding on to me, he couldn't bring his hand up, so he balanced himself on my finger."

To get the idea of elastic elbows in the posting trot, place your hands on the horse's withers and keep them there as you go up and down. You'll feel the elbows flex and extend as the hands stay steady. If you find it difficult to get the timing, try it at the halt. Keep your hands on the withers and notice how your elbows open as you stand and bend as you sit. Once you have some muscle memory, try again at the trot.

It's easy to experience the difference between elastic and locked elbows in the posting trot. Make your elbows elastic and notice how your hands stay still. Then lock your elbows and note how they move up and down.

8.14 and 8.15

In these two photos you can see that Ruth Poulsen has locked her elbows in posting trot. As a result, her hands go up and down as she goes up and down. Because her arms feel rigid to her horse, Mastermind, he stiffens his neck and braces against her hands.

8.16 and 8.17

In these photos of Ruth at the posting trot, the contact is more inviting. When she sits in the saddle, her elbows are softly bent by her sides. As she rises, her elbows open like a hinge. Notice that they open to the same degree as her knees do. Because her arms feel elastic, her horse willingly accepts the contact with her hands by relaxing his neck and softening his jaw.

<u>8.18</u>

Because the rider is stiffening his elbows through this canter-to-trot transition, the horse protests against the "rude" contact by throwing his head up and tensing his back.

Keeping Elastic Elbows While Doing Transitions

Practice elastic elbows in each pace. Then ride transitions from one pace to another and concentrate on maintaining elasticity during the strides right before and immediately after the transitions. These are critical moments when most riders tend to lock their elbows. If you stiffen your elbows during a transition, your horse might do one of several things. He might stop coming forward with his hind legs during the transition; he might protest by throwing his head up; or perhaps he'll evade the contact altogether by overbending his neck and ducking behind it instead of seeking the contact.

Your horse isn't being disobedient if he does any of these things. He is simply finding it impossible to go forward through a blocking and non-allowing contact during those transitions (fig. 8.18).

I had an auditor at a clinic tell me that she knew her mare very well, and if she took a firm contact as I suggested, the horse would rear. I told her I agreed with her if she took a firm contact with rigid elbows. But I

8.19

The rider won't be able to offer her horse an even contact because one hand is higher than the other.

believed that the mare wouldn't even object to a very heavy contact as long as the connection remained elastic.

The auditor was still pretty skeptical when she left the clinic, but two weeks later I received a note from her. Not only did her mare accept the firm, elastic contact, but she was happily working in a much **rounder** frame (see page 14 for my description of "round") than she ever had before.

SYMMETRICAL HANDS

The last quality of contact that we are going to look at is evenness in the rein. This means that you should feel equal weight in each hand, and should not allow your horse to hang on either rein. You need to offer an inviting, symmetrical contact with your hands softly closed around the reins, thumbs the highest point of your hands, and one hand the mirror image of the other.

The contact is not symmetrical and, therefore, not inviting if:

1. One hand is higher than the other (fig. 8.19).

2. The hands aren't equidistant from the rider's body (fig. 8.20)

3. The position of one hand looks different than the other (fig. 8.21).

8.20
When one hand is drawn closer to the saddle, it blocks the activity of the hind leg on the same side.

8.21
Here the thumb is no longer the highest point of the left hand. The position of one hand should always be the mirror image of the other.

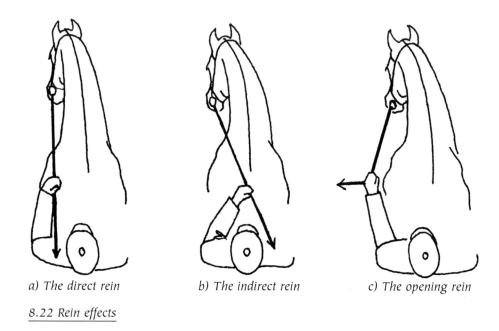

a) The direct rein   b) The indirect rein   c) The opening rein

8.22 Rein effects

Do this exercise to give yourself the correct feeling of symmetrical contact. First, you need to have your hands close together so you'll be able to tell if they look identical. Then, keeping the reins the same length, put both of them in one hand for a few strides and follow with an elastic elbow. With the reins in one hand, your only option is to offer your horse the same feeling on both sides of his mouth. Now put the reins back in both hands. Try to give your horse the same feeling in his mouth as you did when the reins were in one hand. See how close together and symmetrical your hands are? Once you feel comfortable with this hand position and it becomes automatic, challenge yourself by maintaining it during changes of direction and transitions.

The Rein Effects

The different signals and the way that you use the reins to communicate with your horse are called the "**rein effects**". There are actually five rein effects, and they include the *opening rein,* the *indirect rein,* the *direct rein of opposition,* the *indirect rein of opposition in front of the withers,* and the *indirect rein of opposition passing behind the withers.*

If you wish to learn more about these rein effects than I am including here, they are described very well in Anthony Crossley's book entitled, *Training the Young Horse*. I'll only be referring to three rein effects in this book. That's all you'll need for the moment to get the job done (fig. 8.22). The common denominator with all of these actions of the reins is that your arms never move backward toward your body. To do so would have a negative, stopping effect on your horse's hind legs.

Our three rein effects include:

1. The *direct rein* follows an imaginary line drawn from your hand to your hip on the same side. For example, your left hand is directed toward your left hip.

   You can use your direct rein in a variety of ways, such as closing it in a fist, bending your wrist so that your fingernails come closer to your body, or vibrating the rein by squeezing and releasing it as if you're wringing water out of a sponge.

2. The *indirect rein* follows an imaginary line drawn from your hand to your opposite hip. That is, your left hand is directed toward your right hip. You also want to turn your fingernails up toward your face so that your "pinky" finger rather than your thumb points toward your hip. Imagine that you have a key in a door and you're turning the key to unlock the door (fig. 8.23).

   Your hands still stay side by side. This is a momentary adjustment. After you've given the aid, your hands should go back to the symmetrical position.

   When you use the indirect rein, it's essential to remember two things. First, always use your driving aids at the same time that you use your rein. Many instructors are reluctant to teach the indirect rein, and rightly so, because they find that students start using it to replace their legs. If you always use it in conjunction with your leg, you'll be fine.

   Next, it's important to keep in mind that although your hand comes as close to your horse's withers as possible, it never crosses over to the other side of his neck. Each hand must work independently on each side of his body.

3. The *opening rein* or "leading" rein, as it is sometimes called, involves moving your hand laterally, away from your horse's neck. So, for an opening left rein, your left hand moves to the left.

8.23

The indirect rein: turn your fingernails up toward your face so your "pinky" finger, rather than your thumb, points toward your hip. To feel this, imagine you are turning a key to unlock a door.

KEY POINTS

🐎 Your reins serve as transmitters from your brain, through your hands to your horse's mouth, allowing you to affect his hindquarters.

🐎 Your goal is to establish a sympathetic and inviting link with your horse's mouth so that he wants to step into, and accept, a contact with your hands.

🐎 The five qualities that make up correct contact are:

1. A straight line from the bit to your hand to your elbow
2. Firmness
3. Consistency
4. Elasticity
5. Symmetrical hands

🐎 The variations in the ways that you can use the reins are called the "rein effects." In this book, I focus on three of them—the direct rein, the indirect rein, and the opening rein.

NUTS &
BOLTS

In the next two chapters I'll look at basic flatwork—or the "nuts and bolts" of classical training that most horses in any discipline will be capable of doing. The chapters are divided into work on a **single track** (going straight forward) and **two-track** lateral movements (forward and sideways at the same time). I'll examine the movements and exercises technically in terms of description, purpose and aids. Then I'll incorporate imaging to enhance skill development.

You'll see that the movements aren't necessarily an end in themselves. Sometimes exercises can be done to lay a foundation for more advanced work or to break through current mental or physical blocks. For example, if your horse habitually runs with short, quick, sewing machine-like strides when you ask him to lengthen, you can use leg-yielding to loosen, supple, and stretch his muscles. The leg-yields will develop a greater range of motion sideways and, in turn, when you send him straight forward again, he'll be able to cover more ground with each stride.

Or, let's say your horse always gets crooked in a canter depart by swinging his haunches to the inside. You can ride shoulder-fore—one of the easier lateral movements which I describe in Chapter Ten—before the transition to give him the idea of staying **engaged** and keeping that inside hind leg stepping under his body.

Start thinking like this and you'll wonder why you ever thought flat-work was boring. Plus, you won't feel stymied by a problem. Just figure out what your horse already knows how to do, and use it to overcome obstacles.

If you don't have a regulation dressage arena (see appendix for details), mark out a rectangle in a field or in your ring. The short sides should not be any shorter than 60 feet. The long sides can be two to three times longer (120-180 feet) than the short sides. Place four markers directly across from each other in the middle of each side of your arena. A and C are placed in the middle of the short sides, and B and E are in the middle of the long sides. (See a diagram of an arena like this on page 180, fig. 10.20.)

You'll notice that each new movement I describe has a section called "Aids." You use **aids** to communicate with your horse non-verbally. Basically, you have two seat bones, two legs, and two hands with which you can give aids. It is the way that you combine these six aids as well as the various actions of seat, leg, and hand that allow you to be very subtle and specific with your requests. When the lines differentiating the movements are precise, "disobediences" that are really miscommunications are rare. This is because one combination of aids means one, and only one, thing. When you want to ask for something different, you have a different set of aids. As a result, your horse doesn't have to play multiple choice. The language is very clear.

Although I will describe the aids for each new movement and exercise, I want you to remember that once you've given the aids to *start* a movement, your horse should continue doing it on his own until you give him the aids for a different movement. Now, that's the ideal! But the reality is that you'll probably have to remind him to continue from time to time. However, you don't want to fall into the trap of bugging him with your aids every stride. Find moments where you can just relax and ride in harmony. Constant nagging with the aids will not only wear you out but it'll backfire because your horse will eventually tune you out.

For many of the movements and exercises, I'll talk about **inside** and **outside**—both in reference to the aids and to the horse's body. Some of you might think that when you're in an arena, the "inside" is always the side closest to the center of the ring, and the "outside" is the side closest to the rail. This isn't always the case. The horse's inside and outside is always determined by the **flexion** and bend. Specifically, the inside is the direction toward which the horse is flexed (also known as "positioned at the poll") and bent through his body.

In order to make your aids clear to your horse, it will be helpful for you to think that he *always* has an inside and an outside. So even when you're out riding straight along the trail, imagine you are on an enormous circle. Flex and bend your horse ever so slightly in one direction so that you can establish one side as the inside of his body and the other, his outside.

Once you have learned the aids for each movement you can use your imagination to go beyond the mechanics and produce a beautiful picture. Your subconscious mind consists, in part, of a goal-striving mechanism that seeks to accomplish the pictures that exist in your mind. What's more, your subconscious can't tell the difference between what's real and what's vividly imagined. So *perfect* practice...makes perfect. In your imagination you never miss. You're an Olympic rider on an Olympic caliber horse that can do anything, or you've just won the Super Horse title at the World Quarter Horse Show.

Create the perfect picture in your imagination, and you and your horse will soon reach that ideal. Whatever you repeatedly see in your mind's eye in great detail, eventually becomes reality. So pretend you're a champion! See your skills as already in existence and your subconscious has no option but to make it so. For more on this process, read about the theory of **psychocybernetics** in my book *That Winning Feeling! Program Your Mind for Peak Performance.*

CHAPTER NINE

Straightforward Flatwork

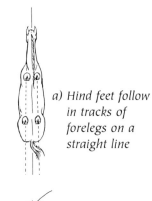

a) Hind feet follow
in tracks of
forelegs on a
straight line

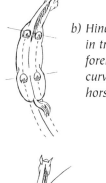

b) Hind feet follow
in tracks of
forelegs on a
curve requiring
horse to bend

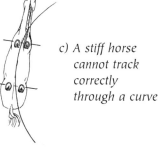

c) A stiff horse
cannot track
correctly
through a curve

9.1
Straightness: spinal alignment

I n this chapter, we'll look at all the movements and exercises that you can do with your horse while riding straight forward on a single track—that is, with your horse's hind feet following directly behind the hoof prints made by his front feet. These movements include circles and corners, upward and downward transitions, backing up, lengthenings in trot and canter, and counter-canter. Once your horse has been introduced to these gymnastic exercises, he'll be ready to start work on **two tracks** covered in Chapter Ten.

Circles and Corners

DESCRIPTION

No matter what your riding discipline, at some point you're going to have to ride a corner or a turn. From a practical standpoint alone, you can hardly keep going straight forever! But there is another reason to ride circles and turns. And that reason is **bend**.

Bend is the common denominator for all varieties of curved lines. And correct bending is essential because (confusing as it may sound) it's a requirement for a *straight* horse.

In Chapter Six I explained that in order to be straight, a horse must be straight on straight lines and bent on curved lines. In both cases the horse's spine corresponds to, and overlaps, whatever line he's on. As a result, his hind feet follow the same tracks as those made by the front feet (fig. 9.1).

In order to improve your horse's ability to *bend* so that he can be *straight*, incorporate circles and other patterns that involve bending, such as figure-eights, shallow loops, and serpentines, into your work.

As a general rule, when you make large circles or gentle loops in the trot, you have the option of posting or sitting. Smaller circles, however, are usually done in the sitting trot.

9.2

For bending, think of your outside aids as the anvil, your inside aids as the hammer, and your horse as the shoe.

The Aids For Bending

The marriage of inside and outside aids creates a horse that bends while turning along a prescribed line. Your inside rein asks your horse to look in the direction he's going and your inside leg asks him to bend through his side. Your outside rein supports and limits the amount of bend in your horse's neck. Your outside leg prevents his hindquarters from swinging out and, therefore, helps bend his body around your inside leg.

To remind yourself to use a complementary influence of the aids, think of how a farrier shapes and bends a shoe. He puts the shoe against the anvil and hits it with the hammer. He cannot bend the shoe with just the anvil or the hammer. He needs both. So, your outside aids are the anvil, and the inside aids are the hammer, and the horse is the shoe (fig. 9.2).

As you ride circles and turns, be sure to look directly between your horse's ears. Riders often have the tendency to turn their heads and look too much to the inside of the line they're on. If this has become a habit, retrain yourself by overcompensating for a while and look at your horse's outside ear on circles and turns.

The aids for a circle or turn to the left (counterclockwise) are as follows:

Seat: weight is on the left seat bone.

Left leg: on the girth as a pole for the horse to bend around and to maintain the activity of the inside hind leg (fig. 9.3).

Right leg: behind the girth to help bend the body around the inside leg and prevent the quarters from swinging out. The degree that the outside leg is back depends on the size of the figure. For a large circle or loop it only comes back an inch or two. On a very small circle, the outside leg might be a few inches behind the inside leg (fig. 9.4).

Left rein: vibrates for flexion at the poll to the inside. The rider should just barely be able to see the inside eye or inside nostril of her horse.

Right rein: steady and supporting to limit the degree of bend in the neck. It also functions as the turning rein as it brings the horse's shoulders around the circle or corner.

9.3
The inside aids on a large circle to the left. Deb's left leg is on the girth so Rapunzel can bend around it. Note that the stirrup leather is perpendicular to the ground. The inside hand is active while the outside hand is steady. Even though the action of the two reins is different, both hands remain side by side.

9.4
It's easier to see that Deb has her weight correctly on her left (inside) seat bone by looking at her seat from the outside of the circle. Note that on a large circle, her outside leg is only slightly behind the girth. You can tell it's back because the stirrup leather is a bit behind a perpendicular line drawn to the ground, and you can see a little more of the horse's barrel between the girth and her leg.

9.5

Rider is bending horse's neck only, not evenly through the body.

• *Helpful Hints* •

Even if you ride an accurate circle with the perfect size and shape, you won't develop your horse's flexibility if he doesn't bend properly.

One issue you face in your quest for correct bend is the fact that horses bend more easily in the neck than in the rest of the spine (fig. 9.5). It's vital to maintain a uniform bend from poll to tail.

Another issue is that, like people, horses are stronger on one side and weaker on the other. With a horse, the strong side is known as the **stiff side**; it is more difficult for him to bend on this side. This is partly due to the muscles on the other side of the body, which are short and tight due to lack of suppleness. These shortened muscles need to be gently stretched and elongated so they allow the horse to bend more easily around the leg on his stiff side.

The weak side is the **soft side**. A horse finds it easier to bend on this side. Riders often describe the soft side as the "good" side because it feels better, or more comfortable, to ride in this direction. However, the soft side is not necessarily the "good" side. This is because the horse is often not using his hind leg on the soft side as actively as he does the hind leg on his stiff side. As a result, the hind leg on the soft side becomes weaker.

Dressage riders usually call the horse's soft side his **hollow** side. However, I'm going to call it the soft side because I don't want to confuse you with a second usage of the word "hollow" that refers to a horse who is not connected over his back. But don't worry too much about this for now. We'll get into that in depth when I discuss putting your horse "on the bit" in Book Two.

Your job is to make your horse bend equally on both sides. You really have your work cut out for you because if you look at your horse when he's just standing in his stall, he probably has his body curved more in one direction than the other. There is a theory that this curve in the horse's spine is related to the position of the horse in the womb. However, whatever the reason, you only have an hour or so each day to undo what your horse does with his muscles naturally. (I will give you some exercises to help you with your horse's stiff and soft side later in this chapter, on page 135).

THE NEED TO INCREASE INFLUENCE OF THE BENDING AIDS

If the horse is bending and turning easily, the inside aids are slightly active and the outside aids stay fairly passive, as I've discussed. When one part of the horse's body is not bending correctly, the appropriate aids become more active. In the following exercises, I'm still referring to a circle (counterclockwise) to the left, as I explain how to increase the aids. As you circle to the left, your inside is the left side and your outside is the right side:

1. If your horse leans on your left leg and doesn't give in his rib cage, or is lazy with his left hind leg, make your left leg active by squeezing and releasing at the girth. You might have to use more active inside aids when you're riding your horse on a circle and his stiff side is on the inside. Here's an image that might help you with this. Think of your left leg pushing your horse's barrel way over to the right to encourage him to bend (fig. 9.6)

2. If your horse's hindquarters swing to the right and are outside the arc of the circle, his hind feet are not following the tracks of his front feet. In this case, press a bit more strongly with your right leg behind the girth. Here's an image that should give you some incentive to use your supporting right leg: pretend you're riding on the edge of a cliff. If you don't keep the hindquarters in line, they'll fall off the edge! (fig. 9.7).

3. If your horse doesn't want to look in the direction he's turning, flex him to the left by activating the left rein. First, gently squeeze and release the rein. If your horse still ignores you and positions his head to the outside of the turn, you can give several small indirect rein aids (fig. 9.8)

9.6
If your horse is leaning on your left leg and doesn't give in his ribcage, "think" of your left leg pushing his barrel to the right—all the way!

9.7
If you need an incentive to encourage you to use your supporting right leg, pretend you're riding on the edge of a cliff. If you don't keep the hindquarters in line, they'll fall off the edge!

9.8
This horse isn't looking in the direction he's turning. He's circling to the left and looking to the right.

9.9

To prevent your horse from bending his neck too much to the left and "popping" his shoulder out to the right, take a firmer hold on the right rein and soften your left hand.

4. If your horse bends his neck too much to the left and his shoulder falls out to the right, take a firmer hold on the right rein. Remember that horses are more flexible in the neck than elsewhere in the spine, so be sure to limit and control the amount of bend in the neck by supporting with the outside rein (fig. 9.9).

Imagine that your right rein together with your arm act like the side reins you use when longeing. A correctly-adjusted outside side rein prevents the horse from bending his neck too much to the inside and stops his shoulder from falling out sideways. As a result the horse can be **axis-straight** (see p. 83).

MARRY YOUR INSIDE AND OUTSIDE AIDS!

Have you ever had a situation while riding on a circle, where your horse just leaves the circle and runs off to the other end of the ring? For instance, you're circling to the left and your horse runs off to the right. If you had an instructor there she might yell, "Outside rein!" which is your right rein. But every fiber in your being tells you to pull on the left or inside rein to get back to your circle.

The problem here is that if you only use the inside or left rein to direct your horse back to the circle and you don't also support with the outside or right rein at the same time and to the same degree, you'll only pull your horse's head and neck around and his body can continue going where he wants.

Remember the marriage of the inside and outside aids! When you're increasing your inside rein to bring your horse back to the circle, you must also increase the outside aids for support so you can limit the amount of bend in the neck and control the outside shoulder.

These same dynamics exist when you ride a circle that isn't quite the right shape. I frequently see circles that aren't truly round because the horse's shoulders are escaping and drifting to the outside of the arc of the curve in much the same way (though to a lesser degree) as the above example where the horse is running off. If you want round circles—and who doesn't—make sure you have a complementary influence of inside and outside aids.

a) Correct lateral
flexion: at the poll

b) Incorrect lateral
flexion: tilted head

c) Incorrect lateral
flexion: in neck

9.10 Correct and incorrect lateral flexion

LOOSENING THE POLL ON THE STIFF SIDE

The first step in riding a circle or corner is to have the horse looking in
the direction he's going. To do this, the horse must flex at the poll. The
poll is actually the top of the horse's skull, (the first vertebra located just
behind the ears) but in common dressage usage, "flexion at the poll"
refers to the closing of the two joints immediately behind the poll. When
I talk about "lateral flexion" or "position to the inside" on a curved line,
I'm specifically referring to flexion of the second cervical (neck) joint (fig.
9.10).

Sometimes flexing a horse at the poll is difficult because he feels
"locked" there. Usually it's harder to flex him laterally on his stiff side.
However, occasionally a horse is simply locked in the poll and it's difficult to flex him either left or right. To loosen your horse in the poll, give
several small indirect rein aids on the locked side; as I mentioned earlier
in the section on rein effects (p. 122), turn your wrist as if you're unlocking a door, or scooping a spoonful of sugar out of a bowl. Your hands
should stay side by side while your fingernails face upward and your
baby finger points toward your opposite hip (fig. 9.11). *Never* draw your
inside hand across the horse's withers.

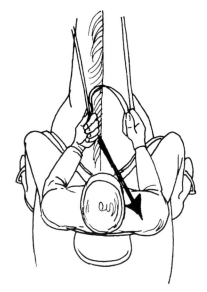

9.11

To flex your horse at the poll
use an indirect rein. Left
indirect rein: left hand rotates
and angles towards the rider's
right hip.

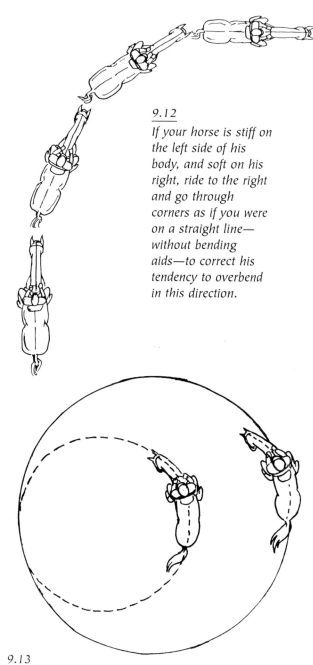

9.12

If your horse is stiff on the left side of his body, and soft on his right, ride to the right and go through corners as if you were on a straight line— without bending aids—to correct his tendency to overbend in this direction.

9.13

To help soften your horse's stiff left side, first ride a small circle to the left. Then go onto a large circle but keep the bending aids on as they were when you were asking your horse to curve his body along the arc of the smaller circle.

EXERCISES TO HELP STIFF AND SOFT SIDES

The following are some exercises to help you with a horse that shows a marked stiffness on one side of his body.

1. The first exercise is to compensate for this one-sidedness by bending your horse too much on the stiff side and not at all on the soft side until he becomes more even. Do this while riding both on straight lines as well as on curved lines.

   For instance, let's say your horse is stiff on the left side of his body and soft on the right. When you go right (clockwise) around an arena, a field or a circle, don't use your bending aids. Ride as if you're on a straight line (fig. 9.12). Riding a corner without any bending aids will prevent the horse from "collapsing" or "curling" on his soft right side.

   Alternatively, when you go left around an arena to his stiff side, use bending aids as if you're on a curve even when you're on the straight lines. By doing so, you get more practice time stretching the shortened muscles on the soft side—the outside of your horse's body.

2. Here's another bending exercise to help soften the stiff side. Ride a large circle and then a smaller circle inside and touching it (fig. 9.13). Adjust your bending aids for the smaller circle and stay on it until your horse bends easily. Then keeping your aids on as if you're still on this small circle, go back to the larger circle. Visualize the outside of your horse's body—his soft side where the muscles are shortened—stretching and lengthening to allow him to bend around your inside leg. Even if you can only do this in the walk for a while, the exercise helps your horse to bend on his stiff side. When he becomes more flexible, you can do it in the trot and then in the canter.

RIDING CORNERS AND CIRCLES CORRECTLY

Many riders just cruise through corners and turns without thought. When correctly ridden, each corner gives you a chance to develop your horse's ability to bend. Every corner in an oblong arena should be ridden as if it's one-quarter of a circle.

A circle is the first gymnastic exercise that we teach a horse on the longe line. By making a round circle, he learns to bend laterally through his side and to bend the joints of his inside hind leg. So every correctly ridden corner presents an opportunity to do the same thing. In a rectangular area, you're given this chance to "gymnasticize" your horse four times as you go once around the ring!

A good rule of thumb is to go into the corner only to a depth that your horse can handle without losing his rhythm and balance. However, once he can easily negotiate a shallow corner, challenge him by going into the corners a bit more "deeply." By "deeply," I mean rather than getting lured into following the well-worn track while riding around the corner, make a new path by riding slightly outside the old track and a bit closer to the fence.

Sloppy corners and circles begin with the rider, but eventually develop as a way for the horse to physically escape the demands of bending and, therefore, be subtly disobedient. If you allow your horse to do as he chooses because you're being careless, he'll begin to make more decisions—a situation you wisely want to avoid.

Transitions

DESCRIPTION

Generally the word **transition** applies to any sort of change. In training, a horse can show the following kinds of transitions:

1. Transitions from one pace to another, such as going from walk to trot or from trot to canter.
2. Transitions within a pace, such as from a working gait to a lengthening of that working gait.
3. Transitions from movement to movement, such as from a leg-yield into a lengthening.

All transitions should be made quickly, yet must be fluid and smooth. The regular rhythm of the pace as well as the tempo is maintained right up to the moment when the pace is changed or the horse is asked to halt.

This next section deals specifically with the transitions from one pace to another. I'll discuss both upward transitions, in which the horse is asked to go from the halt or from a slower pace into a faster one, as well as downward transitions, in which the horse is asked to go from a faster pace to a slower one, or to the halt.

The Aids for Upward Transitions

The following is a list of general aids for all upward transitions, although later in this chapter I address some of the problems connected specifically with transitions to the canter under the section called Helpful Hints For Canter Departs.

1. Halt to walk; walk to trot:

Seat: use a "driving" seat, where you give a little push with your seat as if you're trying to move the back of the saddle toward the front of the saddle.

Legs: close both legs equally on the horse's sides.

Hands: maintain a soft, equal contact with the horse's mouth.

2. Canter depart from walk or trot (left lead):

Seat: weight on left seat bone.

Left leg: squeeze on the girth to promote "forward."

Right leg: swing behind the girth once in a windshield wiper action to signal the outside hind leg to begin the first beat of the canter.

Left rein: vibrate to position the horse's head just enough to the inside so you can see the inside eye. This positioning is called flexion. (Flexion is discussed in detail on page 171.)

Right rein: hold it steady to support and limit bend in the neck to the left, as well as to keep the horse from going faster in the walk or trot.

As far as upward transitions are concerned, you shouldn't have to push or drive your horse into the next pace. You should be able to give a signal with light aids. If you feel like nothing is happening and you want to squeeze harder, you need to go back to the Basics and put him "in front of your leg" again, as I described earlier on page 80.

The Aids for Downward Transitions

Canter to trot; trot to walk; walk to halt:

Legs: first close both legs as you did for upward transitions. You do this to keep the hind legs active and stepping well under the horse's body.

Reins: momentarily close both hands into fists to contain that energy and stop the horse from going faster.

Be sure not to use the reins for downward transitions without using your legs at the same time: any use of the reins without equal use of your legs will discourage the horse's hind legs from coming under his body. The flow and balance will be interrupted and the horse's frame will change. The problem with this is that you usually get some of the result you're looking for. Therefore, you continue to do the same thing and it becomes a habit. You know the cycle! The goal: to get from trot to walk. The method: pull on the reins. The payoff: you're walking. Now you're trained (and the horse too) to pull on the reins for downward transitions.

Seat: using a **"stilled seat"**—that is, sitting with equal weight on both of your seat bones and use your back in a stopping, non-following, or retarding way, think about stretching tall and tightening your stomach muscles the way you would when doing a sit-up. This will cause you to brace your lower back. Keep your back braced while you stop your hips from following the motion of the horse.

To practice this, sit on your horse in the halt and focus on the immobility of your seat. Then, when you want to do a downward transition, mimic the stillness that your seat had when you were in the halt. Pick a particular point in the ring or on the trail and as you pass that spot, make your body immobile (figs. 9.14 and 9.15).

9.14

I'm sitting in a "ready" position to use my back. I'm stretching up with my shoulders directly above my hips and there is a gently curve in the small of my back.

9.15

Here, I've "stilled" my seat for a downward transition. I tighten my stomach muscles as if I'm doing a sit-up. As a result, the curve in my back has gone. Note that my shoulders remain over my hips—it's important not to lean back when you "still" your seat.

9.16

You're saying "whoa," and your horse continues to creep along. Instead of resorting to the reins, turn him toward the wall or rail. He'll stop—I guarantee it!

After you learn how to "still" your seat, you need to educate your horse so you can use your seat as the primary aid for downward transitions. To do this, combine your stilled seat with your voice. Your horse already knows simple voice commands from work on the longe line. If you want to go from canter to trot, tighten your stomach muscles to brace your lower back, "still" your seat, and say "Terrot" in the same way you do while longeing.

If your horse doesn't listen to your voice and back, take advantage of the walls of an indoor arena or a high rail outside. Let's say you want to go from walk to halt. You're "stilling" your seat, saying "Whoa," and he continues to creep along, not halting. Instead of resorting to the reins at this point, turn him toward the wall. When he meets the wall or rail, he'll stop and you can then praise him and try again without the wall (fig. 9.16).

Sometimes I find that riders get overly concerned that they aren't using their backs "correctly." There's no need to worry. We all have different bodies that move in different ways. As long as you use *your* back the *same way* each time, somehow get the response by combining the use of the back with a voice command that the horse knows, and then praise the result, your horse will learn to respond to your back—believe me!

What is necessary for your back to work for you is that you must be sitting in the correct position with an independent seat so you have a "ready" back. Regardless of the style of riding you do, you want to be centered and in balance. As a Western, Saddleseat, or dressage rider with longer stirrups, you need to sit vertically so that a plumb line attached to your ear will pass through the tip of your shoulder, hip joint, and ankle, straight through your center. Stretch up tall so there's a gentle curve in the small of your back. If you ride hunters, jumpers, or combined training horses with shorter stirrups for jumping, you need to bring your upper body forward in order to be in balance. A plumb line dropped through your center would also pass through your feet. Your hips stay behind the plumb line to offset the weight of your forward-reaching head and shoulders.

When you tighten your stomach from this balanced and "ready" position, and stop your seat from following the movement, the horse will do the downward transition.

• *Helpful Hints for All Transitions* •

Both upward and downward transitions should be clear and distinct but not abrupt. They should be done in a fluid manner. The horse should go directly from working gait to working gait. While teaching, I often see a rider allow her horse to take steps that are lazy, little, or in a different rhythm. Many times the horse even rushes off into the new gait. Remember, there shouldn't have to be any adjustment to build energy back up or steady the horse's tempo back down to a good working gait. For the most part I've found that simply making a rider aware that she needs to put her full attention into maintaining the quality of the working gait—before and after the transition—is enough to fix the problem.

Sometimes this extra awareness isn't enough, and you'll find it necessary to do an exercise to give both you and your horse the feeling of maintaining energy as you start the next gait. Ride a few transitions from medium walk into a lengthened trot, or from working canter to a lengthening in the trot, in order to make the trot after the transition more energetic. Then, when you do an upward or a downward transition, pretend you're going to do a lengthening rather than the normal working trot, and you should end up with good energy at the working trot. You can do this for the walk and canter, as well.

• *Helpful Hints for Downward Transitions* •

Some horses tend to rush off after a downward transition—particularly when going from the canter to the trot. If your horse does this, immediately halt. Praise him by patting or using your voice by saying, "Good Boy!" to explain to him that he's done the right thing by stopping. Although the halt should be done fairly sharply, your goal is not to punish but to educate. So the reward is essential! Do this several times until you feel that your horse chooses to do the downward transition into a controlled and balanced working trot.

Later in this book (Chapter Thirteen) I'll show you how you can also use backing up, small circles, and leg-yielding to explain to your horse that he's not to rush off after a downward transition.

• *Helpful Hints for Canter Departs* •

Frequently, I see horses who don't do a distinct upward transition from the walk or the trot into the canter. The horse hobbles through the first canter stride in almost a four-beat rhythm.

The problem here is usually a lack of energy. To make the transition more distinct, change the emphasis of your aids. You'll still give the signal for the strike-off by swinging your outside leg behind the girth, but now focus more on your inside leg, which is on the girth. Give a sharper squeeze with this leg than you did before, to remind him to go energetically forward.

There's another common situation that you might run into during a walk-to-canter or trot-to-canter transition that we will deal with in the next chapter. There are times when a horse will swing his haunches toward the inside of the ring to avoid the engagement of his inside hind leg. You can help the horse avoid this tendency by riding him in a shoulder-fore position, which I describe in Chapter Ten.

Another canter problem that you will run into with a young or uneducated horse is picking up the wrong lead. Often this happens in one direction more frequently than in the other. Keep in mind that the horse will pick up whatever lead he's bent and positioned toward at the moment of departure. Sometimes, the rider has the horse nicely bent around the inside leg, but in the moment of the depart, the horse counter-bends and ends up picking up the wrong lead. The solution is to maintain active bending aids—vibrate your inside rein and squeeze with your inside leg—*right through the moment of the transition.*

If you need help maintaining the correct bend to the inside, first spiral in to make the circle smaller. Then, increase the size of the circle by pushing the horse back out to the larger circle with your inside leg which is on the girth. This is an example of leg-yielding—a lateral movement which I'll describe in detail in the next chapter. Keep your inside leg on the girth and feel the horse give in his rib cage and bend around your inside leg while he's stepping sideways. Do this several times until he's softly bending correctly. Then, when you've enlarged the circle almost back to its original size and while you're still leg-yielding, ask for the canter depart.

The previous helpful hints have been directed toward correctly preparing *the horse* for transitions to the canter. The next two hints are for you, *the rider.*

If you pull on the inside rein during a canter depart, you interrupt the horse's flow and balance, and he can't go forward through the transition. He feels blocked by your hand and takes a short step into the canter. If you tend to do this, you should exaggerate when correcting this riding problem until it's resolved. While asking for the depart, put slack in your inside rein by placing your inside hand several inches toward the horse's mouth. When this becomes your new habit, don't actually loosen the rein, but just think about softening your hand forward (fig. 9.17).

Here's another hint for you to keep in mind when you ask for a transition into the canter. The signal for the canter depart is to swing the out-

9.17
To teach yourself not to pull on the inside rein during a canter depart, for a while exaggerate softening your inside hand by putting it forward as your horse steps into the canter.

side leg behind the girth in a windshield wiper-like action. But because horses are often dull to the aids, a rider often gets into the habit of bringing that outside leg back and holding it there for a few seconds until the horse finally answers. This sets a bad precedent, because horses should be trained to respond immediately to any aid.

If this has happened to you, you need to put your horse in front of your leg again. Swing your outside leg back and forth once. If your horse does not immediately strike off into the canter, give him a sharp kick or tap him with your stick to chase him forward. Then retest his reaction to your leg by once again swinging your leg back to signal the transition to the canter. You might have to do this several times until you "retrain" your horse to react more quickly to the aid.

9.18

If your horse tends to drag his feet when he backs up, imagine that he is stepping up over poles on the ground.

9.19

In the rein back, lighten your seat and point your seat bones toward the back of the saddle, as if pushing a stool out from underneath you.

Backing Up (The Rein Back)

DESCRIPTION

No matter what type of riding you do, at the very least you need to be able to tell your horse to stop, go, turn left, turn right, and back up. Your horse needs to be able to understand and do those things in order to be an enjoyable and obedient riding mount.

In dressage, backing up is called the **rein back**. It's a movement which is shown in competition and judged by some very specific criteria. We can use some of these criteria as guidelines for improving how your horse backs up.

In the rein back the horse steps straight backward by raising and setting his feet down *almost* simultaneously in diagonal pairs. To the naked eye it appears that the legs move in diagonal pairs, and in classical training it's considered a fault if the horse goes back in a four-beat rhythm. The fact is, however, that each front foot is raised and set down an instant before the diagonal hind foot, so that on hard ground sometimes four separate beats are heard. But you shouldn't be able to see this.

During the rein back, the horse must be active and energetic and should pick up and set down his legs clearly and deliberately without dragging or stepping wide with his hind legs. In your mind's eye, picture your horse stepping up over ground poles as he goes backward (fig. 9.18).

The Aids for Backing Up

Seat: lighten your seat by tipping forward slightly and pointing your seat bones toward the back of the saddle as if pushing a stool out from underneath you (fig. 9.19).

Legs: close both legs slightly behind the girth.

Hands: close in fists, then when the horse begins to step back, soften them. If the horse resists the reins, you can softly vibrate them.

• *Helpful Hints* •

INTRODUCING THE REIN BACK FROM THE GROUND

While teaching the rein back, I've seen a lot of uneducated horses who absolutely refuse to back up. They don't necessarily rear or fuss, but they remain rooted to the ground. In desperation, the riders start yanking on the reins. Not a pretty sight!

When I have a horse like this, I go through several stages. I start teaching the rein back from the ground, and say the word "Back" as I place my hand on his chest and gently push. When he steps back, I praise with treats or a pat. (It's a good idea, by the way, to take advantage of every opportunity you have when handling your horse in the barn to teach him the word "Back.")

Then, transfer this idea to your mounted work. Start with an assistant who can press on his chest just as you did with your ground work while you give the aids and say the word "Back." The assistant can gradually move a bit further away from the horse and just stand there while you ask the horse to back up. If your horse doesn't move, she can walk up to him and press on his chest again. Eventually you'll be able to back up without help but still using the voice command combined with your aids. Finally, back up simply from the aids alone without the use of your voice (fig. 9.20 and 9.21).

9.20
Use an assistant who can press gently on your horse's chest to give him the idea of stepping backward.

9.21
Gradually wean your horse away from needing help from the ground by having the assistant stand further away. If he stubbornly refuses to move back, the assistant can take a step or two towards him to remind him of what he's supposed to do.

INTRODUCING THE REIN BACK FROM THE SADDLE

Making Your Horse Wait

Sometimes the difficulty with a horse that's just learning to back up is that he begins to anticipate and back up every time you halt. For this eager horse who tries too hard to do what he thinks you want, do a lot of transitions to the halt without asking him to back up. When he doesn't take the initiative anymore, do the occasional rein back.

This problem may be caused by the rider, so always make your horse wait several seconds after halting before giving the command to back up.

Along the same lines as the horse that anticipates backing up, is the horse that rushes backward. One of my students, Ruth, had a lovely well-schooled Hanoverian gelding that she was showing in upper-level dressage competitions. All of his work was of a very high quality except for the rein back. He was absolutely panicked by it and would rush backward when asked to perform it. We weren't sure why he did this. Maybe there were some "skeletons in his closet" from an earlier bad experience. Whatever the reason, we had to explain to him that he didn't have to run backward frantically.

To overcome his tension, Ruth used tactful aids and asked him to go back only one or two steps before stopping and praising a lot. While stepping back, she quietly said, "Whoa, whoa." She would intersperse these short rein backs here and there throughout a schooling session until it became part of his daily routine, and it was no big deal anymore. To help keep him calm, Ruth imagined him taking deliberate, methodical steps in slow motion while he carefully picked his feet up out of deep mud and placed them back down again (figs. 9.22 to 9.26).

Backing Up Straight

Sometimes horses don't back up in a straight line. This is often because one hind leg is weaker than the other and the horse avoids placing the weaker hind leg underneath his body. I once spent an entire competitive season compensating for this weakness in a young horse by riding the rein back with my left leg placed further back than the right. Sometimes I could just leave it there passively to guard against him swinging his haunches to the left, but sometimes I actually had to press with it in order to get him to back up straight.

When I was at home I often worked on correcting this problem by schooling him in an indoor arena. I tracked right so that his left side was next to the wall when I asked him to back up. Eventually he understood, and as his hindquarters became stronger, it was easy for him to keep his left hind leg underneath his body, so I was able to return to positioning my legs side by side.

9.22 to 9.26
Rein Back Sequence

<u>*9.22*</u>
Before backing up, come to a balanced halt. Although Mastermind isn't absolutely square at the halt with his legs side by side, he's in pretty good balance here.

<u>*9.23*</u>
To start backing up, Ruth tips her upper body slightly forward, brings both legs a bit behind the girth, and closes the fingers of both hands in fists.

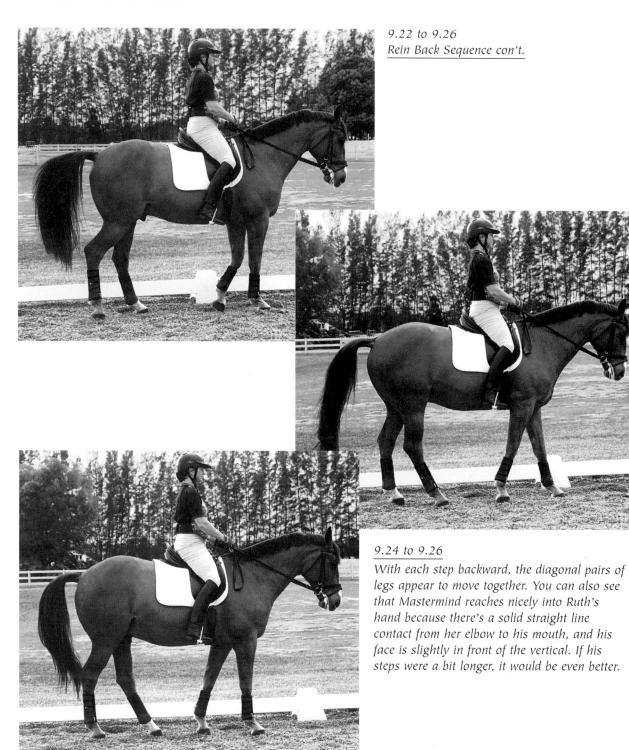

9.24 to 9.26
With each step backward, the diagonal pairs of legs appear to move together. You can also see that Mastermind reaches nicely into Ruth's hand because there's a solid straight line contact from her elbow to his mouth, and his face is slightly in front of the vertical. If his steps were a bit longer, it would be even better.

If you find that your horse consistently doesn't back up straight, make sure the rein pressure is even. If you have a stronger feel on the right rein, for instance, he will step to the left.

Having said that, there are times when you will purposely ask your horse to go sideways while backing up. It's helpful to do this with the horse that backs up a step or two but then stalls out and refuses to go back anymore. For this type of horse, push him sideways by placing one of your legs further back than the other and pressing with it. Pushing him sideways helps to keep him in motion as you back up. When he has finally learned to step back for as many steps as you ask—crooked or otherwise—you can then start backing up on a straight line again.

Teaching Your Horse To Take Better Steps

I often see horses that back up by taking very short steps. Because the steps are short, the horse's back drops, and he sticks his head and neck up in the air. This is uncomfortable for both horse and rider.

If your horse does this, I suggest that you continue backing quietly until your horse takes his first longer step. Even if you can't feel the longer step or the subsequent raising of the back, you'll see your horse's head and neck begin to lower. His lowered head and neck mean that the steps are getting longer. As soon as this happens, stop and praise him. Walk forward for a few strides and start the process again, always stopping and rewarding him when he takes some long steps. While doing this, picture his hind legs staying well under the body as if he's stepping forward *toward* your hand, even though you're going backward. Soon your horse will learn to back up with long strides.

Sometimes you'll find that your horse takes long steps when you ask him to back up but he drags his feet. Ride some brisk trot-to-halt transitions. These transitions will engage his hind legs underneath his body so that the backward steps are crisp and active. Make sure you apply your driving aids as the horse steps into halt, so that the hind legs are well underneath the body, and he has a better chance of moving the legs back in diagonal pairs.

Lengthenings

DESCRIPTION

The horse that is working at the basic levels in dressage should be able to show two "gears" in his trot and canter—a working trot and canter, and a **lengthening** of both paces.

In a correct lengthening of the working trot and canter, two things visibly change. While maintaining the same rhythm and tempo (the rate of repetition of the rhythm) of whichever gait he's working in, the horse

9.27

An active, lively working trot, clearly showing the horse stepping into his tracks.

elongates both his stride and the frame of his body to the utmost that he is capable of doing at this stage of his development. All horses should learn how to lengthen their strides and bodies because it's a great way to promote suppleness.

A lengthening can be developed from the working trot and the working canter. During the lengthening of a gait it's of the utmost importance for your horse to maintain both the same regular rhythm and the same tempo that was established when he was in the working gait. The sound of his footfalls should not change. What does change is the length of his stride and his frame so that he's covering more ground with each stride (figs. *9.27* to *9.30*).

For the sake of clarity and for some of you readers who know a bit about dressage, I'd like to mention here that there is a difference between a *lengthening* in trot and canter and what is called in dressage vernacular a *medium* or an *extended* gait. Riders often incorrectly use these terms interchangeably. That's probably because they do share some similarities, specifically that the horse's strides and frame of his body elongate while the rhythm and tempo of the gait stay the same. However, there is a major difference: in a medium or extended gait, the horse's balance and center of gravity are in quite a different place than when he just performs a lengthening.

9.28
When Special Effects lengthens his working trot, he covers more ground with each stride so that his hind foot touches the ground in front of the place that his front foot left the ground. Note the greater spread between his hind legs and the elongation of his entire frame.

9.29
Deb and Galen showing a well-balanced working canter.

9.30
A lengthening of the working canter. Notice how active the mare's inside hind leg is and how far it reaches under her body. The entire frame gets longer, and the balance is well maintained rather than shifting to the forehand as so often happens when you ask a horse to lengthen.

9.31

In an extended trot (rather than a lengthened trot) the horse's center of gravity is more toward the hindquarters. As a result, his balance seems to be going uphill, like an airplane taking off.

A lengthening is developed from a *working* gait. In a working gait the horse's balance and center of gravity are somewhat on his forehand, so it's reasonable to assume that the horse's balance in a lengthening is also somewhat toward his forehand.

A medium or extended gait, on the other hand, can only be developed from a *collected* gait. In a collected gait, the horse's hindquarters are lower than in a working gait, and they support a greater proportion of his weight than his front legs. The horse's center of gravity, therefore, is more toward the hind legs. (This is the aim of **collection** or **self-carriage**). During a medium or an extended gait, the horse's center of gravity remains more toward the hindquarters, just as it was in the collected gait. As a result, his balance and silhouette seem to be going uphill, like an airplane taking off (fig. 9.31).

For now I'll only be dealing with lengthenings which are developed from the working gaits. In Book Two I'll discuss collected, medium and extended gaits more fully for those who are interested.

Lengthenings can be done on both straight lines and circles. But keep in mind that because of the bend and the demands being made on the inside hind leg when you're on a curved line, lengthenings on a circle are physically harder than those ridden on a straight line.

I suggest you add lengthenings to your horse's education once he is fairly steady and balanced in his working gaits. Some people delay starting lengthenings with their horses for several years, and I believe this is a mistake. Think of how a gymnast needs to stretch and elongate her muscles when she's young. If she doesn't develop her suppleness early on, it will be very difficult to find that elasticity later.

Your horse's working gaits should already contain sufficient energy for him to be able to do lengthenings easily in trot and canter. If they don't, you need to first make your horse more active so he has enough power to lengthen. You can do this by checking that he is forward—both forward over the ground as well as "hot off your leg," which I discussed earlier in the book (see page 80).

The Aids for Lengthenings

When you're ready to ask for an upward transition to a length-ening, the aids applied simultaneously, are as follows:

Seat: use a driving seat, as though you're pushing the back of the saddle toward the front of the saddle.

Legs: press lightly with both legs to signal your horse to express his energy forward over the ground in longer strides.

Reins: soften your hands a bit forward, but keep a contact with your horse's mouth and a bend in your elbows. Do not "throw the reins away."

• *Helpful Hints for Lengthenings* •

Here's an image that will help you under-stand the type of suppleness you're devel-oping when you practice lengthenings. Think of your horse's body as a rubber band that can easily stretch and contract. Not only will this quality make him more athletic, but it's also extremely useful for all disciplines of riding (fig. 9.32). Take show jumping, for in-stance. Just think how many jumping faults could be avoided if your horse's stride were easily adjustable like this!

MAINTAINING THE TEMPO OF THE WORKING TROT

As with most new work, when you begin to incorporate lengthenings into your training, you start in the trot. It's a bonus if you have a horse that can naturally lengthen his trot. Many Warmbloods and Arabians have this ability, but I've worked with a lot of Thoroughbreds, Con-nemaras, Morgans, and Quarter Horses who really need help developing their lengthenings in the trot.

If you ask your horse to lengthen in the way I've described and the tempo gets quicker because he runs with short, fast steps, you need to systematically develop his lengthenings. Part of his difficulty may be purely physical. He may lack the suppleness and strength that he will gain in time by basic dressage training. But part of the problem may be that the horse just doesn't understand that he is to take longer strides

9.32

To help you understand the type of suppleness you need when doing lengthenings, think of your horse's body as a rubber band that can easily stretch and contract.

9.33

When asking for a lengthening, I picture my horse floating, with his feet never touching the ground.

in the same tempo. He actually thinks he's being obedient when he rushes off because he feels you close your legs, and he responds eagerly by immediately going forward.

I often find that I can help him understand that he is to lengthen his strides without speeding up, by asking for the lengthenings while going up hills. Once he gets the idea, I go back into the ring and see if he can transfer this concept of lengthening in the same tempo on the level footing.

Sometimes I do something a bit unusual with the horse that tends to quicken his trot tempo when asked to lengthen. Since it takes time to develop the lengthening, I go out in a big field or I go all the way around the ring and round off the corners so that I don't have to slow down for them. First, I take up a heavier contact than normal. In this way, I can temporarily act as the horse's "fifth" leg and purposely support him so he doesn't lose his balance. Then I ask for a lengthening in posting trot. While posting to the trot, I rise very high and stay in the air a fraction of a second longer than normal. I pretend that I can hold the horse in the air with my body. And, in my mind's eye, I picture him floating over the ground with his feet never touching the ground (fig. 9.33).

I ask my horse to give me a greater and greater effort and eventually one of two things will happen. The first is that he realizes that his legs can't go any faster, and he "shifts into overdrive" and takes some longer, slower steps. At this point I immediately stop, praise him, and let him walk on a loose rein.

In my experience I've found that the first time, I might have to go all the way around a ring once or twice before I get a couple of longer, slower steps. But after the reward, the next effort yields results much sooner. And the same for the next attempt.

The other thing that might happen is that he loses his balance and falls into the canter. This isn't the disaster it seems to be. If my horse hadn't lost his balance and cantered, his next trot step probably would have been a bit longer. So I reestablish the trot and *immediately* ask for a lengthening. It's in that moment that I'm most apt to get a longer stride in a better tempo. And once again if I get even one or two better steps, I stop and praise him. The reward helps the horse to understand that by doing something different, even if initially he doesn't understand what it is, he'll be praised.

Once I can get two or three better steps as soon as I ask for the lengthening, I leave them for another day. During each session the horse builds his understanding of what's being asked, and over time he physically gets strong enough to lengthen in a good tempo for a greater number of steps.

HEAR THE TEMPO

Use some good auditory images to help you while you're teaching your horse to lengthen in the same tempo as his working gait. Pretend you're standing by a paved road and your eyes are closed. Because the tempo stays exactly the same, you can't tell from the sound of the footfalls whether your horse is in the working gait, lengthening, or doing the transition in between.

Here's another auditory image to help you teach your horse to lengthen the trot in the same tempo as his working trot. Pretend you hear a metronome ticking. The tempo stays exactly the same both when you're in the working trot and when you're in the lengthening (fig. 9.34). (Even though I'm discussing trot lengthenings at the moment, you can use the same type of auditory image if your horse quickens his tempo in a canter lengthening. "Hear" the tempo as if your horse is moving over the ground with big, ground-covering bounds in slow motion.)

If your horse still tends to quicken his tempo when you ask him to lengthen, overcompensate by imagining that you "hear" the tempo get slower. Pretend that the tempo gets slower because your horse stays suspended in the air for a long time. If you're doing a posting trot, try rising and sitting more slowly to see if you can be the one to set the pace rather than automatically posting at the speed that your horse chooses.

USE FIRMER CONTACT FOR SUPPORT

Don't be surprised if the contact with your horse's mouth during lengthenings becomes somewhat heavy. Remember that lengthenings are developed out of a working gait and the weight in your hands is somewhat firm to begin with. (I discussed contact in Chapter Eight). In addition, while your horse is learning how to balance himself during lengthenings, his center of gravity might shift even a bit further to his forehand. Don't be alarmed by this. It's a stage of his training, and it's fine to temporarily support him by maintaining a firmer contact. Later on, if you decide to go on to more advanced work, you'll develop "uphill" extensions out of collected gaits. Because the horse will be in self-carriage when he's in a collected gait, the contact will be lighter.

However, there's a fine line between a solid, supporting contact and one in which your horse is leaning so heavily on your hands that your arms ache. Here are some things you can try to improve a contact that is too heavy. Before you even begin to ask for a lengthening, make sure you drive the horse's hind legs more under his body by closing both of your legs. In order to carry himself, your horse needs to have his hind legs underneath him. If his hind legs are trailing out behind his body, he can't support himself in the lengthening, and he has no option but to lean on your hands (fig. 9.35a).

9.34

Pretend you hear a metronome ticking. The tempo of the lengthened trot should not change at all from the "ticking" you heard in his working trot.

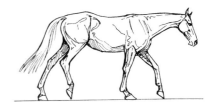

a) Horse trotting with hind legs trailing out behind his body

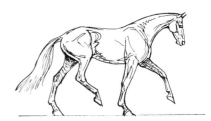

b) Horse trotting with hind legs under him

9.35 *The activity of the hind legs directly affects the horse's balance.*

a) *Correct lengthening: the toe of forefoot points toward the spot where it will touch down. The foreleg cannot touch down in front of an imaginary line drawn down from an extension of his profile to the ground.*

b) *Incorrect lengthening: the horse's toe flips up; his back is tense and his front foot has no option but to retract before he can place it on the ground.*

9.36 *The position of the head and neck affects the quality of the lengthening.*

You can also ride some quick transitions: from trot to halt and back to the trot again or from the canter to the walk and back to the canter again. This will help to rebalance your horse and make the weight in your hands more comfortable.

Another reason the contact can get too heavy is that you may be asking for too many lengthened strides at one time before your horse is ready. Doing well-balanced lengthenings with his hind legs underneath his body for only a few strides at a time is much more valuable for your horse than lengthening for many strides with his hind legs pushing out behind his body.

Remember that when you do the downward transition back to the working gait, be sure that you close your legs to send his hind legs under his body. It might feel natural to ask for the downward transition from the lengthening to the working gait by just using the reins. But, as you know by now, if your goal is to rebalance your horse and improve the contact, you need to *add* hind legs while doing the downward transition (see Aids for Downward Transitions, page 138).

ALLOW THE FRAME TO ELONGATE IN LENGTHENINGS

In trot lengthenings, the front feet should touch the ground on the spot toward which they are pointing when each leg is at its maximum extension. When a horse has to draw his front legs back toward his body before placing them on the ground, or his toes flip up in front, it usually indicates that he hasn't been allowed to lengthen his frame (fig. 9.36).

Sometimes a rider makes it difficult for the horse to lengthen to his utmost. Although I said earlier that you shouldn't be concerned if the contact is a bit too firm, you want to be sure that you're not making it heavy because you're cranking his neck in. If you keep your horse's neck short by restricting him with strong or non-allowing hands, he has to draw his foreleg back before putting it down (fig. 9.37). Allow your horse to lengthen his neck and point the tip of his nose more or less forward. To help you to do this, think about "opening the front door" by softening your hands a bit toward your horse's mouth and by cocking your wrists upward in a way that allows your little fingers to go more forward (fig. 9.38).

9.37

I'm cranking Woody's neck in and he finds it difficult to lengthen his stride in the trot. Note how his toe flips up in front—a sure sign that I'm restricting him with the reins. See the diagram on previous page (9.36b) which is almost identical to what is happening here.

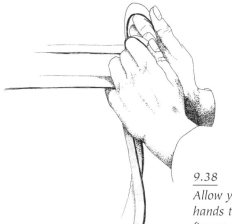

9.38

Allow your horse to lengthen his neck by "opening the front door." Soften your hands toward his mouth, and cock your wrists upward to allow your little fingers to go more forward.

Sit Upright

When you use your driving seat to ask for the transition into the lengthening, don't try to "help" your horse to lengthen by leaning back. Even though you might feel that you can drive him forward this way (and I see many dressage riders doing this in lengthenings and extensions), you'll just end up driving his back down and making it hollow. Stay vertical at all times.

I learned this lesson the hard way while trying to qualify for the Olympic Festival with Jolicoeur at a competition that was being held at Knoll Farm in Brentwood, New York, back in 1987. One of the finest international judges in the world, the late Mr. Jaap Pot, was there. He was a stickler when it came to the correctness of the rider's seat. I remember Jo and I doing huge extended trots for him. I thought we had done really well until my score sheet came back with extremely low marks for the extensions and the simple comment—rider leaning behind the vertical. Believe me, it made an impression.

Counter-Canter

DESCRIPTION

Counter-canter—also known as "false canter"—is an obedience and suppling exercise. Up until the point that you introduce it, all of your horse's education has been to canter with the inside foreleg leading—the "correct" lead. This is known as "true" canter.

In counter-canter you ask your horse to canter on what is considered the wrong lead. For instance, while riding to the left, ask your horse to stay on the right lead. This is contrary to everything he's been taught about the canter to this point. He might initially become confused and think he's doing the wrong thing by cantering with his outside foreleg leading. He might also feel a bit awkward and uncomfortable until he develops the strength and balance to negotiate this movement (figs. 9.39 and 9.40).

The Aids for Counter-Canter

For counter-canter on the right lead while going to the left (counterclockwise): the aids are those used for right lead canter:

Seat: weight on right seat bone.

Right leg: on the girth.

Left leg: slightly behind the girth.

Right rein: vibrates for flexion.

Left rein: supports to prevent the neck from bending too much to the right.

9.39

Deb, riding Monique, canters across the diagonal in true canter on her right lead.

9.40

Deb keeps her on the right lead after she reaches the long side (she's now in counter-canter) by keeping her weight on her right seat bone, her right leg on the girth, and her left leg slightly behind the girth.

a) Suspension   b) First beat: right hind   c) Second beat: lateral pair (left hind
                                                                          and left fore)

d) Third beat: right fore   e) Pushing off; horse is on left lead behind and right lead in front

9.41
*Faulty canter: a disunited, or
cross-canter sequence with the
horse going to the right.*

To avoid confusion, understand that when you hear the words "inside" and "outside" in relation to counter-canter, they refer to the lead you're on rather than to the direction you're going. The leading leg is always on the inside. So, when you are riding to the left in counter-canter on the right lead, the right side of the horse's body is the inside even though it's the side closest to the fence.

TEACHING COUNTER-CANTER

Introduce counter-canter gradually. It's best to start on a straight line or a very gentle curve, rather than on a circle or in tight turns or corners. By following a systematic plan, you can minimize problems such as stiffening, breaking to the trot, switching leads, or cross-cantering (also known as a "disunited canter"). A horse cross-canters when he canters on one lead with his front legs and the other lead with his hind legs (fig. 9. 41). For instance, when you are trying to canter correctly on the right lead and your horse cross-canters instead, the sequence of his legs becomes right hind, then the lateral pair of left hind and left fore together, and finally the right fore. Essentially, he's on the left lead behind and on the right lead in front. When a horse cross-canters, he looks and feels awkward and out of balance. (See the drawings on page 105 for a correct canter).

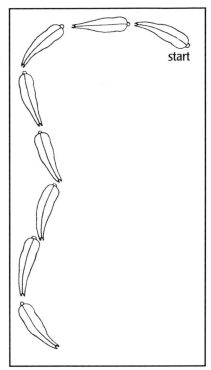

9.42
Counter-canter exercise no.1: ride to the left in true canter. Arc gently away from the track on the long side, and back on to it again. You are doing counter-canter for the few strides when you change direction and begin to head back to the long side.

The following are counter-canter exercises starting with the simplest and progressively increasing in difficulty. Don't attempt a more difficult pattern until your horse can negotiate the earlier one confidently.

1. Start by going to the left (counterclockwise) while in left lead canter—a true canter. After coming through the second corner of the short side of the ring, arc gently off the track (fig. 9.42). Canter three or four strides toward the middle of the ring and then turn back toward the track before the next corner. In this exercise you'll only be doing counter-canter for a few strides—the strides during which you're changing direction and beginning to head back toward the long side that you were on originally.

2. Once again, start by riding to the left (counterclockwise) in true canter. Go across the diagonal of the ring, but don't change your canter lead as you do normally. Instead, stay on the left lead through the short side and go back across the next diagonal (fig. 9.43). This exercise is somewhat more demanding than the previous one because you're asking your horse to stay in counter-canter throughout the entire short side. However, be sure not to go into the corners too deeply because that will greatly increase the degree of difficulty, and your horse is apt to lose his balance at this stage.

3. Ride all the way around the ring in counter-canter, making sure not to go into the corners too deeply.

4. Do a large circle in counter-canter (at least 20 meters or 66 feet in diameter).

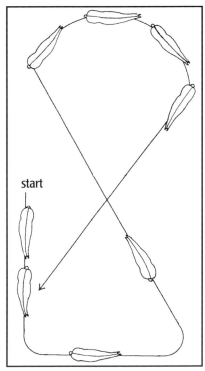

9.43
Counter-canter exercise no.2: ride to the left in true canter. Go across the diagonal but don't change your canter lead as you do normally. Stay on the left lead and go back across the opposite diagonal.

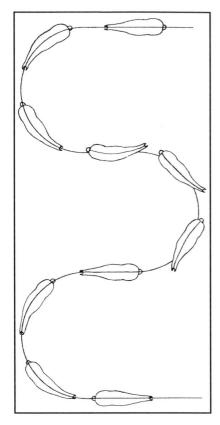

9.44

Counter-canter exercise no.3: ride a series of three large loops—a serpentine—staying on the same canter lead.

5. Ride a series of three large loops (a serpentine), staying on the same lead (fig. 9.44).

6. Increase the number of loops on the serpentine.

Once your horse understands counter-canter, as an obedience exercise try picking up the counter-canter lead while you're on the long side of your arena. Some horses and riders find it difficult to pick up the counter-canter lead while close to the rail because it makes them feel claustrophobic. So, if either you or your horse has this psychological block to picking up the counter-canter lead on the track around your arena, try working a few feet away from it. Then, when you're going to the left and you go to pick up counter-canter on the right lead, think of it as a true canter and that you are going to turn toward the rail on your right, canter right through it and out of the arena! (See fig. 9.45).

• *Helpful Hints for Counter-Canter* •

In the following examples you'll be in counter-canter on the right lead while you're riding to the left (counterclockwise). Your horse maintains his natural flexion at the poll to the right and he is also slightly bent to the right toward the side of his leading leg. Most of these hints will help you stay out of your horse's way.

First, consider your reins. If you hang on the inside (right) rein, you'll block your horse's inside hind leg and he'll probably break to the trot. Think about softening your inside hand forward and, if necessary, use an active inside leg to maintain the canter. Keep your arms elastic and your elbows moving so you can push your hands forward toward your horse's mouth on the third beat of the canter.

Next, think about how your upper body normally rocks back and forth with the motion of the canter. Ideally, you want to rock behind the vertical with each stride because if you come in front of the vertical, you'll be putting more weight on your horse's forehand. "See" yourself rocking backward with each stride so you can think about cantering your horse "up" in front of your body rather than letting his hind legs escape out behind your seat and his body. Be sure to stop the motion of your body when you're on the vertical. Don't allow your shoulders to come even slightly in front of the vertical. If you do, you'll give your horse an escape route that allows him to lose his balance and fall on his forehand.

Here's an image that might help you with this concept of leaning back so you can help your horse lower his hindquarters and "sit down behind" so that he's "up" in front. Pretend that you're sitting on a see-saw and each time you lean back and push your end down, the other end goes up (fig. 9.46).

9.45
If you have a mental block about picking up the counter-canter lead while going left on the long side of your ring, pretend you're going to pick up true canter and circle your horse right out through the rail.

9.46

Lean back when riding counter-canter to help your horse lower his hindquarters—"sit down behind"—so that he is "up" in front. Pretend you are sitting on a see-saw and that each time you lean back and push your end down, the other end goes up.

Finally, feel the same roundness and impulsion in each counter-canter bound as you have felt in true canter. Experience the same ease, balance, and comfort in counter-canter that you have in true canter. Stay loose by convincing yourself that you're really riding true canter and the arena wall or rail just happens to be on the other side. Remember to breathe deeply and rhythmically. If you get tight and hold your breath, so will your partner.

COMMON PROBLEMS

The most common mistake that I see when a rider starts counter-canter is that she bends her horse's neck too much toward the side of his leading leg (the "inside" leg) so that his shoulders fall to the outside of the line they're on (fig. 9.47).

In other words, when the horse is going left in counter-canter on the right lead and the neck is overly bent to the right (inside), he ends up leaning on the left (outside) rein and falling sideways on his left shoulder. In this position he is no longer **axis-straight**. In order to be in good balance, he needs to have his shoulders straight between the reins.

In counter-canter on the right lead, the right hand vibrates for flexion but the left hand must support to limit how much the horse bends his neck to the right. Keep in mind that the balance and position in counter-canter should be identical to that of true canter.

Sometimes I'll help my students understand this feeling of keeping the shoulders between the reins rather than letting the horse fall sideways onto his outside shoulder by doing the following exercise. While in the counter-canter, I have them counter-flex their horses at the poll. For example, while riding left in counter-canter on the right lead, they'll vibrate the left rein to position their horses so they can just see the left eye. By doing this, the horse's shoulders slide back to the right, and they end up between the two reins. In this way, both horse and rider learn the feeling of being straight in counter-canter.

9.47
Here Deb has made Monique crooked in counter-canter by bending her neck too much toward her leading leg (the right leg). As a result, her shoulders fall to her left and her hindquarters drift to the right.

Frequently, when learning counter-canter, a rider allows her horse to pick up speed. If your horse goes too fast, his hind legs will sprawl out behind him. Once again he'll lose his balance by either running onto his forehand or breaking to the trot. Do several transitions from the counter-canter to the walk and back to the counter-canter again to help him keep his hind legs underneath him. The transitions will help rebalance him. In Book Two you'll learn how to use half-halts to control the speed and maintain balance.

The rhythm of the horse's canter should stay exactly the same in counter-canter as it is in true canter. Sometimes, however, the rhythm of the canter gets labored and degenerates into four beats. This often happens because the rider is too restrictive with the reins or because the horse's body gets long and strung out so that his hind legs are no longer well underneath him. When this happens, freshen and restore the rhythm by riding more forward into a lengthening and then make an effort to maintain this crisp rhythm while in counter-canter.

KEY POINTS

🐎 This chapter has contained movements and exercises that most horses, being ridden in any discipline, will be able to do.

🐎 The movements are useful not just as an end in themselves to make your horse more athletic, but they can also be used to lay a foundation for more advanced work or to work through a problem.

🐎 Transitions are a good indicator of a horse's suppleness. They should be prompt, fluid, and smooth without either any rushing or any decrease of power.

🐎 Correct bending on circles, turns, and corners improves your horse's ability to be straight.

🐎 A horse's one-sidedness causes him to bend more easily in one direction. The goal is equal bending on both sides of his body.

🐎 The marriage of inside and outside aids enables a horse to bend while he's turning along a prescribed line.

🐎 An obedient riding horse needs to be able to back up as readily as he goes forward.

🐎 In a lengthening, the horse elongates his stride and his frame while maintaining the same rhythm and tempo he had in the working gait.

🐎 If a working gait is powerful and energetic, it already contains sufficient activity to do a lengthening.

🐎 Counter-canter is used as an obedience and suppling exercise.

CHAPTER TEN

Going Sideways—Lateral Movements

With the information you've acquired to this point, you and your horse are laying the groundwork to excel in any riding discipline. You now have a horse who moves forward obediently in all three paces. He does fluid transitions from one pace to another. And, his increasingly supple body allows him to lengthen and shorten his frame and stride within each pace like a rubber band, as well as bend equally through his side to the left and to the right.

So, what's the next step in your horse's education? Well, it's time to start teaching him to go sideways. In dressage jargon all of the sideways movements are called "lateral work," or work on **two tracks**, and it is this phrase that compels me to digress for a few moments here and discuss the word "tracks."

TRACKS

We use "tracks" in so many different contexts. So, in the interests of clarifying this word, I'm going to describe all the different ways we use it.

First of all, you know the path that you make in the dirt as you go 'round and 'round your arena? Sure you do. That's the dip you have to rake by hand to fill it in when it gets too deep. That's a "track."

In Chapter Seven you learned about the working trot. In the working trot, your horse should "track up." In other words, if you looked on the ground, you should see that the hoof print made by the hind foot steps directly into the track of the hoof print made by the front foot.

Then again you can be traveling around your ring with either your left or your right leg on the inside. In this case we refer to the way you're going as "tracking to the left" or "tracking to the right."

So far, those usages of the word "tracks" are pretty clear-cut. But when I introduce leg-yielding and shoulder-fore later in this chapter, I get into the more complicated uses—fun stuff known as lateral work.

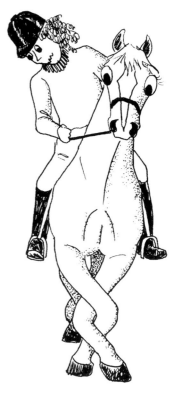

How many tracks? Which way? Help me!

Track to the right, on two tracks, in the track!

To begin, let's consider the concept of *direction*. When you're just riding on a straight line you're working on a **single track**. In this case the "single track" refers to the fact that you're only going in one direction—forward.

When you do any type of lateral work, you'll be working on **two tracks**. The phrase "two tracks" refers to the fact that you're going in *two directions* at once—forward *and* sideways.

Not only can you use the words "single track" and "two tracks" to describe how many *directions* you're going, you can also use the word "tracks" to describe how many *legs* you see coming toward you if you are standing directly in front of a horse.

For example, both the **leg-yield** along the track (see fig. 10.26), and **shoulder-fore** (fig. 10.1), both *two-track* lateral movements, are done on "four tracks". They are called this because if you stand in front of the horse and watch his legs, you see all four of them—unlike the situation where the horse is being ridden on a *single track* and you just see his two front legs (his hind legs being hidden from your view).

With the more advanced two-track movements that I describe in Book Two (**shoulder-in, shoulder-out, haunches-in,** and **haunches-out**), the horse is described as being on "three tracks" because you can only see three of his legs coming toward you. For example, in a shoulder-in counterclockwise to the left, you would see the right hind, the right fore, and the left fore. You would not see the left hind because it's hidden behind the right foreleg (fig. 10.2).

Now that I've thoroughly confused you about "tracks" I'll try to sum up:

Single-track movements: you see two legs coming toward you when standing directly in front of the horse.

Two-track movements: you see either three or four legs coming toward you.

10.1

During shoulder-fore the horse is on four tracks. Each one of his four legs can be clearly seen traveling on its own track.

10.2

During shoulder-in the horse is on three tracks. Only three legs can be clearly seen because the inside hind leg is directly behind the outside foreleg.

Lateral work will greatly enrich your training program. To begin with, it enables you to expand your horse's understanding of, and obedience to, the leg. Up until this point, you've only used your leg to ask your horse to go forward. Now, he'll learn that with a slightly different placement of your leg, you will be telling him to do something else–go sideways as well.

I use lateral work for everything from loosening and stretching my horse's muscles during a warm-up to strengthening a weak hind leg. The important point to remember is that lateral work is not an end in itself. In other words, you don't decide to go sideways because you're bored going straight forward and want to do something different. Lateral movements are a means to an end. Depending on what your horse needs,

10.3 Engagement

a) A horse with his hindquarters engaged

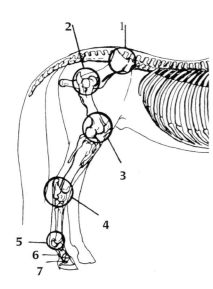

b) The specific joints of the hindquarters:
1. Lumbosacral joint
2. Hip joint
3. Stifle joint
4. Tarsal (hock joint)
5. Fetlock (ankle) joint
6. Pastern joint
7. Coffin joint

you'll pick the relevant and appropriate lateral movement to solve a problem or develop a particular quality, such as strength or straightness.

I've seen many riders who become obsessed with going sideways when they start lateral work, forgetting they *must* still go forward! Never go sideways at the expense of the quality of the horse's paces. Always strive to maintain "forward" movement over the ground with energy, and in a regular rhythm. If you lose any of these qualities, stop trying to go sideways. Instead, ride straight ahead and re-establish whatever you lost before resuming the lateral movement.

Lateral movements can be subdivided into two groups. They are differentiated by whether the horse is "straight" with no bend but just flexed at the poll, or asked to bend all through his body.

The first category of lateral movements, where the horse's body remains straight with no bend, includes the **turn on the forehand** and **leg-yielding**. These two movements are the easiest to perform because the horse is ridden *without* bend, and there are not a lot of physical demands made on his hind legs.

I will describe turn on the forehand and leg-yielding in this chapter, along with shoulder-fore. Shoulder-fore is one of the movements from the second group, the group which includes the lateral movements with bend. Even though shoulder-fore has a greater degree of difficulty than a turn on the forehand or a leg-yield, it can be done in a working gait. At this stage of your horse's training, he should be ready to start it.

The second category of lateral movements are all exercises where the horse is asked to go sideways *with* bend through his body. They include shoulder-fore, shoulder-in, haunches-in (also known as **travers**), haunches-out (also known as **renvers**), half-pass, walk pirouettes, and canter pirouettes. But, as I said earlier, the only one in this category that you need to deal with at this stage of your horse's training is the shoulder-fore.

All these lateral movements with bend are more difficult for the horse to perform than a leg-yield. This is because you're asking your horse to bend through his body at the same time as you are asking him to go sideways. This requires him to bend the joints of his hind legs more than he's ever had to do before.

This increased bending of the joints of his hind legs is referred to as **engagement**. When the horse "engages" his hind legs, he **flexes** the joints of the hind legs and of the lumbosacral area and lowers his hindquarters (fig. 10.3). I know this might sound a little complicated for you right now, but I wanted to mention it. This way you can file it away in your mental computer and by the time you get to learn about **self-carriage** (in Chapter Three of Book Two), the information will be easy for you to retrieve from your memory bank.

With that to look forward to, all you need to know for now is that the more the horse engages his hind legs, the more he changes his balance and can carry himself through whatever movements you ask of him (fig. 10.4). In the meantime I am including shoulder-fore in this chapter because I want you to use it now, not so much as a way to change your horse's balance, but as a way to make your horse **straight**.

FLEXING AND FLEXION

The Closing of Joints

I also need to take a moment here to discuss and broaden our usage of **flexion** (another word that can be confusing). Generally speaking, "flexion" refers to the closing of a joint so that the angle between the bones is decreased.

You first heard this word in Chapter Nine where I discussed riding circles and corners to explain inside positioning at the horse's poll. That is, a horse is flexed or looks in the direction he's going (for example, he looks left while going counterclockwise to the left) on curved lines. The rider should just be able to see the horse's left eye or left nostril. This type of flexion refers to the closing of the second cervical (neck) joint and is specifically called "lateral flexion." This is the "flexion" that you'll be most concerned with at this stage of your horse's education.

Another use of the word involves the closing of the joints of the horse's *hindquarters*, thus lowering them. This promotes the "engagement" I discuss above.

In Book Two I'll also be talking about a slightly different kind of flexion at the poll. You'll see that when a horse flexes "in" (rather than left and right, as above), he closes the joint between his head and neck. This is specifically called "longitudinal flexion." So when I get to talk about giving a **half-halt** and putting your horse **on the bit**, you'll see that part of the **round** frame achieved by working on the bit includes flexion "in" at the jaw and poll. (Another part of your education to look forward to!)

How Lateral Flexion Relates To "Inside" And "Outside" of the Horse

It's important, before I give the details about riding turns on the forehand, leg-yields, and shoulder-fore, that I review the use of the terms "inside" and "outside" as they relate to the horse. We use the horse's flexion and bend to determine which side of the horse's body is referred to as his inside and which is his outside. The inside is always the direction toward which the horse is flexed or bent. Some of you might still be under the impression that the inside rein, leg, or side of the horse always refers to the side toward the center of a circle and that the outside rein, leg, or side of the horse's body is either furthest from the center of a circle or is the side closest to the rail. So far, in this book, this has been the case. However, with lateral work, what we call inside and outside may change.

10.4 Balance in turns

a) *The joints of the inside hind leg engaging as the horse bends along the arc of a circle*

b) *The joints of the inside hind leg engaging in a turn at speed*

For example, as you begin to ride leg-yields in various patterns, you'll see that the inside and the outside of the horse often changes. You don't have to be confused by this. Just remember that even though the horse's body doesn't bend in leg-yielding, he is asked to *flex* at the poll. So, the inside is always the side toward which he is flexed, even if it's not the side closest to the inside of the ring (fig. 10.5).

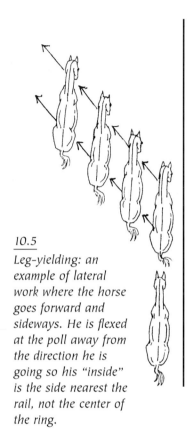

10.5

Leg-yielding: an example of lateral work where the horse goes forward and sideways. He is flexed at the poll away from the direction he is going so his "inside" is the side nearest the rail, not the center of the ring.

Turn on the Forehand

DESCRIPTION

If your horse has never done any lateral work, you might like to introduce the concept of going sideways by teaching him how to do a turn on the forehand. I say "might like" because there are disadvantages as well as advantages to having your horse learn this movement, which I'll discuss in a moment. In a turn on the forehand, the horse learns to yield away from the rider's leg when he is at a standstill. His front legs remain more or less on the same spot, while his hindquarters make a 180 degree turn around his forehand so that he ends up facing the opposite direction (fig. 10.6).

The advantages of learning this movement include introducing the uneducated horse to the sideways-pushing aids. The turn on the forehand also has a practical use when you're out hacking and you want to open and close a gate without getting off your horse.

However, once a horse understands the idea of yielding sideways to the leg, most riders hardly ever use the turn on the forehand again. This is because of the disadvantages of riding this movement. With every other lateral movement that you teach your horse, you'll ask him to go forward as well as sideways. But with the turn on the forehand, the horse doesn't go forward–he starts and finishes the movement in the halt. Some people think that the absence of forward movement is sufficient reason to avoid teaching the turn on the forehand.

An even greater drawback is what the movement does to your horse's balance. Think about the name of the exercise: turn *on the forehand*. Because the hindquarters are mobilized around a stationary forehand, the horse's center of gravity gets shifted more toward his front legs. But what we're striving for in dressage is to get horses *off* of their forehands!

So consider using the turn on the forehand only in the very beginning stages of teaching your horse to go sideways. Once he understand how to move away from your legs, don't use it for training anymore.

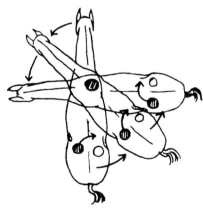

10.6

Starting the turn on the forehand.

10.7

Start the turn on the forehand from the halt. Ideally, Special Effects should be standing with "a leg in each corner," but this halt is fairly well-balanced. He'll do a 180-degree turn to change direction by pivoting around his right front leg.

10.7 to 10.12 Turn on the Forehand

10.8

Just before asking the horse to move his hindquarters to the left, flex him at the poll to the right.

The Aids for the Turn on the Forehand

For a turn on the forehand to the left (figs. 10.7 to 10.12):

Seat: sit squarely and balanced over the middle of your horse.

Right leg: a couple of inches behind the girth for sideways movement.

Left leg: on the girth for support and to prevent the horse from turning sideways too quickly.

Right rein: vibrate for flexion at the poll.

Left rein: steady and supporting to keep the neck straight.

10.10
Note that Amy is using her left rein quite firmly to prevent her horse from trying to bend his neck to the right.

10.9
Stay centered over the middle of the horse's back. Here, Amy gets slightly left behind the movement and leans to the right.

10.7 to 10.12
Turn on the Forehand con't.

• *Helpful Hints* •

If you ask your horse to do a turn on the forehand and he just refuses to move away from your leg, start to teach him from the ground. Stand by his head, facing backward toward his hindquarters. Hold the rein closest to you with the hand that's nearest to the horse. You can position his head so that his neck is slightly bent toward you.

Place your other hand on his barrel a couple of inches behind the girth area, where your sideways pushing leg will be when you're mounted. Push with this hand. When your horse moves sideways in response to the pressure of your hand, praise him.

10.11
A good angle from which to see how wide the hind legs are stepping.

10.12
Almost done. Note how well the joints of the right hind leg are bending and how that leg steps over and in front of the left hind leg. Although he responds obediently to the rider's aids, Special Effects loudly expresses his negative opinion about the exercise through the excessive swishing of his tail!

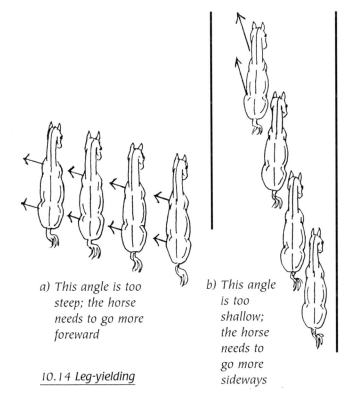

10.13
*Leg-yielding:
correct angle to the
rail. A horse needs to
travel in this position when
leg-yielding on a diagonal line.*

a) *This angle is too
steep; the horse
needs to go more
foreward*

10.14 *Leg-yielding*

b) *This angle
is too
shallow;
the horse
needs to
go more
sideways*

Leg-Yielding

DESCRIPTION

Leg-yielding is the lateral movement in which the horse's *inside front* leg and *inside* hind leg pass, and cross in front of, his *outside* legs. His spine is straight, and he is flexed at his poll in the opposite direction from the way he is moving. For instance, if you ask your horse to move sideways to the left, you want him to flex or "look" to the right.

Because there's no bend through the whole body, only flexion at the poll, leg-yielding doesn't increase self-carriage like the exercises in the second group of lateral movements mentioned on page 170. However, it is a good loosening, stretching, "toe-touching," warm-up exercise for the horse that is doing any discipline and any level of dressage. In addition, it teaches the horse to obey the rider's leg when asked for sideways movement. Finally, it gives the rider an opportunity to learn coordination of aids for lateral movements (figs. 10.13 and 10.14).

I've already mentioned, on page 142, how you can use leg-yielding to help your horse pick up the correct canter lead. And in Chapter Thirteen I'll show you ways to incorporate leg-yielding into your program to help solve many different training problems. Leg-yielding as an exercise is extremely beneficial because of the way it affects the horse's hind legs. The bottom line in riding is the saying "He who controls the hind legs, controls the horse." The hind legs are the horse's engine, and all work should be directed to them. The more the hind legs are active, engaged, and underneath your horse's body, the easier it will be for him to balance himself and do what you ask of him.

Leg-yielding can be done at the walk, the posting trot, and the sitting trot. Depending on a horse's personality, you might decide to introduce the leg-yield at one pace rather than another. Sometimes a tense horse benefits from this exercise being explained in the walk because it's quieter, and he has more time to understand. You can use mental images to help this type of horse relax, by picturing his eye remaining calm and his back staying relaxed. On the other hand, another horse might build tension in the walk so the trot would be a better choice to start leg-yielding. The trot is also preferable for a lazy horse because there's more natural impulsion in this pace.

The Aids for Leg-Yielding

For a leg-yield over to the right (figs. 10.15 to 10.17):

Seat: sit squarely and balanced over the middle of your horse (fig. 10.18).

Right leg: on the girth for forward movement.

Left leg: behind the girth for sideways movement. Both legs are passive unless the horse needs to be sent either more forward or more sideways. In that case, the appropriate leg squeezes and releases.

Left rein: vibrates for flexion at the poll.

Right rein: steady and supporting to keep the neck straight.

10.15 to 10.17
Leg-Yielding to the Right on a Diagonal Line in the Walk

10.15
A very nice start. Deb flexes her horse, Monique, at the poll to the left while keeping the rest of the mare's spine straight. However, Deb should turn her head to the right to look at the point she's riding towards.

10.16
You can clearly see the difference in the position of Deb's legs. The right one is at the girth to insure forward movement and the left one is behind the girth to ask the horse to step sideways. However, she seems to be pushing too hard with her left leg as her toe is turned out.

10.17
The horse is still doing a good leg-yield, but we have a couple more clues that the rider is working too hard. Her left leg is now drawn up as well as back, and she's collapsed the left side of her waist causing her shoulder to drop.

10.18
Rider's position
during leg-yielding

a) *When leg-yielding, sit squarely and balanced over the middle of your horse*

b) *If you lean and twist your body, you'll make it difficult for your horse to go sideways*

As with every other movement you do with your horse, all of your aids have a role to play. Some aids are active, and some are passive, but they're all important. They all need to be coordinated in order to do a good leg-yield.

Remember that leg-yields are a blending of forward and sideways movement. If the horse leg-yields easily, the rider's legs stay quietly placed on his sides. The leg on the girth indicates forward movement while the leg behind the girth asks for sideways movement. If either quality is lacking, make the appropriate leg more active by squeezing and releasing with it on the horse's side.

The aids described above should be given in the following sequence: take a moment to center yourself so you're sitting in the middle of the saddle. Ask for flexion at the poll to the left. Then bring your left leg slightly behind the girth to initiate sideways movement. Those are the active aids. While you go sideways, continue to think about supporting with the passive aids—the right rein and right leg.

Shortly, I'll discuss all the places and patterns that you can leg-yield. But before I do, I want to make a point about the alignment of your horse's body when you leg-yield on a diagonal line or increase the size of a circle. For the most part, your horse's body is parallel to whatever line you're leg-yielding toward. However, his forehand should be just slightly ahead of his hindquarters, so it meets the track or final arc of the circle first. (The reason for teaching this positioning of the horse's body in the leg-yield is to make it easy and familiar when you go on to teach the half-pass, which is introduced in Book Two.)

It's often the rider's tendency, or the horse's desire, to lead with the hindquarters so they reach the destination before the forehand. Be aware that this often happens in one direction more than the other, so make the necessary adjustment to align your horse's body correctly.

A good way to think of this is to pretend someone is going to take a photograph of you at several points during your leg-yield. When the horse's body is aligned correctly, every single picture should show the forehand slightly in advance of the hindquarters (fig. 10.19).

PLACES AND PATTERNS FOR LEG-YIELDING
You should aim to become adept at leg-yielding in many different places in the arena. It can be done on diagonal lines, straight lines or circles. Mix and match leg-yielding for variety and fun.

Leg-Yielding on a Diagonal Line
Leg-yield from the middle of the ring over to a specific point on the rail or from the rail toward the center of the ring. The pattern you make on

The finish of a good leg-yield on a diagonal line in the trot. Although the horse's body is basically parallel to the rail, we can clearly see that the forehand will reach the track ever so slightly ahead of the hindquarters.

10.20

Leg-yield on a diagonal line from the middle of the ring over to a specific point on the rail, or from the rail towards the center of the ring.

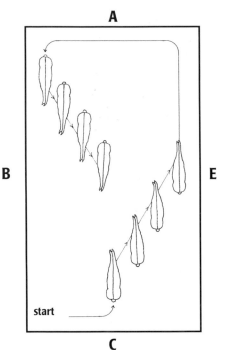

the ground is a diagonal line, since you're going both sideways and forward (fig. 10.20). While leg-yielding on a diagonal line, remember that the horse's body is almost parallel to the rail, with the forehand slightly more toward the rail than the hindquarters.

Leg-Yielding Along the Track

You can leg-yield along the track in two different ways—in the **head-to-the-wall** position, and the **tail-to-the-wall** position (figs. 10.21 and 10.22). In both cases the angle of displacement of the hindquarters is about 35 degrees. At a 35-degree angle, the horse's body forms almost half of a right angle to the rail.

1. Walk your horse forward with his forelegs on the track and move his hind legs away from the rail. This is known as leg-yielding in the head-to-the-wall position (figs 10.23 to 10.25).

When you do this in posting trot, switch your posting diagonal. You want to be sitting in the saddle when the inside hind leg is on the ground. Remember our discussion of "inside" being determined by the horse's flexion? If you are riding to the left (counterclockwise), you flex your horse to the right and move his hindquarters away from your right leg. Since your horse is flexed to the right, this now becomes his "inside," even though this is the side closest to the rail. So, to be on the correct diagonal for influencing his right hind leg, you should be sitting in the saddle when the diagonal pair of right hind leg and left foreleg is on the ground, and posting in the air when that same diagonal pair is also in the air.

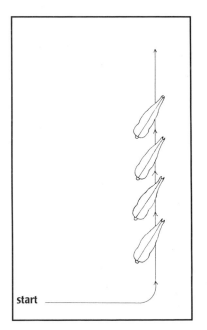

10.21

Leg-yielding along the track in the "head-to-the-wall" position.

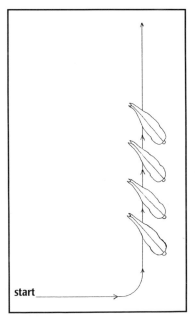

10.22

Leg-yielding along the track in the "tail-to-the-wall" position.

10.23 and 10.24
Note how the Special Effects is slightly flexed at the poll to the right, but his spine remains straight. This is correct.

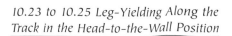

10.23 to 10.25 Leg-Yielding Along the Track in the Head-to-the-Wall Position

10.25
A different view of the leg-yield in the head-to-the-wall position. Amy is nicely centered over her horse's back.

10.26

Leg-yielding along the track in the tail-to-the-wall position. Special Effects' spine is nicely straight, but you can see that his head is tipped (spoiling his position) because his ears are not level.

2. You can also ride a leg-yield with the horse's tail-to-the wall (fig. 10.26). If you're in a ring that has a rail or fence, first bring the horse's forelegs slightly to the inside of the track so that he has room to move his hindquarters over toward the rail without hitting it. Then displace his hindquarters toward the fence at about a 35-degree angle.

When you ride this pattern in posting trot, stay on the normal diagonal. This is because the inside and the outside of the horse don't change in the tail-to-the-wall position as they do in the head-to-the-wall position. When riding to the left, the horse remains flexed to the inside (left) and his hindquarters are moved sideways to the right.

Leg-Yielding Along the Arc of a Circle
Leg-yielding can also be done along the arc of a circle. This pattern significantly increases the difficulty level of the movement, so make sure your horse is comfortable leg-yielding along a diagonal line, or the track, before you try this. In all of the examples below, your horse is circling to the left (counterclockwise).

1. Put the horse's front legs on the track of the circle and move his hindquarters out at a 35-degree angle to the circle. Your horse remains flexed to the left and his hindquarters are displaced to the right. His front legs stay on the original track of the circle and his hindquarters describe a larger circle (fig. 10.27).

2. Put the front legs on the track of the circle and move the hindquarters *in* at a 35-degree angle. Change your horse's flexion so that he looks to the right and move his hindquarters to the left toward the center of the circle. His front legs stay on the original circle and his hindquarters describe a smaller circle (fig. 10.28). If you do this exercise in posting trot, change your diagonal for the reason given under "Leg-Yielding Along the Track," on page 180.

Increasing The Size of the Circle

When increasing the size of a circle in leg-yielding, your aids are slightly different from the ones described for all of the previous leg-yields. In the following examples, rather than bringing your leg behind the girth to ask your horse to go sideways, keep that leg on the girth because in this exercise, that leg has two functions: asking the horse to move sideways, *and* asking the horse to bend around the leg as he goes sideways. Remember, your horse needs to *bend* on a circle in order to be *straight*: a *straight* horse is straight on lines and bent along the arc of curves (see Chapter Six).

So, it's still true that you want to keep your horse straight during all leg-yields. But to be straight as he increases the size of a circle, your horse must be bent!

You might wonder how your horse can distinguish between the inside leg that tells him to bend but stay on the circle, and the inside leg that tells him to bend but increase the size of the circle. The answer is actually a combination of several things: telling him to go sideways by the amount you use that leg; sitting in the direction of movement by stepping down into the outside stirrup; looking where you want him to go; and guiding him with your mind. If you find yourself feeling skeptical that these subtle signals will work, try it—you'll like the result.

Remember, also, to maintain the correct alignment of your horse's body to the line of the circle in the same way that you do when leg-yielding on a diagonal line. The forehand and the hindquarters basically stay parallel to the arc of the circle, but the forehand leads slightly and reaches the final circle just before the hindquarters do.

To increase the size of the circle in leg-yielding, apply your aids as follows: if you're circling to the left, your horse remains flexed to the left and his entire body moves to the right, away from your left leg that stays on the girth (fig. 10.29 and see photo 13.8).

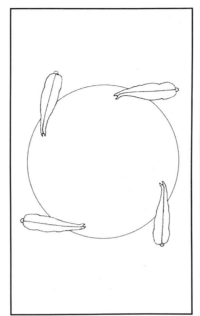

10.27
Leg-yielding: hindquarters out on a circle.

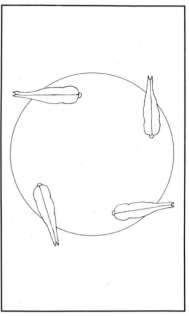

10.28
Leg-yielding: hindquarters in on a circle.

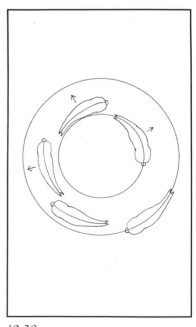

10.29
Leg-yielding: increasing the size of a circle.

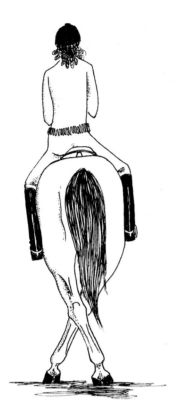

10.30

If you tend to lean to the right when you leg-yield to the left, imagine you have three-quarters of your body weight on the left side of your horse's spine, so that you end up sitting squarely.

• *Helpful Hints for the Rider* •

USE LIGHT LEG AIDS

Be sure not to use strong leg aids when introducing the leg-yield to your horse. The well-trained horse moves sideways from the *placement* of your leg, rather than the *pressure* of your leg. If this isn't the case, you must get the horse to listen to your leg. First, place your leg back. If he doesn't move sideways eagerly, either take the leg off and kick vigorously enough to get a reaction, or use the whip. Support enough with your other aids so that the kicking or tapping sends him sideways rather than forward. Then *retest* by moving the leg back again. If he moves away immediately, praise him. If he reacts sluggishly or if you're tempted to squeeze hard, chase him sideways again and then test again. You shouldn't have to force your horse sideways with strength. Through training, he should learn to move sideways easily from the position of your leg.

SIT SQUARE AND CENTERED

There is another reason you don't want to use a strong pushing leg: the importance of sitting squarely. If you push hard with your right leg, your body has the tendency to lean to the right, and this makes it even harder for your horse to move sideways to the left.

Some people lean because they get left behind the movement: if you have this tendency, use some exaggerated images to help you counteract it. As you leg-yield to the left, imagine you have three-quarters of your body weight on the left side of the horse's spine (fig. 10.30). Or think about putting your right seat bone in the middle of the saddle—this will help you end up in the middle.

• *Helpful Hints for the Horse* •

INCREASE THE CROSSING OF THE LEGS

Your horse may try one of several evasions so that he can avoid crossing his legs. Prevent his escape by checking the following four criteria. You'll notice that the first three of these are part of the foundation for all training. They are:

1. Forward: maintain energy and forward motion over the ground.
2. Straight: keep the horse's neck straight.
3. Rhythm: maintain regular rhythm and consistent tempo.
4. Achieve Sufficient Angle: it should be 35 degrees when you leg-yield along the track or along the arc of a circle.

It's only when all four of these qualities are present and correct that the horse will be crossing his legs sufficiently for the leg-yield to be of benefit as a loosening and suppling exercise (fig. 10.31).

INCREASING FORWARD MOTION AND ENERGY

As I said earlier, good lateral work is a blending of forward and sideways movement. Sometimes a horse loses his forward momentum because he's not quite physically ready to do a lot of lateral work. Other times the rider causes the loss of forward motion by asking the horse to go sideways at too steep an angle, restricting the horse with her hands, or doing too much lateral work without interspersing work on straight lines to renew the horse's desire to go forward. Whatever the reason, going sideways should never be done at the expense of going forward with energy.

The following are some ideas to help you if your horse needs to be encouraged to go more energetically forward while leg-yielding.

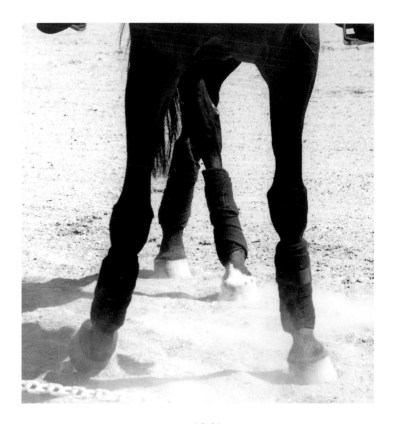

10.31
This leg-yield shows good form. The horse is crossing his hind legs up by his hocks. His front legs should cross up by his knees.

1. If lack of agility is causing your horse to lose his forward motion, introduce leg-yields by asking for less than the normal 35-degree angle. Maintaining forward movement is more important than going sideways, so ask for less angle. As your horse becomes more agile, gradually ask for more angle in stages. At each stage, check that your horse is still easily going forward before increasing the angle any further. Eventually you need good energy and forward movement at a 35-degree angle for the leg-yield to be beneficial. But, it might take several weeks or more to get to that point.

2. If lack of strength is the issue, try riding fewer sideways steps until your horse gets strong enough to maintain his energy. Leg-yield for a few steps at a time only; then go straight forward and ask for a lengthening to relax his muscles and renew his desire to go forward, then go sideways again for a few steps.

3. Try leg-yielding in a "staircase" pattern. Start a diagonal-line leg-yield for a few steps, then ride straight forward parallel to the rail. Repeat the pattern until you run out of room in your ring (fig. 10.32). This is also a good exercise to check your horse's responsiveness to your legs. The leg that's on the girth says "Go forward"

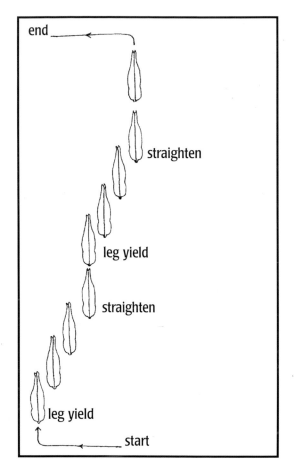

10.32

To help your horse move more energetically forward, leg-yield in a staircase pattern. Start a diagonal-line leg-yield for a few steps, then ride straight forward parallel to the rail to freshen the trot. Repeat the pattern until you run out of room.

and the leg that's behind the girth says "Go sideways." Your horse should respond immediately and appropriately to whichever leg becomes active.

If are doing your leg-yield in the sitting trot and losing energy, overcompensate for this loss of activity by leg-yielding while lengthening in the posting trot. Post very high while you're leg-yielding, to encourage your horse to take long strides. When you eventually go back to sitting the trot, pretend that the exercise you're doing is really leg-yielding in the lengthened trot rather than leg-yielding in the working trot.

KEEPING THE HORSE'S NECK STRAIGHT

The most common mistake that i see in leg-yields is a bend in the neck to the inside rather than just flexion at the poll. Remember, in a leg-yield to the left, the right (inside) rein asks for flexion *only* at the poll while the left (outside) rein supports to keep the neck straight. If the influence of the two reins isn't correct and there's too much emphasis on the right (inside) rein, the horse will bend his neck to the inside rather than only flexing at the poll. This overuse of the right (inside) rein without a supporting left (outside) rein makes it impossible to keep the horse **axis-straight**. In other words, his neck bends too much and his shoulders don't stay lined up directly in front of his hindquarters. The more the horse's shoulders pop out to the left, the more his hindquarters trail to the right (figs. 10.33 and 34).

If the neck is bent and the horse is not axis-straight, the legs don't cross well and the purpose of the exercise is lost. Because it's difficult for the horse to respond to the rider's sideways pushing leg when his body is in this contorted position, the desperate rider usually resorts to "rein yielding." She "rein-yields" by using an indirect rein to try to move the horse sideways, when she should be keeping the horse's neck straight and insisting that the horse move away from her leg.

If you see your horse's neck bending, relax the inside (right) rein toward his mouth and support more with the outside (left) rein. Feel the heaviness of this supporting outside (left) rein and imagine that this rein is a side rein keeping your horse's neck straight and providing a physical barrier to prevent his shoulder from falling out.

Here's something else to consider when keeping your horse's neck straight. Often when you leg-yield away from a horse's soft side, he bends his neck even if you are trying to use equal influence of the two reins. As a correction, ride the leg-yield in that direction either with *no*

10.33

Deb has Galen nicely positioned as they start this leg-yield. Galen's body is straight and she is ever-so-slightly flexed away from the direction toward which she is moving. (She is flexed to the right while moving to the left).

10.34

However, because Galen is soft on the right side of her body, she bends her neck too much to the right. Her shoulders pop to the left, her hindquarters trail to the right, and she is no longer straight and parallel to the rail.

10.35

During the next leg-yield, Deb corrects Galen's tendency to bend too much in the neck by flexing her at the poll to the left. Changing the flexion helps to keep Galen's body straight.

flexion at all or with a little flexion toward the direction you're going. For example, if your horse is stiff on the left side of his body and soft on the right side and you want to leg-yield over to the left, don't flex him to the right at all (fig.10.35).

MAINTAINING RHYTHM AND TEMPO

Sometimes you have to deal with a horse wanting to change his tempo by speeding up when you start to leg-yield. It's important that the speed and the regular rhythm of the working gait stay the same as you change from moving straight ahead into the leg-yield.

If the horse speeds up either because of tension, confusion, or to avoid the difficulty of the exercise, here are a couple of things you can do in the head-to-the-wall position to slow him down.

First, you can momentarily increase the angle to greater than 35 degrees until it becomes too difficult for your horse to run. As soon as your horse slows down, praise him and decrease the angle back to 35 degrees.

Or, you can do transitions from trot to walk and back to trot again while still leg-yielding, until he anticipates slowing down rather than running.

Another advantage of doing head-to-the-wall leg-yields in an indoor ring or facing a high rail is that you can ask the hind legs to cross over more, and you don't have to deal with your horse going faster when you use your leg. In the head-to-the-wall position, the wall or rail slows him down. When doing leg-yields in other patterns and the horse runs forward, a rider often resorts to pulling on the reins. This stops the hind legs from coming forward and you're worse off than if you hadn't done a leg-yield at all, because it's difficult for the horse to be in good balance if his hind legs aren't stepping well underneath him.

Here are some images and ideas to help you maintain the rhythm and the tempo of the working gait while leg-yielding. Support your aids by "hearing" the rhythm of the footfalls remaining regular and even—every step the same before, during, and after the exercise. Imagine the horse's frame (his **outline** or **silhouette**) staying the same or improving as you change from moving straight ahead to going sideways. Repeat to yourself words like "free," "flow," or "loose" to capture the feeling of the movement.

ACHIEVING SUFFICIENT ANGLE

Even if you think you're correctly coordinating the reins, sometimes it's difficult to know if the horse's legs are crossing enough. As I said earlier, there's little value in doing a leg-yield if the inside legs aren't crossing (or are barely stepping) in front of the outside legs. This point applies particularly to the hind legs as you'll see later when I give you leg-yielding exercises directed specifically to influencing the horse's hindquarters–his engine.

Most people introduce their horses to leg-yielding by doing it on a diagonal line such as from the middle of the ring over to the track. Often it's difficult to feel if the horse is crossing enough when the leg-yield is done in this pattern. You feel like you're accomplishing your purpose because you manage to get from point A to point B, but that doesn't necessarily mean your horse is crossing his legs sufficiently.

What you need to do is develop a "feel" for how much your horse is crossing his legs. You can do this by changing from the diagonal-line pattern and instead leg-yield with your horse's head to the rail along the track. First, ride around the ring to the left and establish good energy and rhythm in your working gait. Next, flex your horse right, toward the rail, and displace the hindquarters to the left, toward the center of the ring so that they are at a 35-degree angle to the rail (slightly less than half of a right angle). Then, make sure you keep your horse's neck straight by supporting with the left rein.

When all three elements are present—the rhythm and energy correct, hindquarters at a 35-degree angle to the wall, and the neck is straight—then there's usually good crossing of the legs. Once you get a feeling for what your horse does when he's crossing sufficiently, go back to the leg-yield on the diagonal line. See if you can make that leg-yield "feel" the same as the good leg-yield that you did in the head-to-the-wall position.

If you're in the head-to-the-wall position going to the left and you still can't get enough angle, use a quick, opening, inside (right) rein. Move your hand laterally (your right hand moves directly to the right) for one stride and then immediately place it back in riding position. Then if you need to, you can open it again (fig. 10.36). Keep in mind that the opening rein won't have the desired effect unless the outside (left) hand is low and supporting so that the shoulder doesn't pop out to the left. If the two reins are properly coordinated, the action of the rein will go to the inside (right) hind leg, and this leg will be sent sideways to the left.

USING BOTH HIND LEGS EQUALLY
Many horses and riders have better sideways or forward motion in one direction than the other. It's important that you ride the leg-yields the

10.36
Use a quick opening rein aid to increase the horse's angle to the rail sideways. Deb brings her right hand directly to the right for one stride without pulling backwards on it. At the same time, she keeps the horse's body straight by supporting firmly with the left rein.

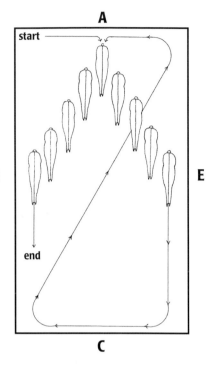

A

start

B

E

end

C

10.37

To encourage your horse to use both hind legs equally, try this exercise. Ride to the right, turn at A, and leg-yield to E. Change direction, turn at A, and leg-yield to B.

10.38

Note the difference in bend and angle required for the shoulder-fore compared to the shoulder-in. In shoulder-fore the horse is on four tracks, and in shoulder-in, on three tracks.

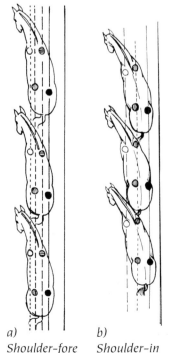

a)
Shoulder-fore

b)
Shoulder-in

same in both directions, so that you're sure that your horse is using his hind legs equally. If your leg-yields don't look the same to the left as they do to the right, there is an exercise you can do that will make them more equal.

In your arena marked with letters as I described at the beginning of Stage Two (page 126) turn down the centerline at A, and leg-yield to E. Then, change direction across the diagonal and turn down the centerline at A again, but this time leg-yield to B (fig. 10.37). You can do many variations on this theme.

In one direction your horse might want to go too much sideways and you get to the side of the ring before the E marker. In the other direction, it may be more difficult to go sideways, and you end up beyond your mark for B. Riding leg-yields accurately to specific points insures that your horse uses both hind legs equally.

It's also possible that if you're having difficulty going sideways in one direction and not the other, it may be you, the *rider*, causing the problem. Maybe you're getting left behind the movement—the horse is going sideways to the left and your upper body leans to the right—making it hard for your horse to move over. If this is happening, here's an image that may help. Visualize stepping down into the outside (left) stirrup or falling off the outside of the horse (see fig. 10.30).

Shoulder-Fore

Now that you've learned how to ride a leg-yield—a lateral exercise *without bend*—I'm going to discuss an exercise from the second category of lateral movements, the ones *with bend*. This exercise is called **shoulder-fore**. Please be aware that I'm discussing shoulder-*fore* here, not shoulder-*in*, which is a more advanced lateral movement that I'll introduce in Book Two (fig. 10.38).

I know I told you earlier in this chapter that because lateral movements *with bend* help a horse develop self-carriage, they are usually done with an animal that is more advanced in his schooling. But, it's important for you to know how to ride shoulder-fore now, not as an exercise to promote self-carriage, but as a way to make your horse *straight*—an issue you deal with everyday.

Besides, the amount of bend required in shoulder-fore is so slight that your horse should be able to cope with it. The bend is actually no greater than the arc of a large, 20-meter (about 60 feet) circle. If you look at a nine-foot segment of this circle—the approximate length of your horse's body—you'll see that the curve is barely noticeable (see fig. 10.38).

In Chapter Six on *forward* and *straight*, I emphasized that straightening your horse is one of the most fundamental rules of all kinds of riding. Dealing with weight on his back and the confines of a ring often increases your horse's struggle with his balance and he can become even more crooked than he is in freedom. Most often, your horse expresses this crookedness by carrying his hindquarters to the inside of the ring and leaning out with his shoulders toward the rail, so that his hind feet don't follow directly in the tracks of the front feet (fig. 10.39).

DESCRIPTION

In shoulder-fore, the horse is slightly bent around the rider's inside leg, which is the one closest to the center of the ring. The rider brings the horse's forehand a small amount in off the track so that his inside hind leg steps between his front legs. If you were to watch a horse coming straight toward you in the shoulder-fore position, you would be able to see all four of his legs (see fig. 10.40).

Riders often mistakenly feel that they have to make a huge adjustment to position their horses in shoulder-fore. It's actually a very small displacement of the forehand. To make this point, I tell my students to look at the distance between their horse's front feet. Then I ask them to tell me how many inches they'll have to move their horse's shoulders over to cover half that distance. The answer is usually only about four inches—a very small amount, indeed! So, don't be intimidated by the idea of doing an "advanced dressage" movement. The challenge is more about making the adjustment subtle enough, rather than how to do it at all.

During shoulder-fore the horse looks in the opposite direction from the way he's moving. In other words, if you are riding to the left, your horse is flexed and looks to the left, but his legs and body move to the right. This movement can be ridden in all three paces—you can easily ride shoulder-fore in medium walk, working trot, and working canter.

Shoulder-fore can be done on both straight and curved lines. Keep in mind when you introduce any new movement that you must always increase the degree of difficulty systematically and gradually. In other words, it's easiest for your horse to start shoulder-fore in the walk on a straight line. When he can do this willingly, ask for it in the trot on a straight line. Then, place him in shoulder-fore in the canter on a straight line.

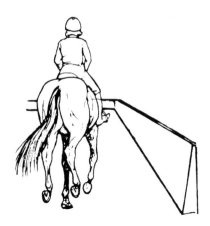

10.39
Most often, a horse expresses his crookedness by carrying his quarters to the inside of the ring and leaning out with his shoulders towards the rail. His hind feet don't follow directly in the tracks of his front feet.

10.40

A good shoulder-fore with the horse clearly on four tracks. Deb should look straight ahead and make sure that her inside leg stays forward on the girth rather than drawing it up and back.

Once your horse can easily cope with the demands of shoulder-fore in walk, trot and canter on a straight line, ask him on a circle starting from the walk and gradually advancing to the trot and canter. After that, you ask him to hold this position during transitions from one pace to another—once again starting on straight lines and progressing to doing the transitions on a circle.

The Aids for Shoulder-Fore

For left shoulder-fore:

Seat: weight left seat bone.

Left leg: on the girth for the horse to bend around as well as to ask for engagement of the inside hind leg.

Right leg: slightly behind the girth to help bend the horse around the inside leg and to prevent his hindquarters from swinging out toward the rail.

Left rein: vibrate for inner flexion.

Right rein: steady and supporting to prevent too much bend in the neck.

Both reins: move laterally a couple of inches to the left to lead the forehand in. Both hands stay equidistant from your body.

• *Helpful Hints* •

When you first attempt to straighten a horse who is used to carrying his hindquarters to the inside, I guarantee you that he's going to look for an escape route. This is because it's a lot easier for your horse to let his hindquarters drift to the inside of the line he's traveling on, than it is to bend the joints of his inside hind leg and step toward his center.

There are three common ways that horses try to evade the difficulty of the shoulder-fore. In the following examples, we're still traveling to the left (fig. 10.41).

Your horse's first escape route will probably be to try to bring only his head and his neck to the inside (left in these diagrams). When he does this, his shoulders are able to fall out to the right toward the rail and his hindquarters might actually drift even more to the inside of the ring than they were before you tried to straighten him. So he ends up being even more crooked then when you started!

Here's how you can block off this escape route and at the same time learn the feeling of moving his shoulders to the inside rather than just his head and his neck. First, counter-flex him at the poll: vibrate the right rein and see his right eye. Then, bring both of your arms laterally to the left to move his shoulders to the left. Counter-flexing your horse will make it more difficult for him to escape by popping his shoulders out toward the rail. Once you learn the feeling of controlling his entire forehand, go back to flexing him correctly—to the inside. While you have him correctly flexed, check that the shifting of his forehand to the inside feels the same as it did when he was counter-flexed.

Once you are able to move your horse's forehand to the inside, he'll probably look for his second escape route by stepping to the inside of the ring with his entire body. You'll know this is happening when you end up on a different track than the one you started on. For example, if you started on the track near the rail, after ten or fifteen steps you might end up further from the rail than where you started. Or, suppose you started on a large circle and after several strides you find yourself on a smaller circle.

The correction here is to use a strong inside leg at the girth to drive your horse's inside hind leg toward his center. Make sure you don't try to hold him over on the track or out on the larger circle by bringing both of your arms to the outside. If you do, you'll end up with your horse in the same "head and neck-in with shoulder falling out" position that he was in the previous example.

If you manage to block off both of the previous escape routes, your horse's third and final effort to avoid the difficulty of the exercise will probably be to lose energy and slow down. In that case use your driving aids actively. Give some sharp squeezes with your inside leg and push with your seat as if you're trying to move the back of the saddle towards the front of the saddle. Also, imagine that you're riding shoulder-fore in a lengthening of whatever pace you're in. This will get both you and your horse *thinking* forward.

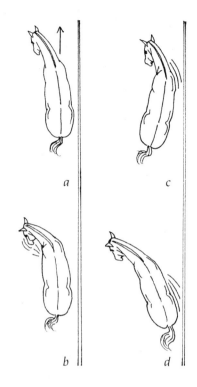

10.41

Three common evasions to the shoulder-fore position:

a) correct shoulder-fore
b) head and neck in
c) shoulders falling out
d) haunches drifting out

ADDITIONAL USES FOR SHOULDER-FORE

Straightening your horse is my primary purpose for introducing the shoulder-fore at this point. However, there are other benefits to learning how to ride this movement now.

Riding your horse in the shoulder-fore position will not only straighten him but will also strengthen and increase the carrying, rather than the pushing, power of the inside hind leg. This is because in shoulder-fore the horse's inside hind leg is asked to step further under his body, move more in the direction of his center of gravity, and carry weight. Therefore, if you choose to continue with his dressage education beyond the basics, you'll be laying a foundation for more advanced work such as shoulder-in.

Shoulder-fore is also very useful as an exercise to improve the regularity of rhythm with a horse who has a "lateral" walk (see page 99). Ask him to go sideways in shoulder-fore until the rhythm becomes regular. Then, straighten him for only as many steps as the rhythm remains regular and four-beat. As soon as the rhythm starts to degenerate into a lateral walk, immediately place him in the shoulder-fore position again. In this way, you explain to your horse that his only option is to walk in an evenly spaced four beats. He never gets the chance to do a lateral walk because as soon as the rhythm changes, you keep it regular by going sideways.

In the trot a common fault occurs when a horse hurries so much that his foreleg comes to the ground before his diagonal hind leg. Two separate hoof beats can be heard instead of the one together. This is because the horse is carrying most of his weight and that of his rider on his shoulders. You need to shift this horse's center of gravity back toward his hind legs. Riding shoulder-fore will help this situation.

Finally, shoulder-fore is useful when a horse swings his haunches in toward the inside of the ring to avoid engaging his inside hind during the canter depart. You can correct this by riding shoulder-fore in walk or trot just prior to asking for the canter as well as during the canter depart itself. Use an active, inside leg and a firm, outside rein to keep your horse in the shoulder-fore position through the transition. If you don't hold him in shoulder-fore during the depart, he'll become crooked to make the job easier for himself.

KEY POINTS

- In lateral movements, the horse moves forward and sideways at the same time.

- There are two groups of lateral movements. The first group includes turns on the forehand and leg-yielding. The horse is *not bent* during these movements. The second group includes shoulder-fore, shoulder-in, haunches-in, haunches-out, half-pass, walk pirouettes and canter pirouettes. These movements are more difficult because the horse is *asked to bend* as he goes sideways.

- Flexion refers to the closing of a joint so that the angle between the bones is decreased. A horse can flex at the poll left, right, and "in." Flexing the joints of the hind legs and lumbosacral area is called "engagement."

- Turn on the forehand is the only lateral movement done from a halt. It is a useful exercise to teach a green horse the idea of moving away from the leg.

- Leg-yielding is a good warm-up exercise because it loosens, stretches, and relaxes the horse's muscles.

- Shoulder-fore is the main exercise used to straighten a crooked horse.

CHAPTER ELEVEN

Suppling for Balance and Harmony

I n a perfect world, all horses are relaxed, supple, athletic, and obedient. The reality is, however, that few of us ride horses that show all of these qualities all of the time (or even some of the time!).

In Book Two, *More Cross-Training*, I'll teach you how to give a half-halt, to help you deal with the less-than-perfect horse. This is the most valuable tool I can give you to control and communicate with your horse. With this half-halt you'll be able to cope with any number of situations that arise during training. It can help you reduce your horse's tension, loosen his stiffness, teach a resistant horse acceptance of the rein, connect your horse from back to front, bend him on his stiff side, as well as ask him to pay attention to you when he's distracted.

As a preliminary exercise to the half-halt, I'm going to teach you a simple exercise that I call **suppling**. Please take a moment to look at figs. 11.2 to 11.6 starting on page 199, so you'll have an idea what suppling looks like before I explain further. Done correctly, suppling can help you deal with all the training issues that I mentioned above. But I want to emphasize that using suppling to deal with training problems is a temporary stage. Once you and your horse have learned about half-halts, they will be all you will need to improve his balance, attention, and harmony.

The advantages to suppling are that it's easy to learn to do and enormously effective for loosening very stiff or resistant horses in a short period of time. There is a disadvantage, too. Unlike the half-halt, which is an invisible aid, suppling is very obvious to an onlooker. It's quite apparent that you are bending and straightening your horse's neck. Not only do we always strive to ride with the most discreet aids possible in training, but from a practical point of view, suppling is too visible to be done in most competitive events.

Suppling is easy for anyone to do and that's one reason why I'm explaining it before we get to the half-halt. The other reason is that I see countless *distorted* versions of suppling being done by riders in all disciplines. For example, a rider will bend her horse's neck to such an extreme degree that rather than loosening him, she knocks him off balance. Or, she'll waggle her horse's head back and forth dramatically and repetitively.

The worst-case scenario, however, is when it is used as a way to punish a horse. Unfortunately, I've seen advanced riders as well as novices guilty of doing this. Suppling a horse in an abusive way is *never* acceptable. Because of the widespread confusion about how to supple as well as misuse of suppling, I feel compelled to include a section about it in this book.

To get started I'll show you how you can supple a horse to make him less stiff, both laterally (through his side) and longitudinally (over his back). In the next chapter, I'll show you how you can use suppling to do all sorts of problem solving.

First, let's consider the dilemma of the uneducated horse when he's asked to cope with a rider's weight on his back. This horse finds it simple to be in good balance when he's in freedom. But, when a rider sits on him, he naturally contracts his back muscles and drops his back to hollow it away from that weight. When the rider picks up the contact, he stiffens his neck and pokes his nose forward (fig. 11.1b). In this posture he uses his neck as a balancing rod in much the same way as you hold on to a banister for balance when you go down a flight of stairs.

As long as your horse moves over the ground in this position, his body feels stiff as he shuffles along with short, tight steps. His back seems frozen and the only thing that appears to move are his legs. I call this being a "leg-mover" and, in this case, your goal with suppling is to unlock and loosen this horse so he can move gracefully through his whole body.

a) When a horse's back is loose and round, he can move freely and gracefully

b) When his back is stiff and hollow, his movement will be choppy and unathletic

11.1 A supple back and a stiff back

The Aids for Suppling

When you supple your horse, you'll actively use the leg and rein aids on one side of your horse. However, it is essential that you place equal emphasis on the passive supporting aids that are on the other side. The goal is to supple the horse between the active and passive aids, not just away from the active aids (figs. 11.2 to 11.6).

The other thing to remember is that even though the visible part of suppling is the bending and straightening of your horse's

11.2
Look at how Moxie carries herself before suppling. Her steps are short, her back is low, her neck and head are short and high, and she is resisting Deb's hand. Notice how similar her body is to the horse in 11.1b.

11.3
Deb begins suppling her horse by closing her inside leg as she bends Moxie's neck to the inside.

11.2 to 11.6 Suppling con't.

11.4

As soon as Deb has bent her horse's neck, she immediately straightens it with the other rein. She is careful to maintain the contact with Moxie's mouth on the inside rein as she straightens her with the outside rein.

11.5

As Deb continues to straighten the neck, Moxie begins to lengthen and lower it.

11.6
The final result of effective suppling. The hind leg reaches further underneath the body, the whole topline is longer, and Moxie has a happier expression on her face.

neck, you should never just work a "part" of your horse (the neck in this case). Always ride the whole horse from back to front by using your leg each time you bend his neck with the rein. To check that my students are thinking along the right lines, each time they supple their horses, I'll have them say out loud, "My leg sends my horse's hind leg forward towards my hand." This reminds them to work their horses from their leg forward into their hand.

Suppling can be done in all three paces and either to the inside or the outside of the ring. For clarity of aids, however, right now I'll assume we're riding to the left and you're going to supple your horse to the left, which is the inside.

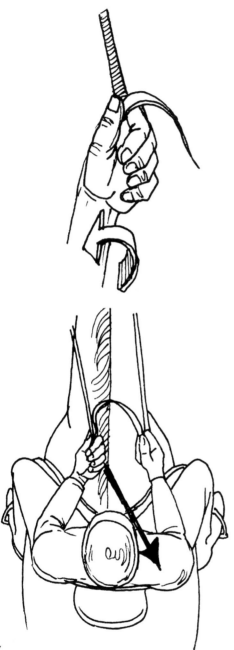

11.7

Use an indirect rein aid when suppling your horse. Your hand comes as close to the withers as possible without crossing over it. Turn your knuckles up toward your face so that your pinkie finger points toward your right hip.

Aids for Suppling to the Left

Active aids:

Inside rein: use as an indirect rein. The action of the rein is toward your opposite hip. Your left hand comes as close to the withers as possible without crossing over. Turn your knuckles up toward your face so that your pinkie finger points toward your right hip (fig. 11.7).

Inside leg: each time you bend your horse's neck to the left, close your left leg on his side. This way you'll be sending his left hind leg forward into your left hand. I'm assuming, of course, that your horse is "in front of your leg." If he isn't, as far as he's concerned, you're just riding him with your hands and you need to go back and review how to put your horse in front of your leg (page 80).

Passive Aids:

Outside rein: the outside right rein is steady and supporting at all times. Many riders mistakenly feel that they must let this hand go forward toward their horse's mouth when they bend the horse with their inside hand. Keep your hands side by side at all times.

Outside leg: steady and supporting to prevent the horse from swinging his quarters to the outside. It's placed on the girth if you're on a straight line and behind the girth if you're on a curve.

As you use your inside rein, bend your horse's head around to a degree that would be between 10 and 11 o'-clock if you were looking at a clock with 12 o'clock straight ahead. If you bend his neck more than that, you'll knock him off balance, causing him to stiffen even more to save himself.

Be sure to maintain a consistent contact with his mouth before, during, and after you bend him. Often riders drop the contact and put slack in the rein as they straighten their horses' necks (figs. 11.8 and 11.9). Your horse won't object when the rein is slack, but you'll be jerking him in

<u>11.8</u>
This is a good start to suppling.

<u>11.9</u>
But here Amy drops contact with the inside rein as she straightens her horse's neck with the outside rein. She needs to maintain the straight line from her elbow to the bit at all times.

the mouth when you establish contact again. Stay connected to him. Imagine having a dance partner holding on to you firmly but gently as he guides you around the dance floor. It's a solid, secure feeling and the last thing you want your partner to do is let go of you as he lowers you into a dip!

The timing of the act of bending and straightening should be fairly quick, but very smooth. It does not have to be in the rhythm of the gait. Bend your horse's neck around in a two or three second span of time and then immediately straighten him with the other rein. Pretend that you're giving him a massage. Pleasantly manipulate his neck in a smooth, continuous motion—not too fast or too slow.

When you meet resistance and the horse locks his jaw, don't hang on to the rein. If you feel a marked stiffness or resistance in the beginning, it doesn't matter. You must straighten him by using the outside rein as soon as you've bent him, whether he resists or not. Otherwise, the relief that you get from the stiffness, comes from just flexing him in the jaw. And remember that we always want to work the horse's entire body from back to front, not just his jaw.

If your horse is so stiff that he resists by stopping, jigging, or swinging his hindquarters sideways, ease your way into suppling by bending his neck less. Once he's loose enough that you can "take his neck away" a little, try to bend it to between 10 and 11 o'clock again.

Supple your horse three times and then relax for at least seven or eight strides before you start another series of three "supples." Don't just supple continuously. Give the horse's body a chance to react, and then evaluate whether or not he feels looser.

TESTS OF SUPPLENESS

After you've done several series of three "supples," you'll find that your horse will begin to relax his back, lower his head and neck and take longer, more fluid strides. This is what you're looking for. But you might ask how long you need to continue suppling, and if it's okay to only supple one side of the horse's body regardless of the direction you're going. To answer those questions, I'll give you three ways to determine when your horse has become supple.

1. Before you start to supple your horse, take a moment to evaluate how much weight you have in your hands when your horse's neck is straight. Then ask yourself how much power it takes you to bend his neck around to between 10 and 11 o'clock. You might find the weight increases from two pounds to five, or even fifteen, pounds. When your horse is supple, you should be able to bend his neck around without using any strength. This doesn't happen overnight.

But, if you initially had to use fifteen pounds of power and now you only need thirteen pounds, you know your horse is becoming somewhat more supple. Little by little, the strength you need to bend him will decrease from thirteen pounds to ten to eight to five until eventually the weight of the rein stays the same before, during, and after the "supple."

This usually happens on one side of his body before the other. So concentrate on suppling the side that's crying for attention. You might end up suppling your horse 80% of the time to the left and 20% of the time to the right. Or, perhaps you'll always need to supple him to the right regardless of which direction you're going. Listen to what your horse tells you and do what he needs.

2. It's a good sign that you're successfully loosening your horse when he lowers his neck after you've suppled him three times. But ideally you want to see him lower his neck *while* you're bending him (see photo 11.5 in earlier suppling sequence). If he lengthens and lowers his neck and stretches toward your hand each time you bend him, he's showing marked suppleness.

3. When you do this exercise with a supple horse, his neck is the only thing that deviates from the line you're on. As you bend his neck, his body continues to overlap the line of travel even if you do not support him with strong outside aids. You know your horse is stiff when you use the inside rein and the action of the rein ricochets through his body so that his hindquarters swing to the outside.

SUPPLING THE POLL

You can also do a more subtle version of suppling in order to loosen your horse just in his poll rather than his whole neck. You can use this when you have trouble flexing your horse on a circle, he's locked against your hand, or he's tipping his head. You'll know you need to do this exercise if you find it difficult to flex him to the inside when you're circling, turning, or leg-yielding (figs. 11.10 and 11.11).

Go on either a circle or a straight line in the walk and ask your horse to flex to the outside and then to the inside for a few strides each. Do this by turning your wrist a couple of times as if you had a key in a door and you were unlocking the door. (It's the same movement with your wrist that you need to do for an indirect rein aid, which I explained earlier on page 123). When your horse is supple in his poll, he will keep looking in whichever direction you flex him all by himself, even when your wrist is back in its normal position. Once you've flexed him, he should keep looking in the direction you've indicated until you specifically ask him to look straight ahead or flex the other way. You shouldn't

11.10
Suppling the poll to the inside. Note that the rest of the horse's body stays straight and overlaps the line she is on.

11.11
Suppling the poll to the outside. The only thing that has changed is the direction toward which Galen is looking. The mare's body is still straight and on her line of travel.

have to hold him in flexion with your hand. Once you can do this in the walk, try it in the trot and the canter.

When you supple the poll, remember to use a passive supporting rein on the other side. Otherwise your horse will bend further down his neck (which is the suppling I described earlier in this chapter) and the value of this particular exercise is lost because you won't be isolating and loosening his poll. When your horse is flexed either left or right, the position of his neck should look exactly the same—straight on lines and bent along curves. You should merely see his inside or outside eye.

Here's an image for you to think of when you do this poll suppling exercise. Imagine that your horse is so loose in his poll that his head is attached to his neck with a spring like those little toy dogs that people used to put in the back of their '57 Chevys—their heads loosely bouncing around! (See fig. 11.12.)

11.12
When suppling the poll, imagine that this joint is so loose that your horse's head is attached to his neck like the toy dogs you see in the back windows of '57 Chevys!

KEY POINTS

- Suppling can be used to relax, loosen, and connect your horse, as well as teach him to accept your hand.

- Always supple by actively using your leg at the same time that you bend your horse's neck. For example, think of your left leg sending your horse's left hind leg forward into your left hand.

- Make sure that you support with the passive aids so that you supple the horse between the active and passive aids.

- Time your suppling so that it is done fairly quickly but very smoothly.

- When he's supple, a horse meets the following requirements:

  1. You don't need to use strength to bend his neck.

  2. His neck gets longer and lower as you supple him.

  3. His legs stay on the line of travel.

CHAPTER TWELVE

Putting It All Together— Sample Schooling Session

You now have a lot of information about the Basics and the various exercises you can do with your horse as you begin your dressage program, but you might be wondering how to put it all together in a logical sequence. I know from experience that you're not alone with this quandary because at clinics I'll often see versions of the following three scenarios.

A rider leads her horse from the stable to the ring and mounts. She shortens the reins right away, walks around for a minute or two, and then warms up by doing transitions back and forth from the walk to the trot.

A rider will warm-up her horse by walking, trotting, and cantering around for five minutes on a totally loose rein. Her horse trucks along with his head stuck straight up in the air, and his back muscles rigid and contracted.

Then, there's the rider who takes a 45-minute lesson with me and because she wants to "practice," takes her horse into another ring afterwards and drills him for another hour!

Because these hypothetical schooling sessions are, in fact, quite common, I'd like to give you some guidelines about how to put the information that you've learned to this point together in a way that makes sense and is in your horse's best interest.

TIME FRAME

First, let's talk about a sensible weekly program and then decide how to organize your daily work. As far as a weekly program is concerned, even those who specialize in dressage don't spend every single day working in the ring. A normal week for a dressage specialist includes five days of work, one day off, and one "play" day. Playing can be anything from hacking, to jumping low fences, to galloping on the track that we're fortunate to have available. The play day is normally scheduled sometime in the middle of the work week so that our horses don't work in the ring five days in a row. This plan keeps the horses mentally fresh and enthusiastic about their work. Plus, since muscles get stronger when they're at rest, doing something totally different from the "weight lifting" that is required by dressage horses allows these muscles time to rest, repair, and get stronger. So, you see, play is just as important as work.

My combined training riders have a built-in variety to their weekly program. They usually devote two or three days each week to their flat work. The other days they warm up as they would if they were going to work on the flat, and then they do whatever is on their schedule—stadium jumping, a cross-country school, a gallop for wind, or a conditioning hack.

As far as daily work goes, if I'm going to concentrate totally on flat work, my sessions usually last somewhere between forty-five minutes to an hour. This time includes walking, both at the beginning and the end of the ride. With a very young horse, like a three year old, my sessions are often as brief as twenty minutes and definitely no longer than half an hour.

When I work with students who are planning to jump or condition during their ride that day, we'll spend perhaps fifteen minutes doing a warm-up which I'll describe shortly, and then they'll go on to the rest of their program. You'll need to modify both your daily and your weekly routine depending on your particular specialty. Always keep in mind that your horse is an athlete; in order to work productively and reduce the risk of injury, most athletes divide their training sessions into three stages—warming up, work, and cooling down.

WARMING UP

In their natural state, horses mosey around, graze, and rest. They do this pretty much continuously over the course of a day. Nowadays, however, these normally roaming creatures live in stables for the most part. It's unfair to take a horse who has been standing around in a stall and expect him to go directly to work. So, for the first five or ten minutes after you get on, give your horse a chance to just walk around on a loose rein (fig. 12.1).

After walking around "on the buckle" for several minutes, pick up a contact so you can begin your warm-up.

When I think of warming up, the key word that sticks in my mind is *relaxation*. As far as I'm concerned, any work done in tension is pretty much a waste of time. So I spend as little or as much time as necessary relaxing my

12.1

Warm-up: for the first five or ten minutes after you get on, give your horse a chance to walk around on a loose rein.

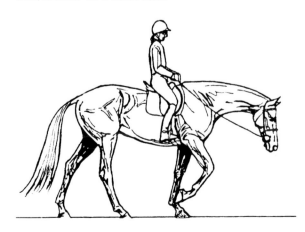

horse both physically and mentally before I go on to the work phase of my ride. I'm sure you can imagine that with certain horses on particular days, my entire ride consists only of the warm-up!

As I mentioned in the chapter on suppling, it's easier to relax a horse physically first. Once his body is relaxed, his mind usually follows suit. So after I pick up a contact with a young horse, I'll go directly to the posting trot. I do this because it's easy to ruin the quality of the walk by working a young horse on contact in the walk (see Chapter Seven, page 97 on paces, gaits, and rhythm). Then I'll begin to loosen my horse's body by suppling him. If my horse is further along in his education, I'll start suppling in the walk. Then, when he's relaxed in the walk, I'll go on to the posting trot. I'll supple him while trotting both to the left and to the right, and once he's relaxed in both directions, I'll do the same thing in the canter.

12.2
I think of the warm-up as the loosening, stretching, "toe-touching" part of my horse's schooling session!

I like to think of the warm-up as the "toe-touching" part of my schooling session (fig. 12.2). After each series of three "supples," I'll let a few inches of rein slip through my fingers so that my horse can stretch his head and neck forward and down toward the ground (fig. 12.4).

Remember that the length of your reins determines the length of your horse's neck. So the longer your reins, the more he can stretch. However, it's important to maintain the contact with his mouth when you do this. So, don't just drop the reins in an effort to get your horse to stretch. Instead, open your fingers slightly and allow your horse to choose how much rein he'll take as he seeks the contact forward and down. You'll often hear people refer to this position as "long and low" (figs. 12.3 to 12.5).

I was giving a lecture once during which I was describing this long and low frame, and a woman raised her hand to ask a question. She said, "When I pick up the contact with my horse's mouth, he immediately dives way down with his head and neck and sucks dirt. Is this good?"

My response to her question was, "Well...there's good 'dirt-sucking' and there's bad 'dirt-sucking.' If his hind legs are still stepping well underneath his body, that's good 'dirt-sucking.' If his hind legs are trailing out behind his body, that's bad 'dirt-sucking.'"

The point that I'm making here is that not all "long and low" is created equal. The important thing is where your horse's hind legs are when you allow him to stretch forward and down to the ground. That determines just how much rein you give him and just how far you let him out.

12.3 to 12.5
Suppling and Stretching

12.3
Warm-up: supple your horse in the usual way by bending his neck as you drive him forward with your inside leg.

12.4
Allow him to stretch "long and low" by opening your fingers and letting him "chew" the reins out of your hands, but don't give him so much extra rein that the reins become loose and you lose contact with his mouth.

12.5
The more you let the reins go, the longer your horse can stretch.

THE WORK PHASE

After you've warmed up "long and low" (for however long it takes!) and your horse is relaxed, give him a break and let him walk on a loose rein for a few minutes. When you pick up contact again, shorten the reins to a more normal working length for you.

Then you can begin to incorporate all the movements you've learned in the preceding Nuts and Bolts chapters—circles, transitions, lengthenings, backing up, leg-yields, shoulder-fore, and counter-canter. Spend a couple of minutes reviewing and refining each exercise. Then "listen" to your horse. He'll tell you what he needs to practice.

In other words, whatever you find difficult to do, that is the work that's crying for attention. Focus on the "needy" movement or exercise until it gets a *little bit better*. This is all you need to do each day to make progress happily and with a minimum of resistance. A "little bit better" and a "little bit better" eventually add up to a "whole lot better." If you expect perfection every day, both you and your horse will end up frustrated.

I'd like to make two other points about your attitude toward training. First, take frequent breaks by walking on a loose rein in between each of your exercises. Not only will this reward your horse, but it actually expedites the training process. You'd be surprised how giving your horse a break when you think he just isn't "getting it," can help him relax and figure things out. Somehow, when you start again, more often than not, he miraculously does a whole lot better.

The other point is to be very generous with your reward. I've seen riders struggle with their horses over a particular movement and when the horse finally improves, they nod their heads as if their horses owed it to them. Well, your horse doesn't owe you anything, and he certainly doesn't know that you're nodding your head. Let him know that he's good by patting, verbally praising or by giving him a brief rest by walking on a loose rein. Telling him he's a "star" becomes a self-fulfilling prophecy. (So is telling him he's a pig!) He'll revel in your appreciation of him and he'll try even harder. Remember, as far as your horse is concerned, *absence of reward is the same as punishment.* So make the following your motto: Ask often, expect little, and praise lavishly.

COOLING DOWN

In order to avoid stiff, sore muscles the next day, every good athlete's training session includes a period of cooling down. Your cool-down is simply a shortened version of your warm-up. Most of my riders do a "long and low" posting trot in each direction until they feel any residual physical or mental tension dissipate. Then they walk on a loose rein for another five minutes or go for a short hack. They dismount before they return to the stable. They loosen the girths and lead their horses the rest of the way back to the barn. (And if you were a fly on the wall in the barn, you'd overhear them telling their horses just how brilliant and perfect they were that day!)

KEY POINTS

- Schedule variety into your program to refresh your horse's mind and to allow his muscles to repair and get stronger.

- Every schooling session should include a warm-up, work, and a cooling down period.

- As far as work goes, always reward him and be satisfied when your horse does a movement or exercise "a little bit better."

CHAPTER THIRTEEN

Trouble Shooting with Basic Flatwork

Now that you're familiar with the nuts and bolts of basic flatwork, I'll show you how you can use that knowledge to troubleshoot some common problems.

In this chapter you'll find that we can solve all sorts of resistances and disobediences by using the information that you've learned to this point. (In Book Two, I'll again deal with training issues, using more advanced dressage movements to solve problems).

Tension

No matter what your riding discipline, in order to do productive and rewarding work you want a relaxed, calm horse. Relaxation should be a priority because for the most part, attempting to train a tense horse is a waste of time and not very pleasant for either one of you.

The first thing to keep in mind is that, like yourself, a horse has both a mind and a body, and it's impossible to separate them. In my experience, I've found that although it can be somewhat effective to calm a tense horse's mind by speaking to him in soothing tones, it's much more effective to first relax the body because then the mind, in turn, becomes more quiet.

With physical relaxation as my goal, I supple my horse as I described in Chapter Eleven. As my horse's body begins to loosen and relax, inevitably I find that his mental stress diminishes. Another thing to remember is that speed and tension are closely related; often I'll relax a tense horse by working him in a very slow trot.

In Chapter Seven, I said that *energy* is one of the criteria of high quality paces. However, when my primary goal is to reduce tension, I do not want energy yet. This is because I think of the word energy as meaning "more." If I ask for energy, I'm going to get *more* of whatever I have. So if I have a tight horse who moves with short, quick steps, asking for "more" will give me a tighter horse who moves with even shorter, quicker steps. So, before I ask for energy, I make sure that I like the qualities I have because that's what I'm going to get more of when I put the energy back in.

Once my horse begins to relax, I carefully add energy. If I find I've asked for too much and the tension creeps back in, I turn the level down a notch. Little by little my horse learns to stay relaxed as I add activity by increments in order to bring his trot back up to a normal, energetic, working gait.

Rushing and Running Away

If your horse tends to rush around out of control and he won't listen to your back and outside rein when you ask him to slow down, turn him onto a small circle. Circles tend to take speed away from a horse so you can slow him down. Remember you never want to pull on the reins, because doing so stops the hind legs. Once you stop the hind legs, your horse's back goes down and his head and neck come up. Pulling on the reins causes a loss of connection from the back to the front.

Here's an exercise for the horse that rushes. Work on a large circle, and as soon as your horse runs, arc onto a smaller circle within that circle. Stay on the smaller figure until he slows down, then melt back onto the larger circle. The moment he speeds up again, whether it's one stride or twenty strides later, turn back onto the smaller circle (see fig. 9.13).

Once you can moderate and control the speed on a circle, challenge the horse by going on a straight line where he might tend to run even more. As soon as he rushes, do a small circle until he slows down. Then, go straight again.

Sometimes it's only in our minds that we think we can't slow down a rushing horse. If this has become a mental block for you, let's look at the situation logically. You know that when you're finished riding, you'll be able to stop your horse in order to get off. Well, if you can come to a complete stop in order to get off, you can certainly give a fraction of the aid that you use to stop, and instead slow your horse down.

So, let's say your horse is racing around in the trot. Apply your aids as if you're going to stop and dismount. Bring your horse almost to the halt and then just before he stops, soften your hands and allow him to trot forward again at a more civilized speed. Do this as often as you need to until he chooses to maintain a steady, controlled pace.

Perhaps you have an off-the-track Thoroughbred who doesn't come forward with his hind legs. Instead he walks and trots with short, quick, tense steps and, as a result, he rushes over the ground at a pretty fast, uncontrolled-feeling clip. Since you know that taking longer strides will slow him down, you close your legs to ask his hind legs to step further under his body. However, his reaction to your aids is just to go faster.

To decrease this horse's speed, ask him to leg-yield. The leg-yield forces him to slow down because his hind legs must take longer strides. As soon as you feel a reduction in his tempo, reward and straighten him. When he begins to accelerate again, push him sideways until he learns to step with long strides whether he's going sideways or straight ahead.

If you have an indoor ring, do the leg-yield in the head-to-the-wall position. Having the wall in front of him will back him off so that you won't have to resort to pulling on the reins.

You can also remind your horse not to rush by backing him up. Remember that one of the reasons that a horse rushes is because his hind legs are too far out behind his body. So, if your horse gets rolling along too fast, halt, back up, and then resume whatever pace you were doing.

Not only will backing up physically get your horse's hind legs further underneath him, but mentally, he'll be anticipating stopping and backing up rather than barreling along.

Another rushing problem is presented by the horse who is confused about changing his canter lead. Let's say you'd like to ride a change of lead through the trot, but as soon as you trot, your horse rushes off or, when he canters again, picks up the same lead as before. (For a change of lead through the trot, you switch from one canter lead to the other by trotting for three or four steps in between each canter.)

Try this exercise (fig. 13.1). Pick up right lead canter. Go across a line that divides your ring diagonally. Trot in the middle and immediately step into left shoulder-fore. In the left shoulder-fore, the hind legs stay on the diagonal line, and you guide the shoulders slightly to the left of that line by bringing both of your hands to the left. Be sure to maintain a firm left leg *on* the girth so your horse doesn't drift to the left of the diagonal. Ride left shoulder-fore in trot for the rest of the diagonal, then straighten before the corner and pick up left lead canter.

Do the same thing on the next diagonal. Riding shoulder-fore prevents your horse from rushing off in trot because the movement engages his inside hind leg and keeps it underneath him. Also, the slight bend of the shoulder-fore helps position him to pick up the correct lead.

The Lazy Horse Who Needs a Lot of Leg

There's practically nothing worse than a horse that doesn't listen to your legs. You use your legs, your horse reacts a little, so you squeeze harder, and he temporarily responds to the aid. Then he gets dull to the stronger aid, and you have to do even more. Pretty soon you're exhausted and you have to take a break. This means that your horse has successfully trained you to let him do less work.

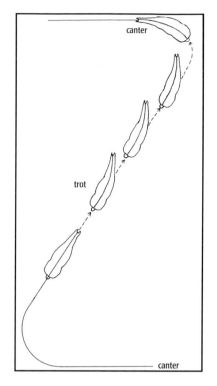

13.1

To help prevent your horse from rushing through a lead change, go across the diagonal in right lead canter, trot in the middle, and immediately step into left shoulder-fore. Straighten your horse before the corner, then ask for left lead canter.

If you've ever been lured into this cycle, the first thing you need to do is resensitize the horse to light leg aids. This is described in detail in Chapter Six).

I remember giving a clinic on the Basics—forward, straight, and rhythm. Shortly after, I received a nice note from one of the participants in which she exclaimed, "I can hardly believe it! This is the first time in three years that I've brought my horse back to the barn and he's breathing harder than I am!" That's the way it should be!

Once you've resensitized your horse to your leg, you can use the movements from Chapters Nine and Ten to ask your horse: "Are you paying attention? Are you listening to refined aids?" It's not necessary to do each exercise very long. It's your horse's initial reaction to your leg that gives you the answer to these questions.

TRANSITIONS

If your horse seems a little dull, ride frequent transitions from pace to pace to put him mentally on the aids. He should feel "hot" off your leg for the upward transition and quick to respond to your back and outside rein for the downward transition. Don't stay in any pace for more than a few strides. It's the frequency of the transitions that makes him more alert. For the lazy horse, pretend you're doing the transition from a working gait into a lengthening of the next gait—from working trot to lengthened canter, for instance—so that you inspire him to go more forward.

By the same token, you can check that your horse is paying attention by doing transitions within a pace. Do several lengthenings and shortenings. You don't have to do a lot of steps. Just ask the right questions. Will you go more forward as soon as I ask? Will you listen to a light aid to come back from a lengthening?

LEG-YIELDING

You can also use leg-yielding to ask obedience-to-the-leg questions. A submissive horse moves sideways just from the position of the leg behind the girth rather than from strong pressure. You don't *make* a 1200 lb. animal go sideways. (Or do anything else, for that matter!) You ask him to do so with a signal, and when the training is correct, he responds. The process of making the horse responsive to a leg that is behind the girth is described in Chapter Ten.

The following obedience-to-the-leg exercises can be done for a few strides each. Once again, you simply want to ask the questions and evaluate your horse's initial response.

1. Walk or trot on a straight line along a track or the rail. Position your horse's head toward the rail, by squeezing and releasing with the

fingers of the hand that's on the same side as the rail, just enough so that you can see his eye. Then slide your leg near the rail back a few inches.

Your horse should immediately swing his hindquarters to the inside of the ring while his forehand stays on the track. If he doesn't, kick him or tap him with the whip and ask again. Imagine that the leg that's behind the girth is an electric cattle-prod or a red-hot poker. As soon as you bring your leg back, your horse should move away from it eagerly (fig. 13.2). As soon as he does, slide your leg back to the on-the-girth position and go straight forward. Then, ask for the leg-yield again. Do four or five of these transitions on the long side of your ring.

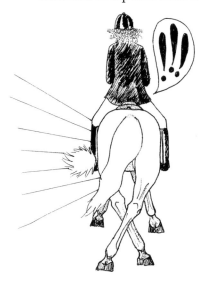

13.2

To help your horse react to your request for a leg-yield, imagine that your leg that is positioned behind the girth is a red-hot poker. As soon as you move this leg back, your horse should move away from it immediately and eagerly.

2. Go on a circle in the walk or the trot and alternate a leg-yield where you move the hindquarters away from your left leg, with straightening for a few strides. Then, move the hindquarters away from your right leg. In all cases, the horse's front legs stay on the original track of the circle and the hindquarters are displaced left and right (fig. 13.3).

3. Leg-yield along a diagonal line and make a "staircase" by moving your horse's whole body sideways away from the long side for a few steps. Then ride him straight forward for a few strides. Then leg-yield again. Your horse should respond immediately to the frequent changes in leg position, from behind-the-girth which asks him to go sideways, to on-the-girth which asks him to go forward (fig. 13.4).

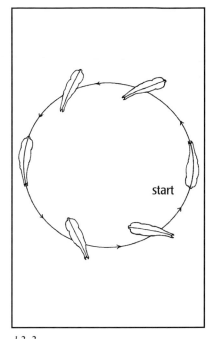

13.3

Go on a circle, leg-yield away from your left leg, straighten, then leg-yield away from your right leg.

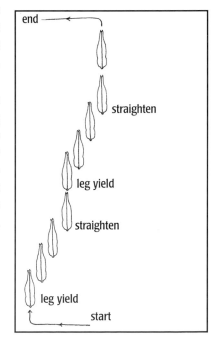

13.4

Leg-yield along a diagonal line and make a "staircase." Your horse should respond immediately to your frequent changes of leg position.

13.5
Support your leg-yielding aids by visualizing that your horse's legs are crossing with wide, long strides.

13.6
Check your horse's desire to go forward by going backward. Put your "gear shift" in reverse for four steps, drive forward for four steps, then go back to reverse. This should be a continuous motion.

Support your leg-yielding aids by picturing in your mind's eye that the hind legs continually are crossing and spreading with very wide, long strides (fig. 13.5).

BACKING UP

You can ask "forward-thinking" questions even when your horse is going backward. Here are three exercises to do to check his desire to go forward.

1. Back up a few steps and then immediately go forward into trot without any hesitation. As soon as your legs change position from behind-the-girth to on-the-girth, the horse should react by trotting forward keenly.

2. Back up a few steps and while still going backward, start to position your horse for a left lead canter depart. Flex him to the left until you just see his eye, put your weight on your left seat bone, and close your right hand in a fist. As soon as your right leg comes behind the girth, your horse should step forward into the left lead canter.

3. Do a "rocker" where your horse takes four steps backward, four steps forward, and four steps backward again. This should be a continuous motion with no halting in between each series of four steps. In your mind's eye, support your aids by "seeing" the automatic gear shift in a car. Put it on "R(everse)"—the horse goes back; move it to "D(rive)," and he goes immediately forward; then shift back to R, and he smoothly steps backward again (fig. 13.6).

Speeding Up and Slowing Down

You can help the horse that goes in fits and starts to maintain a constant tempo if you understand what horses do normally. They generally speed up when leaving a circle or corner, starting across a diagonal, or approaching wide open spaces. And they tend to slow down as they begin circles and turns.

So, anticipate these reactions and train in what I call a benignly antagonistic way by doing the opposite of what your erratically "tempo-ed" horse chooses to do.

For instance, as you start a circle, ask for a few strides of a lengthening. Then as you leave the circle and head into an open stretch, halt. By staying one step ahead of your horse and doing the opposite of what he wants to do, pretty soon he'll begin to wait for your signals rather than making his own decisions about his tempo.

13.7

I'm preparing to pick up the left lead canter from the trot, but Woody is leaning on my inside (left) leg. Because he is flexed to the right, and his rib cage is bulging slightly against my left leg, I'm concerned that he'll pick up the wrong lead.

13.8

To help set him up for the left lead canter, I change his flexion and bend, by leg-yielding him away from my left leg as if I'm increasing the size of a circle. (Although I want him to move to the right, I should not shift my weight so much in that direction as I'm doing here. I need to stay more centered over Woody's back with my left leg on the girth, and my right leg behind the girth.)

Picks Up Wrong Lead

Part of being obedient to the leg includes a willingness to respond immediately and correctly to the aid for the canter. Set the horse up for the canter by vibrating the inside rein for flexion, supporting with the outside rein to keep the neck straight, and putting weight on your inside seat bone. Then your inside leg, which is at the girth, asks for forward movement while your outside leg swings behind the girth in a windshield wiper-like action to signal the outside hind leg to strike off.

Sometimes your aids will be right, but your horse will still make mistakes. Here's how you can use some of the movements you've learned to help him canter on the correct lead.

Maybe your horse is picking up the wrong lead because he's leaning on your inside leg. To remedy this, trot on a large circle. Decrease the size of the circle by spiraling in, and then increase the size of the circle by leg-yielding back out (figs. 13.7 and 13.8). Do this several times. When your horse feels softly bent around your inside leg, ask for the canter at the moment you are back on the larger circle (fig. 13.9).

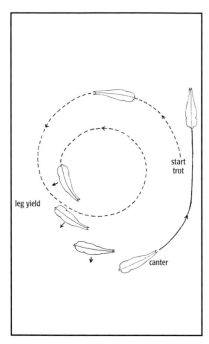

13.9

If your horse is picking up the wrong canter lead, it may be because he is leaning on your inside leg. Trot on a large circle. Decrease the size of the circle by spiraling in, and increase the size of the circle again by leg-yielding back out. Do this several times. When your horse feels softly bent, ask for a canter depart the moment you are back on the larger circle.

Sometimes the problem is a lack of what I call **"throughness."** If that's the case, improve his "throughness" or **connection** by suppling him (see Chapter Eleven). Repeat the spiraling in and leg-yielding out exercise that you just did. But this time while you're leg-yielding back out to the larger circle, "supple" him toward the inside of the circle three times. Give your signal for the canter depart right after the third "supple." This way you can take advantage of the connection or "throughness" you've created from suppling.

Or, perhaps he picks up the wrong lead because he's lazy with the outside hind leg (the strike-off leg). Trot on a large circle and activate the outside hind leg by leg-yielding his hindquarters in toward the center of the circle for a few strides and then straightening. Do this several times to drive his outside hind leg under his body as well as to make him think about this leg. Then be sure you take the time to re-bend him along the arc of the circle before you ask for the depart.

Horse Doesn't Accept Contact

Horses can show non-acceptance of contact in a variety of ways, such as carrying their heads too high, fighting the bit, reacting incorrectly when the reins are used, and ducking behind the contact so that there is slack in your reins. Before looking for a training solution, check that your horse's bit fits him properly and isn't too harsh, and that his teeth are in good shape with no sharp edges, in case these are the reasons for his actions.

I'm going to discuss the first three of these resistances together. When a horse holds his head and neck up in the air, it's called "coming above the bit" (fig. 13.10). This is somewhat uncomfortable for both horse and rider but not as unpleasant as the second resistance, when the horse fights the bit by yanking and pulling on the reins.

The third resistance, a more subtle expression of non-acceptance of the bit, is when the horse allows you to establish a pleasant, elastic contact with his mouth, but as soon as you use the reins to give an aid, he resists by pulling, putting his head up or shortening his neck. It's that unpleasant sensation of feeling like, "I don't dare touch the reins. I can

13.10

Non-acceptance of contact—coming above the bit.

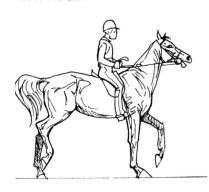

sit up here and look pretty, but I feel like I'm walking on eggs because even the slightest movement will disturb everything." Well, even though you may have been taught to have "good," quiet hands, your reins are part of your aids and you need to be able to use them.

"Suppling" can help you deal with all of these contact issues. When you supple the horse who is above the bit, he lowers his head and neck. When you supple the horse who is yanking at the bit, you take the bit away from him. And as you supple the horse who reacts incorrectly when you use the reins, he learns to lower and lengthen his neck and go toward the bit *as* you touch his mouth. Therefore, you teach him two things—not only can you use the reins but using them helps him to move better!

For the time being, use suppling for all of these resistances. Later on in Book Two, you'll use a more subtle aid, the half-halt, to resolve all of these problems of non-acceptance of the bit.

The fourth contact issue is the horse that ducks behind the bit (fig. 13.11). This horse needs to learn to go forward from your legs and step into your hand. Give him the idea by closing both legs and sending him forward over the ground in a lengthening. Do this several times; once he responds to your legs immediately, close your legs *as if* you want a lengthening but don't actually let him cover more ground. Rather than asking him to go more forward over the ground this time, you're now asking him to go forward through his body. If you're successful, you'll see him raise his head, and you'll begin to feel some weight in your hands. When he does this, praise him lavishly. You're teaching him a very important concept here and he needs to be encouraged for the slightest effort to seek a contact with your hands (see figs. 8.6 and 8.7, page 113).

You can also use a leg-yielding exercise to help your horse accept the reins. At the same time it will enable the action of the reins to go to the hind legs and affect them in a positive way, rather than stopping them and causing the horse's back to stiffen and become hollow as occurs when he resists contact.

Begin this exercise on a small figure-eight in the walk. Put your horse's front legs on the perimeter of each circle of the figure-eight and push his hindquarters to the outside so that they end up making a larger circle (fig. 13.12). Each time you give a little squeeze with your inside leg (the one closest to the center of the circle) behind the girth, use an opening inside rein as described in the leg-yielding section (fig. 10.36, page 189). Go back and forth from one circle to the other. Each time you open a rein and squeeze with your leg, your horse should take a bigger step sideways. In other words, when you bring your left hand to the left and close your left leg, his hindquarters should swing to the right. In this

13.11
Ducking behind the bit.

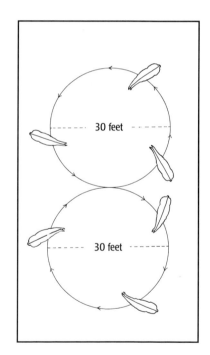

13.12
Non-acceptance of the bit: do the leg-yielding exercise going back and forth between circles, as described in the text. Each time you use an opening inside rein, your horse should willingly take longer strides sideways.

way he learns that you can use your reins positively to help him; his hind legs end up taking longer strides rather than being blocked by the use of your hand.

Stiffness

One of the best ways to loosen a stiff horse is by suppling as I've described in Chapter Eleven. Not only is a supple horse more comfortable to ride, but he can be more obedient simply because his body allows him to respond to your requests more easily.

You can also use some of the movements and exercises from Nuts and Bolts in Chapters Nine and Ten to unlock the stiff horse and make him more supple. The key to developing suppleness through those movements is transitions. Any transition—any change—whether it's from one pace to another, going from a straight line into a leg-yield or from bending in one direction to the other such as on a serpentine, will help you promote suppleness.

TRANSITIONS

When a horse is supple, he can smoothly do transitions from pace to pace or within a pace like lengthenings and shortenings. Your horse's suppleness is directly related to the ease and fluidity with which the transitions are done. If there's no change in rhythm, tempo, balance or frame, your horse is showing marked suppleness. So, ride many transitions until he's very adjustable.

While lengthening and shortening, remember to imagine that your horse's body is like a rubber band. It can easily stretch and contract. Pretend you're on pavement and you can hear the tempo of the steps of each pace staying exactly the same whether he's doing longer or shorter strides. Support the process by picturing smooth transitions that are as soft as a butterfly coming to rest on a leaf.

This reminds me of the time I was in the warm-up area at a big show in Virginia. I was riding Jolicoeur and we were coming up behind Pam Goodrich, noted dressage trainer and member of the United States Equestrian Team at the World Championships in 1986, and her horse, Semper Bene. I did a transition from the trot to the halt, and without turning around Pam said, "That was too abrupt, Jane." Now, I already had great admiration for Pam's talent, but I didn't realize that having eyes in the back of her head was another one of her many assets! When I questioned her about it later, she explained that she could hear that the transition was hard instead of soft.

LEG-YIELDING

Suppose you ask your horse to lengthen, and because he's feeling tight, he runs with quick, short steps. Use leg-yielding to help him. Do several steep leg-yields that have an angle greater than the standard 35 degrees, (perhaps in the walk) to stretch his muscles and increase his range of motion. Then go back to the trot lengthening and see if he feels freer.

You can also develop suppleness by riding a zig-zag in leg-yielding while in rising trot (fig. 13.13). To do one zig-zag, come through the corner, change your posting diagonal so that you're on the wrong diagonal, and leg-yield away from the rail. Just before you're across from the midpoint of the long side, straighten, change the flexion, change your diagonal, and leg-yield back to a point just before the corner.

You can also do two zig-zags, finishing the first one just before the middle of the long side. In this case, don't come too far off the track. The point of this exercise isn't to go sideways for a great distance, but to develop suppleness through the frequent transitions. It's important to do the exercise symmetrically by covering the same amount of ground when you yield to the left as when you yield to the right. This is a way to be sure that there's equal effort from each hind leg.

This is also a very good coordination exercise for the rider. Your posting diagonal is changed because you want to be sitting in the saddle when the inside hind leg is on the ground. At this moment it's easier for you to use your leg, and it's the best time to influence you horse's hind leg.

Hard to Steer

MOBILIZING THE SHOULDERS

If you're circling to the left and your horse ducks out to the right, your instinct usually is to pull on the left (inside) rein to bring him back on the circle. The problem here is that the more you pull his face to the inside, the more his body can fall in the opposite direction. If you turn your horse's shoulders, the rest of his body will follow. But in order to execute this, your horse has to have supple shoulders (i.e. they must be able to move easily in the direction you want to turn).

Often when a horse feels hard to steer it's because he's not very maneuverable with his shoulders. To increase the mobility of the shoulders and make them more supple, do several transitions from shoulder-fore to straight ahead and back to shoulder-fore on each long side of the arena. When the shoulders are mobile, you can easily move them in without an increase in the weight of the reins. If you try to do this exercise and you find it practically impossible to move your horse's shoulders, then his shoulders aren't supple at all, and he needs some loosening exercises directed to that part of his body.

Recently I had a jumper rider bring her horse to me for some help. She explained that her horse was bold and athletic and could even "jump

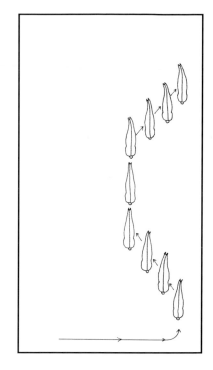

13.13

You can develop suppleness by riding a zig-zag in leg-yielding at the posting trot.

13.14 to 13.17
Mobilizing the Shoulders

13.14

To supple Joffrey's shoulders, Lynda makes a square with four 90-degree corners. To prepare, she rides him on a line that is parallel to the long side of the arena, but a little away from it, and flexes him a bit toward the rail to the right.

a house," but she couldn't turn him well enough to negotiate the courses. After watching him work a bit, it was obvious that he didn't have very supple shoulders.

We did a series of "shoulder-mobilization" exercises to improve his ability to slide his shoulders left and right. We knew we were gaining in the suppleness department when she could move his shoulders around and there was no increase in the weight of the reins.

Following are three shoulder suppling exercises, listed in order from the simplest to the most demanding. They can be done in all three paces. First, make sure that flexion, which is created by vibrating the rein, is opposite the direction you want the shoulders to move. In other words, if you're going to slide the shoulders to the left, you'll want to first flex the horse to the right.

1. Go to the left and make a square that doesn't quite touch the rail on any side (figs. 13.14 to 13.17). In each of the four corners of your square, ask for outside flexion (counter-flexion toward the rail) and then move the shoulders to the inside of the turn by bringing both of your arms in that direction. The hand that is closest to the inside of the square (left hand) is used as an opening rein while the right hand gives an indirect rein aid. During the indirect rein aid, this hand comes as close to the withers as possible without ever actually crossing over them. For a horse whose shoulders are really stuck, you'll need a little leverage, so think of "knocking," "spinning," or "sliding" your horse's shoulders around the turn. As you work your way around the turn, "knock" the shoulders over with a quick but smooth action, then soften the contact for a second. Then "knock" again and soften again. It feels a little like "shoulder-reining" rather than neck reining.

2. On your square, alternate between a turn like the one described above for one corner and a small circle in the next corner—both done in counter-flexion. You'll continue to knock the shoulders in

13.15
She brings both of her hands a little to the left for a moment to slide his shoulders around the turn.

13.16
After she "knocks" the shoulders over, she relaxes the contact for a moment before asking them to move over again.

13.14 to 13.17
Mobilizing the Shoulders
con't.

13.17
They've finished their 90-degree turn and are continuing along the next side of the square. Lynda keeps Joffrey flexed a bit toward the rail so that it's easy for her to move his shoulders around the upcoming corner.

and then soften several times until you work your way all the way around the circle. When you've finished the circle, proceed to the next corner of your square.

3. Ride straight down the long side of your ring or on the trail and ever so slightly slide your horse's shoulders in and out. Flex him to the left and move his shoulders to the right. Then straighten him for a few strides. Then flex him to the right and move the shoulders back to the left. As your horse becomes more athletic in his ability to slide his shoulders left and right, the weight in your reins will stay the same rather than increase. The shoulders only need to move a couple of inches in each direction. If you displace them too far, you'll get the hind legs involved rather than just isolating the shoulders. It's a very subtle exercise (figs. 13.18 and 13.19).

The Wiggly Horse

Do you ever feel like you're wrestling an alligator or trying to hold onto a greased pig instead of schooling a horse? That's what riding the wiggly horse feels like. It's wonderful that he's so supple, but your four-legged friend feels like a centipede (fig. 13.20). Not only is this horse difficult to turn because he's all over the place, but it's just as hard to keep him going forward on a straight line.

I ran into one of these wormy guys recently at a clinic. His rider was trying to correct him by closing her appropriate hand or leg depending on where he was escaping. But as soon as she corrected him, he bounced off her aids and fell out somewhere else. She had fallen into a cycle of correcting her correction and then having to correct her next correction. The two of them looked like they had indulged in "one-too-many!"

I suggested that she make a solid, narrow corridor of her legs and hands and let her horse bounce from side to side between her steady, enveloping aids until he finally was able to go straight

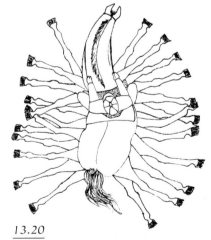

13.20
It's great to have a supple horse, but sometimes this wiggly guy feels like a centipede moving in a hundred different directions at once!

13.18

Deb has flexed Galen to the outside of the ring and has brought her shoulders slightly to the inside. She has moved the mare's shoulders by bringing both of her hands in the direction she wanted the shoulders to go.

13.19

Now, Deb has changed the flexion to the inside and moved Galen's shoulders back toward the rail. Compare the position of Galen's body to the pictures of her when Deb supples her poll (photos 11.10 and 11.11). During poll suppling, her shoulders stay parallel to the chain and only the position of her head changes. In this exercise, her shoulders are moved left and right.

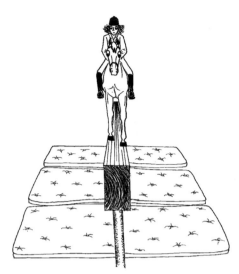

13.21

Imagine that you're on a balance beam that is placed exactly three feet away from the rail. If your horse's distance from the rail changes, you'll fall off the beam.

forward. To help her with this concept, she visualized standing in a hallway and throwing a ping pong ball forcefully against one wall. She "watched" the ball bounce from wall to wall until it finally rolled straight down the corridor.

We went through several stages. The first was to go all the way around the track, keeping him absolutely straight with no bend even when they were in a corner. When they could do that easily in all three paces, they did the same exercise three feet in from the rail with no track to help them. I told her to imagine she was on a four-inch-wide balance beam such as gymnasts use (fig. 13.21). If he got any closer to, or further away from the rail, she'd fall off the beam.

Once they could do that with few "falls," they did several brief lengthenings of five or six strides each while staying on the beam, which was still three feet away from the rail. Eventually they added some circles, starting and finishing the same distance away from the rail and then continuing along the balance beam without getting drawn into the track. The final exercise was to turn onto the centerline, leg-yield over to within three feet from the rail, and then stop the sideways momentum with the outside aids so the horse could continue forward along a line parallel to but not quite in the track.

Good Side, Bad Side

Our goal for all horses is to help them become athletic enough so that they are equally strong and willing to carry weight with both hind legs. When both hind legs are equally strong, you won't feel like your horse has a "better" and a "worse" side. He'll be just as easy to ride to the left as he is to the right.

The catch is that the hind legs can become equally strong only if the horse is **straight.** Most horses aren't truly straight, just as most people are also either right- or left-handed. The solution for "one-sidedness," therefore, is to keep working on everything you've learned in this book, until your horse goes "forward, straight, and in rhythm"–then he will go equally well to each side.

Riders must also recognize that a horse's forehand is narrower than his hindquarters. If his shoulders are taken too close to the wall, he has no option but to become crooked by bringing his hindquarters to the inside to make room for them. This can be the result of "pilot error," or sometimes a young horse will put his shoulders toward the wall in an effort to support himself and maintain his balance.

STIFF VS. SOFT SIDES

This right- or left-handedness leads to the development of what we call stiff and soft sides. The stiff side may feel more difficult to bend, but generally the horse carries the inside hind leg under the body and will bear weight on that side. The soft side feels easier to bend, but the inside hind leg tends to drift to the inside of the ring, and avoids carrying weight. That might explain why a shoulder-fore on the stiff side, where the horse steps into the rein, is easier to do than on the soft side where the horse tends to bring his head and neck in and his shoulders fall out toward the fence.

We can compensate for this tendency by doing the opposite of what the crooked horse wants to do. In other words, ride the stiff side more bent and

13.22 and 13.23 Correcting the Soft Left Side

13.22

Galen's soft side is her left side. It's easy to bend her, but her inside hind leg drifts to the inside of the turn to avoid carrying weight.

13.23

Deb is correcting Galen by doing the opposite of what the mare wants to do with her body. Rather than letting her bend too much when she travels on curved lines to the left, Deb keeps her body absolutely straight—no flexion or bend. Note how riding Galen straight as if she's on a line is helping to keep her inside hind leg underneath her body so it has to bear weight and get stronger.

work the soft side absolutely straight. Let's say your horse is stiff to the right (figs. 13.24 and 13.25). While going to the right, bend him to the right even if you're on a straight line. While riding a large circle to the right, overbend the body as if you're on the arc of a smaller circle.

When riding this horse to the left, keep the soft side absolutely straight. Don't bend your horse at all on either curved or straight lines. When you turn him, pretend his body is as stiff and straight as a bus (figs. 13.22 and 13.23).

You can also use **suppling** to help loosen your horse's stiff side. If he's stiff to the left, always supple him on his left side regardless of the direction you're going (figs. 13.26 and 13.27).

13.24 and 13.25 Correcting the Stiff Right Side

13.24
It's harder to bend Galen on her stiff side—the right. She doesn't flex to the right and her barrel leans against Deb's inside leg.

13.25
To make her more athletic, Deb bends Galen slightly to the right all the time—both on straight and curved lines. She's careful to bend Galen equally from poll to tail rather than letting her "cheat" by just bending her neck.

13.26 and 13.27
Suppling the Left Side

13.26
Joffrey is stiff on the left side of his body and finds it difficult to bend in that direction. While trotting on a circle to the left, Lynda supples him toward the inside of the circle. Note how she keeps him moving forward energetically as she bends his neck to the left.

13.27
They have changed direction and are circling to the right, but since Lynda still wants to work on softening the left side of Joffrey's body, she supples him toward the outside of the circle. Notice that Lynda firmly supports him with the right rein as she supples him to the left. That way his front legs stay on the circle rather than moving to the left and coming off the original arc. Only his neck should move off the line of the circle.

13.28

To help straighten a crooked horse, ride him in shoulder-fore position. Here, we see right shoulder-fore in counter-canter—the right hind leg is driven between the front legs as the forehand is brought toward the chain.

SHOULDER-FORE

Use shoulder-fore to straighten your horse and make his hind legs equally strong. Always straighten your horse by bringing his forehand in front of the hindquarters rather than by pushing his haunches out.

To get comfortable placing the forehand in front of the hindquarters, practice riding around the ring in shoulder-fore, through corners, through transitions, and through school figures, until it becomes automatic and easy for the horse to keep his inside hind leg under his body (fig. 13.28).

You can also ride shoulder-fore as a strengthening exercise for the hind leg that likes to drift to the inside and is more reluctant to bear weight. Use makes the muscle, and the weaker hind leg will get stronger as it's placed under the horse's body (13.29).

Increase the strengthening benefits of the exercise by staying in shoulder-fore throughout transitions. For example, go down the long side in sitting trot and ride several trot-walk-trot transitions while maintaining the shoulder-fore throughout. Be very aware that the horse doesn't drift to the inside (the responsibility of your inside leg), swing the hindquarters out (the responsibility of your outside leg) or decrease the angle (the responsibility of your two hands) at the moment that he steps into the new pace. That's the critical point when the horse will try to escape the difficulty of the movement. The same exercise can be done during canter-trot-canter transitions.

Tripping

If your horse trips a lot, the first thing you need to do is check that he's shod correctly and that his feet aren't too long.

If his feet are in good shape, make him more attentive and get his balance off his forehand and onto his hind legs by doing frequent transitions from one pace to another. Or, increase his energy level and freshen his working gaits by doing frequent transitions to and from lengthenings.

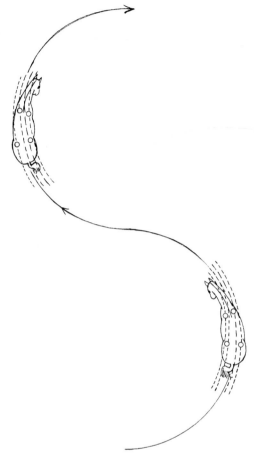

13.29

Use shoulder-fore to straighten your horse and make his hind legs equally strong. Always straighten him by bringing his forehand in front of his hindquarters, not by pushing the hindquarters sideways. Practice on figures and transitions until he's happy to carry weight on his inside hind leg.

KEY POINTS

This chapter has shown you how to use the movements and exercises that your horse has learned to solve some common training problems. For example, you can:

- Relax a tense horse by suppling him.

- Relax a tense horse by reducing the energy of the pace.

- Control a horse that rushes by doing small circles or leg-yielding.

- Wake up a lazy horse by putting him in front of your leg and then keep him sharp by asking for frequent transitions and leg-yielding.

- Help a horse pick up the correct canter lead by increasing his "throughness" with suppling.

- Teach a horse to accept the bit by suppling and leg-yielding.

- Loosen a stiff horse by suppling, doing frequent transitions from pace to pace as well as within the pace, and leg-yielding.

- Make a horse easier to steer by doing "shoulder mobilization" exercises.

- Organize a wiggly horse's body by working on the "balance beam."

- Help a horse go equally well in both directions by working his stiff side with too much bend and his soft side absolutely straight.

- Straighten a horse and strengthen a weak hind leg with shoulder-fore.

Afterword

So what do you think of your first taste of classical training? I bet it's quite a bit more fun and a lot less mysterious than you imagined before you got started.

If you've carefully followed the system that I've outlined in this book, you should now be enjoying a deeper level of communication and understanding with your horse. In essence, you now speak the same language—like my friend, Pat, learned to do with my horse, Hogan.

You see, a few years ago when I had to go out of town for a week and needed someone to exercise my horse, I asked Pat if she'd like to ride Hogan. I assumed it would be a real treat for her because I thought Hogan was perfect, and totally uncomplicated to ride. So, I was quite puzzled when I returned and Pat told me that Hogan "took advantage" of her the entire time. I watched them work one day and quickly saw the problem. Pat's system and signals were totally different from mine. Poor Hogan! I explained to Pat that as far as Hogan was concerned, he only spoke English and she was speaking to him in Russian. He couldn't understand a word she was saying! So I taught her Hogan's language and this "disobedient" horse soon became the paragon I knew he was.

After reading this book, I hope you and your horse enjoy the same kind of understanding that Pat and Hogan eventually developed. I'm not saying that your horse can now be called a "dressage horse." You've just used a little dressage to cross-train. But, now that you know just how much that little bit of classical training can help your horse, whatever job he has in life, I urge you to pick up Book Two, *More Cross-Training: Build a Better Performance Horse With Dressage*.

In Stage Three you'll learn about "The Professional's Secret"—the key to training that allows experts to get their horses to do things with invisible aids. This secret is called the "half-halt."

Then, in Stage Four, you'll get to do some "Fancy Stuff"—extensions, lateral work, and flying changes. You'll be pleased to discover how everything you've done in the previous three stages makes this new work a "piece of cake" for your horse!

I look forward to seeing all of you in Book Two.

Appendix

Arena Diagrams

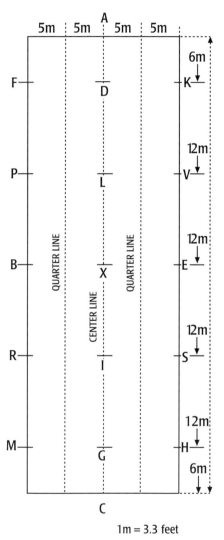

5m | 5m | A | 5m | 5m

F ┤ D | 6m ↓ K

P ┤ L | 12m ↓ V

QUARTER LINE | CENTER LINE | QUARTER LINE

B ┤ X | 12m ↓ E

R ┤ I | 12m ↓ S

M ┤ G | 12m ↓ H | 6m ↓

C

1m = 3.3 feet

Standard Arena

5m | 5m | A | 5m | 5m

6m ↓ F | D | K

40m | 14m ↓ B | X | E

14m ↓ M | G | H | 6m ↓

20m

C

1m = 3.3 feet

Small Arena

Arena Diagrams: 20-Meter Circles

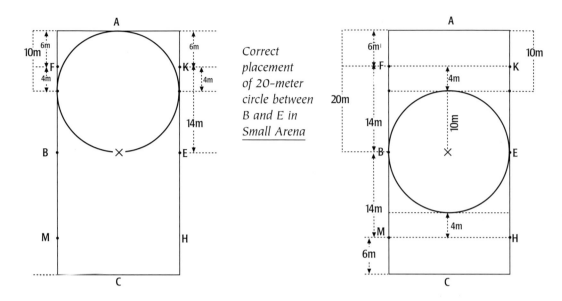

Correct placement of 20-meter circle at A in <u>Small Arena</u>

Correct placement of 20-meter circle between B and E in <u>Small Arena</u>

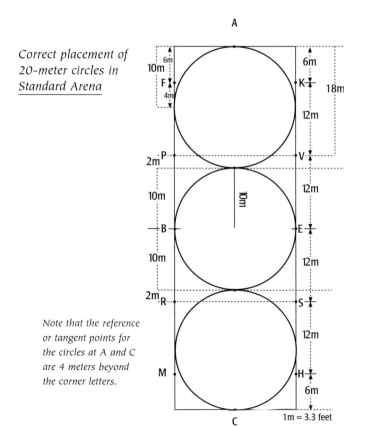

Correct placement of 20-meter circles in <u>Standard Arena</u>

Note that the reference or tangent points for the circles at A and C are 4 meters beyond the corner letters.

1m = 3.3 feet

Arena Diagrams: 15-Meter Circles

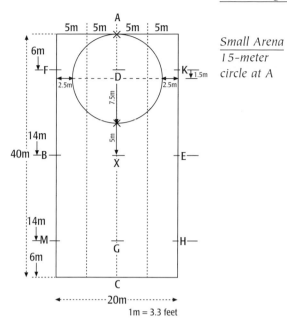

*Small Arena
15-meter
circle at A*

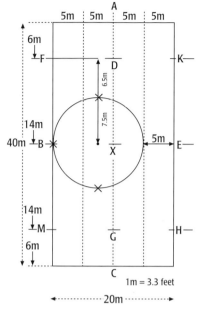

*Small Arena
15-meter
circle at B*

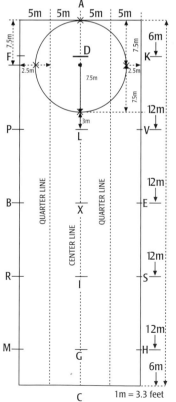

*Standard Arena
15-meter
circle at A*

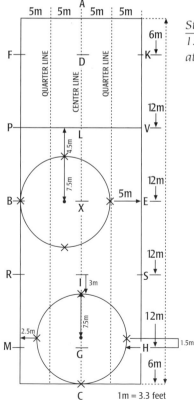

*Standard Arena
15-meter circle
at C and B*

Glossary

aids. Signals—The various combinations and actions of the seat, legs, and hands that allow you to communicate nonverbally with your horse.

axis-straight. The horse's spine overlaps his line of travel. *See* **straightness**

basics, the. Rhythm, Forward, and **Straightness**. The Basics are the foundation for all correct work.

bend. Refers to lateral bending. When the bend through the horse's side is correct, it conforms to the arc of whatever curved line he is on.

collected walk. The horse remains **'on the bit**,' moves resolutely forward, with his head raised and arched and showing clear **self-carriage**. The pace remains regular, marching and vigorous but each step covers less ground and is higher and more active than the steps of the medium walk because all the joints bend more markedly.

collecting/ion. Also called **self-carriage** or gathered together. The horse's center of gravity shifts more toward his legs. The hindquarters lower and carry more weight and the forehand lightens and appears higher than the hindquarters.

connecting/ion. On the bit; a connected horse's back serves as the bridge between the hind legs and the front legs so that energy can travel from the hind legs, over the back, through the neck, into the rider's hands and be recycled back to the hind legs.

consistent. A desirable quality of **contact**. The contact from the rider's hand to the horse's mouth stays constant. The reins never become slack and then tight. This is only possible when the rider's elbows are elastic.

contact. Refers to the horse's stretching forward into the bit and accepting the taut rein as a means of communication with the rider. *See* **rein effects.**

counter-canter. An obedience and suppling movement in which the horse is asked to canter on what is considered the "wrong" lead (i.e. while going to the right he canters on the left lead).

driving seat. The action of the seat that is used to send the horse forward or speed up the **tempo** of a **pace**. To use a driving seat, stretch up and push with the seat as if you are trying to move the back of the saddle toward the front of the saddle.

elastic contact. A desirable quality of contact. Elastic contact is made possible by the opening and closing of the elbows, allowing for the forward and back movement of the horse's neck in the walk and canter and for the up and down movement of the rider's body during posting trot.

engagement/engage. The **bending** and **flexing** of the joints of the hindquarters so that the angle between the bones is decreased. As a result, the croup lowers and the hindquarters bear more weight.

extended walk. The horse covers as much ground as possible without haste and without losing the regularity of his steps, the hind feet touch the ground clearly in front of the footprints of the forefeet. The rider allows the horse to stretch out his head and neck without losing contact with the mouth.

flexes. (Joints of the hind legs). *See* **engagement**

flexion. Refers to bending in the joints, specifically the poll and jaw.

forward. One of **the Basics**. The direction the horse moves over the ground (i.e. forward as opposed to sideways).

frame. The outline or silhouette of the horse's body, showing his posture.

free walk. A pace of relaxation in which the horse is given a loose rein and allowed complete freedom to lower and stretch out his head and neck.

gaits. The "gears" within each pace (i.e. extended walk, working trot, or medium canter). *See* **paces**

half-halt. A hardly visible, almost simultaneous, coordinated action of seat, legs and hands that increases a horse's attention and improves balance and harmony.

haunches-in. (travers). The horse is slightly **bent** around the rider's inside leg. His front legs stay on the original track of the long side and his hindquarters are brought in off the track toward the center of the ring at about a 30 degree angle to the rail. His outside legs pass and cross in front of his inside legs and he looks in the direction he's moving.

haunches-out (renvers). This is the inverse movement of the **haunches-in**, with the **tail to the wall** instead of the head. Otherwise the same principles and conditions are applicable as in haunches-in.

head to the wall. A position for **leg-yielding** in which the horse is **flexed** toward the rail, the forelegs remain on the track, and the hindlegs are moved away from the rail at about a 35 degree angle.

impulsion. Thrust—the horse gives the impression of carrying himself forward and springing off the ground. The elastic springing off the ground begins in the haunches with a bending of the joints of the hindquarters and culminates in very energetic gaits.

inside. Refers to the direction or side toward which the horse is **bent** and/or **flexed**.

lateral walk. A rhythm fault in the walk in which the foreleg and the hindleg on the same side move almost on the same beat, so that there is no longer even spacing between the four steps that make up a stride of walk. This irregularity is a serious deterioration of the walk. *See* **rhythm.**

leg-straight. The hind feet follow in the exact same tracks as those made by the front feet. *See* **straightness.**

leg-yield. A lateral movement in which the horse's inside front and hind legs clearly cross in front of his **outside** legs. The spine is straight, but there is flexion at the poll away from the direction of movement. *See* **two track movements.**

lengthening. A preliminary exercise to extension. The horse lengthens his stride and frame while maintaining rhythm, tempo, and balance.

medium walk. A free, regular and unconstrained walk of moderate lengthening. The horse walks energetically but calmly with even and determined steps, the hind feet touching the ground in front of the footprints of the forefeet. The rider maintains a light, soft, and steady contact with the mouth.

on the bit. The horse moves actively from behind through a supple back and accepts a light contact of the rein with no resistance. He yields in the jaw and poll to the rider's hand, has a "round" outline, and willingly responds to the rider's aids. *See* **connection, round.**

outside. The side of the horse's body opposite from the direction toward which he is **bent** and/or **flexed**.

paces. The walk, trot and canter. *See* **gaits.**

psychocybernetic. Refers to the part of the subconscious mind that is responsible for the goal-striving behavior of human beings.

rein effects. The different ways that the reins are used to communicate. The five rein effects include: opening rein, indirect rein, direct rein of opposition, indirect rein of opposition in front of the withers, and indirect rein of opposition passing behind the withers. *See also* **contact.**

renvers. *See* **haunches-in**.

rhythm. One of **the Basics**. The order of the footfalls or the "beat" of the pace (walk: 4-beat; trot: 2-beat; canter: 3-beat).

round. The shape of the horse's outline or silhouette when the hind legs step well under the body, the back is raised, supple and looks convex, the neck is long and arched, and the horse stretches toward the contact. *See* **connection**.

self-carriage. *See* **collection.**

shoulder-fore. A lateral movement that can be used as a **straightening** exercise. The horse is slightly **bent** around the rider's **inside** leg and the forehand is brought in off the the rail so that the inside hind leg steps in between the front legs.

shoulder-in. A lateral movement that can be used as a **straightening, suppling,** and **collecting** exercise. The horse is **flexed** to the **inside** and slightly **bent** around the inside leg. The forehand is brought in off the rail at approximately a 30 degree angle so that the inside hind leg is lined up directly behind the **outside** foreleg. The inside foreleg passes and crosses in front of the outside foreleg; the inside hind leg is placed in front of the outside hindleg. The horse looks away from the direction in which he is moving.

shoulder-out. A schooling exercise that is the mirror-image of **shoulder-in**. The horse is ridden on a line that is slightly to the inside of the rail. He is **bent** and **flexed** toward the rail and his forehand is brought closer to the rail. All of the same principles of shoulder-in apply.

silhouette. The horse's outline or **frame**.

single track. Work done going straight forward.

soft side. The horse's weaker side; the hollow side; the side that is easier to bend.

stiff side. The horse's strong side; the side that is more difficult to bend.

stilled seat. The aid that is used to signal the horse to slow his **tempo**, steady his **rhythm**, decrease his length of stride or do a downward transition. It is done by stretching up and tightening the abdominal muscles so that the seat stops following along with the horse's motion.

straight/straightness. One of **the Basics**. A straight horse is straight on lines and **bent** along the arc of curves, with his spine overlapping the line of travel and his hind feet stepping into the tracks of the front feet.

suppling. An exercise used to reduce tension, loosen stiffness, teach acceptance of the rein, improve **bending** or enhance **connection**.

tail to the wall. A position for leg-yielding in which the horse is ridden slightly to the inside of the track, is **flexed** away from the rail and the hindlegs are moved towards the rail at about a 35 degree angle. *See also* **head to the wall.**

tempo. The rate of repetition of the **rhythm.**

throughness. The quality of being **on the bit, connected,** and having a **round** frame; the supple, elastic, unblocked, connected state of the horse's musculature that allows unrestricted flow of energy from back to front as well as the receiving of that energy back to the hind legs.

transition. Any sort of change, including from one **pace** to another, within a pace such as to and from a **lengthening**, or from movement to movement such as from working straight **forward** on a **single track** to a **leg-yield**.

travers. *See* **haunches-in**.

turn on the forehand. The horse yields away from the rider's leg when he's at a standstill. His front legs remain more or less on the same spot while the hindquarters make a 180 degree turn around the forehand, so that the horse ends up facing in the opposite direction.

two track movements. Lateral movements in which the horse goes forward and sideways at the same time.

working trot. The trot in which the young or uneducated horse presents himself in the best balance. The horse moves energetically in a regular two-beat **rhythm** and his hind feet step into the tracks made by the front feet.

Suggested Reading

The Achievement Zone, Shane Murphy, Putnam, 1996.

Advanced Dressage, Anthony Crossley, Trafalgar Square Publishing, 1996 (US)/ Swan Hill Press, 1995 (UK).

The Athletic Development of the Dressage Horse, Charles de Kunffy, Howell Book House, 1992 (US)/ Simon & Schuster UK, 1992 (UK).

Carriage Driving: A Logical Approach Through Dressage Training, Heike Bean, Howell Book House, 1992 (US)/ Prentice Hall UK, 1992 (UK).

Centered Riding, Sally Swift, Trafalgar Square Publishing, 1985 (US)/ Ebury Press, 1998 (UK).

The Classical Rider: Being at One with Your Horse, Sylvia Loch, Trafalgar Square Publishing, 1997 (US)/ J.A. Allen, 1997 (UK).

The Competitive Edge, Max Gahwyler, Half Halt Press, 1995.

Drawing on the Right Side of the Brain, Betty Edwards, Putnam, 1989 (US)/ Grafton Books, 1993 (UK).

Feel the Fear and Do It Anyway, Susan Jeffers, Fawcett, 1988 (US)/ Rider, 1991 (UK).

The Glossary of Dressage Judging Terms, United States Dressage Federation, 1993.

Heads Up!, Janet Edgette, Doubleday, 1996.

Horse Gaits, Balance and Movement, Susan E. Harris, Howell Book House, 1993 (US)/ Simon & Schuster UK, 1993 (UK).

Learn to Ride Using Sports Psychology, Petra and Wolfgang Hölzel, Trafalgar Square Publishing, 1996 (US)/ Kenilworth Press, 1996 (UK).

Lungeing and Long Reining, Jennie Loriston-Clarke, Half Halt Press, 1994 (US)/ Kenilworth Press, 1993 (UK).

My Horses, My Teachers, Alois Podhajsky, Trafalgar Square Publishing, 1997 (US)/ J.A. Allen, 1997 (UK).

The New Toughness Training For Sport, James Loehr, Dutton, 1995 (US)/ Atlantic Books, 1994 (UK).

1998-99 Dressage Division Rule Book, American Horse Shows Association, 1997.

101 Arena Exercises, Cherry Hill, Storey Communications, 1995.

Practical Dressage, Jane Kidd, Howell Book House, 1990 (US)/ Prentice Hall UK, 1994 (UK).

Practical Dressage Manual, Bengt Ljungquist, Half Halt Press, 1983 (US)/ Kenilworth Press, 1995 (UK).

Psychocybernetics, Maxwell Maltz, Wilshire, 1973.

The Psychology of Winning, Denis Waitley, Berkeley, 1986 (US)/ Simon & Schuster UK, 1989 (UK).

Ride With Your Mind: An Illustrated Masterclass in Right Brain Riding, Mary Wanless, Trafalgar Square Publishing, 1991 (US)/ Kenilworth Press, 1995 (UK).

Riding for the Rest of Us, Jessica Jahiel, Howell Book House, 1996 (US)/ Prentice Hall UK, 1996 (UK).

Riding Logic, Wilhelm Müseler, Simon & Schuster, 1985.

See You at the Top, Zig Ziglar, Pelican, 1994.

Seeds of Greatness: The Best Kept Secrets of Total Success, Denis Waitley, Revell, 1984 (US)/ Cedar, 1987 (UK).

That Winning Feeling!: Program Your Mind for Peak Performance, Jane Savoie, Trafalgar Square Publishing, 1992 (US)/ J.A. Allen, 1992 (UK).

Training Strategies for Dressage Riders, Charles de Kunffy, Howell Book House, 1994 (US)/ Simon & Schuster UK, 1994 (UK).

Training the Young Horse, Anthony Crossley, Trafalgar Square Publishing, 1994 (US)/ Stanley Paul, 1993 (UK).

What to Say When You Talk to Yourself, Shad Helmstetter, Grindle Press, 1986 (US)/ HarperCollins, 1991 (UK).

Index

Page numbers in *italic* indicate illustrations

Illustration Credits